D1442351

the world of automobiles

An Illustrated Encyclopedia of the Motor Car

COLUMBIA HOUSE/New York

Consultant Editor: Tom Northey
Executive Editor: Ian Ward
Editorial Director: Brian Innes
Assistant Editors: Laurie Caddell
Mike Winfield
Art Editor: David Goodman
Picture Research: Evan Davies
Cover Design: Harry W. Fass
Production Manager: Warren Bright

contributors
RONALD BARKER: Hudson
Isotta Fraschini
GEORGE BISHOP: Humber
Issigonis
Itala
DAVID BURGESS WISE: Howe
Hupmobile
HWM
Imperia
Instruments
Invicta
LAURIE CADDELL: Intermeccanica
EDWARD FRANCIS: Invalid Cars
IAN FRASER: Iso
Ital Design
JOHN JAMES: Indicators
MIKE KETTLEWELL: HRG
Indianapolis
Italian Grand Prix
ROBERT PEMBERTON: Innocenti
Isuzu
L. J. K. SETRIGHT: Hydraulics
Ignition
Jaguar

MIKE TWITE: Hulme
Ickx
Ireland

Picture acknowledgments
Page 961: National Motor Museum—962: National Motor Museum—963: N. Bruce; National Motor Museum—964: National Motor Museum; N. Bruce; National Motor Museum—965: National Motor Museum—966: National Motor Museum; National Motor Museum; N. Bruce—967: C. Pocklington—968: Quattroruote; National Motor Museum; National Motor Museum—969: National Motor Museum; American Motors—970: National Motor Museum—971: National Motor Museum—972: National Motor Museum—973: National Motor Museum—974/975: National Motor Museum—975: National Motor Museum—976: Betti; H. Shell—977: S. Morris; American Motors—978: Boroli; F. Villani—979: G. Mairani; G. Goddard—980: Humber—981: Tony Stone; Boschetti—982: National Motor Museum—983: National Motor Museum (I); Boschetti; National Motor Museum—984: National Motor Museum—985: London Art Tech—986: National Motor Museum; Cherrett; N. Bruce—987: National Motor Museum—988: National Motor Museum (I); National Motor Museum; National Motor Museum—989: National Motor Museum; National Motor Museum; Keystone—990: Betti; National Motor Museum; National Motor Museum; National Motor Museum—991: Gilltraps Auto Museum; National Motor Museum; National Motor Museum—992: National Motor Museum; National Motor Museum; Betti—993: National Motor Museum; National Motor Museum; National Motor Museum; Betti—994: BHRA—995: Fiat; Papetti; Innocenti—996: Fiat; Fiat; Bignozzi; Sauer & Sohn—997: Sauer & Sohn—999: G. Goddard—1000: National Motor Museum—1001: Boroli; G. Goddard—1002: Camera Press; Quattroruote; G. Goddard—1003: Ceci; Ceci; Quattroruote; Quattroruote; Quattroruote—1004: Ceci—1005: Quattroruote—1006: Papetti; Quattroruote; Papetti—1008: National Motor Museum—1009: Quattroruote; National Motor Museum—1010: National Motor Museum—1011: London Art Tech; Di Santo; Camera Press—1012: National Motor Museum; National Motor Museum; Camera Press; National Motor Museum—1013: Quattroruote—1014: Marka—1015: Marka; G. Goddard—1016: Marka—1018: Di Santo; De Vita; Innocenti—1019: Papetti; Nesta; Quattroruote—1020: Quattroruote—1021: Autocar—1022: Quattroruote; Ceci; Quattroruote; Quattroruote; Jaguar; Jaguar—1023: Cherrett; Pininfarina; Italdesign; Quattroruote—1024: Smiths Industries—1024/1025: Quattroruote—1026: Smiths Industries—1027: Ford; Smiths Industries; Smiths Industries—1028: Quattroruote; C. Pocklington; C. Pocklington—1029: Car—1030: Car—1031: E. Francis—1032: N. Bruce; E. Francis; E. Francis—1033: N. Bruce; N. Bruce; Invacar—1034: N. Bruce—1035: C. Pocklington; G. Goddard—1036: National Motor Museum—1036/1037: National Motor Museum—1037: National Motor Museum—1038: London Art Tech—1039: Marka—1040: London Art Tech—1041: Papetti; Quattroruote; Boroli—1042: Quattroruote—1043: Quattroruote—1044: Van der Steen—1045: Boschetti; Boschetti; C. Pocklington—1046: Auselmi; Quattroruote—1047: Betti; Betti; Auselmi—1048: Boschetti—1049: Boschetti; Boschetti; Betti; Quattroruote; Betti—1050: Issigonis; Issigonis; Issigonis; G. Dowson—1051: Orbis—1052: Issigonis—1054: British Leyland—1055: Camera Press; Quattroruote—1056: Camera Press; National Motor Museum—1057: Quattroruote; Quattroruote; Papetti; National Motor Museum (I)—1058: Italfoto; Quattroruote—1059: Quattroruote; Zagari; Italfoto; Quattroruote—1060: Boschetti; Italfoto; Papetti—1061: Quattroruote; Zagari—1062: Car; Ital Design Iguana—1063: Car; Quattroruote—1064: Zagari—1066: Quattroruote—1067: Di Santo; Boschetti; Boschetti; Boschetti; Di Santo; A. Moreland—1068: Boschetti—1069: Boschetti—1070: Boschetti—1071: Boschetti—1072: Boschetti—1073: A. Moreland; Boschetti; C. Pocklington—1074: Boschetti—1075: Quattroruote—1076: A. Moreland—1077: Quattroruote; Quattroruote; L. J. Caddell—1078: Jaguar—1079: Jaguar—1080: Jaguar—cover: Orbis; Issigonis

Contents

Britain's racing statesman

'IF THE SHIP OF STATE WERE A CAR,' said Sir Henry Birkin in a praising speech in 1932, 'Lord Howe would have been Prime Minister long ago . . . of all racing motorists with whom I have ever come in contact, he is, I think, the keenest; he brings to any subject with which cars are remotely concerned an application that nothing will deter'.

Yet, Lord Howe, who was one of Britain's best-known racing drivers of the 1930s, did not take up competitive motoring seriously until 1928, when he was 44. That was, commented Birkin, 'after visiting almost every police court in the land'. Howe, it seems, decided to practise his speed where it would be more appreciated, and exact from the constabulary of the track a licence he had been refused on main roads.

Edward Richard Assheton, Viscount Curzon (he had not succeeded to the title when he started racing), had followed in the wake of his illustrious forebear, the first Lord Howe, victor of the Glorious First of June in 1794, and served with distinction in the Navy during the Great War aboard HMS *Queen Elizabeth* in the Dardanelles campaign.

His light hearted manner concealed a determination to succeed, inspired by his intense patriotism; his cars were always meticulously prepared, because he felt that to start in a race with a scruffy car would be letting the side down. Indeed, Howe's cars always stood out on the starting line because of their driver's brilliant

blue helmet and racing overalls, and the huge Oxford blue umbrella that he always affected in the rain, virtually to the fall of the starter's flag.

The first race of note in which Lord Howe appeared was the 1928 Irish TT at Newtownards; he drove with great skill for the first 150 miles at almost 68 mph, then speeded his Bugatti up until it was averaging over 70. By the halfway mark, he had lapped all the back markers and was gaining rapidly on the smaller cars—which had had a considerable start under the handicap system—with a good chance of winning the race, when his petrol tank burst. The Tourist Trophy remained a regular commitment for Howe: 1930 saw him at the wheel of an ex-Caracciola SSK Mercedes, while the following year he drove his Alfa Romeo. Indeed, 1931 was a very good year for Howe: he won the Gold Star handicap at the Whitsun meeting at Brooklands, beating Cobb and Birkin, then within the month shared an Alfa at Le Mans with Tim Birkin. Because of a last-minute decision to run on pure benzole, the car's pistons had to be replaced, and the work was not finished until 5.30 am on the morning of the race. At first, the car was slowed by plug trouble, but by the end of the sixth hour Howe had moved up through the flying Talbots, Aston Martins and Mercedes to take second position. Then, as midnight struck, he slipped into the lead, a position which the two co-drivers comfortably maintained until, at the

Above: Lord Howe's 1½-litre Delage, an ex-Malcolm Campbell machine, pictured at Brooklands. This car was unfortunately written off at Monza in 1933

Inset: Lord Howe, in his car at the 1934 Dieppe Grand Prix

end of the 24 hours, Birkin thundered across the line at over 90 mph. It was the fastest *Vingt-Quatre Heures* that had yet been held, and the Howe/Birkin combine's average speed of 78.13 mph had broken all records. A couple of weeks later, Howe was at the French Grand Prix, with a different car (Bugatti) and a different co-driver (the Hon Brian Lewis); but this time his luck was out, for an hour and a half was wasted in the pits trying to discover the cause of a mysterious ignition fault, which turned out to be nothing more serious than a chafed-through sparking plug lead. Once this had been rectified, the Bugatti was the fastest car in the race; but it was too late to catch the leaders, and Howe had to be content with twelfth place.

By this time, Lord Howe had acquired one of the famous 1.5-litre Delages from Malcolm Campbell and with this he won his class at the 1931 Grand Prix de Dieppe, despite narrowly missing being involved in a pile-up which

eliminated seven Bugattis. Indeed, he could have won the race outright with his five-year-old car, had it not been for a burst tyre caused, it seems, by an act of sabotage.

The Delage's successful career, however, was cut short at Monza in 1933: Howe entered a bend fast, only to find the track blocked by three slower cars. He braked hard and the servo jammed. With all four wheels locked, the car spun right around and skidded off the road backwards, into the trees lining the track. All Howe could do was duck. 'The next moment,' he recalled later, 'the car was among the trees, and I saw one tree cut a front wheel off like a knife. Then the car turned on its side, something hit me hard on my crash helmet, and we came to rest with an almighty bump. I was still sitting in the car, holding the steering wheel, but the car, on its side, was wrapped clean round the tree, with the front wheel and the rear wheel only six inches apart'.

Although his car had been sliced and wrapped, Howe was unhurt and the remains of the car were pushed into his purpose-built Commer Invader car transporter van, eventually to be dumped in his mews garage near the Dorchester.

Above left: Lord Howe at Brooklands in 1931; during that year he co-drove an Alfa Romeo with Tim Birken to win the Le Mans 24-hour race. He also won the Gold Star handicap race at Brooklands. On the grid, he was instantly recognisable by his vivid blue helmet and overalls

Above right: Lord Howe watching an event at the Goodwood circuit during 1948

In any case, the Delage was not Howe's only car: in 1932, he had driven a 2.3-litre Bugatti into fourth place in the Monaco Grand Prix, beaten only by Nuvolari, Caracciola and Fagioli; his green Bugatti, moreover, had beaten the official team cars, whose drivers numbered just about every immortal name in the Bugatti canon.

Summing up Howe's drive, *The Motor* commented: 'He is incontestably to be classed among the world's greatest drivers, and may be ranked with the Continental champions whose names are household words'.

To prove this point, Howe led the 1934 Le Mans 24-hour race in his Alfa until the failure of his lights and clutch put him out of the running.

Howe, let it be noted, only drove foreign cars because he was convinced that there was not a British car that was truly competitive with the Continentals, although he did essay a few races with an MG Magnette. Leading his class in the Mille Miglia with this car, he slid off the road on a waterlogged S-bend, and knocked down a telegraph pole.

After 1936, however, he seems to have revised his opinion of British cars, for he acquired an ERA, and also drove as a member of the Fox & Nicholl Lagonda team.

His last significant track achievement was a 108.27 mph lap of Brooklands at the wheel of a Lagonda V12, in 1938: no mean achievement for a 54-year-old man. Although his racing days were over after World War II, he continued to support motor racing, both in committee and organisational work and in the House of Lords. He also became President of the British Racing Drivers' Club; his death in 1964 removed one of the last great gentleman amateurs from the racing scene.   DBW

Strictly for the enthusiast

Below: an HRG 1500 taking part in a Lands End trial on Darracott Hill

THE BRITISH HAVE A PENCHANT for doing things out of the ordinary; ironically, it is known as being 'traditional'. The HRG story is out of the ordinary, involving a motor car built to vintage tradition. Its specification remained almost unaltered from 1935 to 1956 when production ceased. The name remained until 1966 and, during the company's 31-year history, a little under 300 cars were built.

H. R. 'Dan' Godfrey collaborated with Archie Frazer-Nash to build the first genuine sporting light car, the GN, in 1910. Eventually, the two partners went their separate ways, Frazer-Nash building chain-driven cars, similar to the GNs, which bore his own name. Godfrey waited a while before combining with two fellow competition drivers, Major E. A. Halford and Guy H. Robins, to produce the HRG. A workshop was established in part of the Mid-Surrey Gear Works factory at Norbiton, Surrey, although a year later new premises were taken at nearby Tolworth in Oakcroft Road. Coincidentally, next door were Nash & Thompson Ltd, who built gun turrets: this company was a new venture of Godfrey's erstwhile partner, Archie Frazer-Nash.

Godfrey, Halford and Robins eschewed the contemporary family and so-called sports cars. Comfort was sacrificed, and an emphasis placed on pure performance. The result was an enthusiast's delight. The first HRG was basically a light and very rigid chassis with quarter-elliptic springing at the front and semi-elliptic astern, giving a hard 'vintage' ride but

firm and precise handling qualities. The no-nonsense two-seater bodywork had an element of charm about it and with its low weight of 14 cwt (1568 lb) it was a strong performer, thanks to the utilisation of the four-cylinder, 1496 cc Meadows overhead-valve engine for which 58 bhp at 4500 rpm was claimed. The specification also combined cable-operated brakes (which could be adjusted from the driver's seat), a crash-type Moss gearbox and a fly-off handbrake.

From the very start, the HRG earned a reputation as a rugged all-rounder, being at home on the race track, in trials and rallies or on the public road. Top speed was a shade over 80 mph and the 'Hurgs', as they became affectionately known, could accelerate from 0–50 mph in under 10 seconds.

Before World War II, the Meadows engine was superseded by the single-overhead-camshaft Singer unit in either 1496 cc or 1074 cc form. The engines were modified by HRG to suit their requirements, featuring a raised compression ratio plus twin SU carburettors. The 1100 engine developed 38 bhp, while the 1500 power unit produced an encouraging 65 bhp at 4800 rpm.

Competition successes were scored in the prestigious

Top: the 1½-litre Meadows-engined 1935 HRG prototype

Above left: a 1937 HRG, competing in a rally

Above right: the 1496 cc, four-cylinder, overhead-valve Meadows engine fitted to the original HRG machines; 58 bhp at 4500 rpm was the output claimed for this engine. Before World War II, this power unit was superseded by the single-overhead-camshaft Singer engine, in either 1496 cc or 1074 cc form

Le Mans 24-hour race which, at that time, catered for production sports cars. In 1937, A. C. Scott and Major E. A. Halford were thirteenth overall and second in the 1500 cc class; the following year, Peter Clark and Marcus Chambers were tenth overall and second in the 1500 cc class; in 1939, Clark and Chambers finished fourteenth overall and won their class.

Following World War II, production of the 1100 and 1500 models continued with but minor revisions, and a new 'aerodynamic' model was introduced. With a sleek, full-width body designed by Marcus Chambers, in conjunction with R. de Yarburgh-Bateson, and built by Fox & Nichols, it sold for just over £100 more than the standard machine—at £991 instead of £882 (including purchase tax). However, its extra weight penalty was not compensated for by the expected increase in speed, due to better aerodynamics and it was withdrawn from the range in 1950. The HRG Aerodynamic has to be considered a pioneer, however, being the first British production sports car to feature full-width bodywork.

Although the factory refrained from entering works cars in competitions, they offered full assistance to HRG owners wishing to take part in motor sport.

Peter Clark was one of the most successful exponents and ran a team of HRGs (two Aerodynamics plus a one-off coupé) in the 1948 Francorchamps 24-hour race in Belgium where they won the *Coupe du Roi* team prize. For 1949, Clark had conventional 'stark' 1½-litre HRGs modified by Monaco Engineering. The bodies were lightened to scale a mere 50 lb and the chassis were developed to cope with rough race-track surfaces. Three cars were entered for the Le Mans and Francorchamps 24-hour races and one, driven by Eric Thompson/Jack Fairman, finished an amazing eighth overall and easily won the 1½-litre class. The Peter Clark/Mortimer Morris-Goodall car suffered a severed water pipe and seized its engine shortly after the first hour, while the Jack Scott/Neville Gee vehicle failed in the middle of the night.

A fortnight later in the Belgian race, despite a multitude of problems, the Thompson/Fairman car triumphed again, not only winning its class but gaining awards for the first British machine to finish, the first British drivers to finish and the team prize with the sister cars of Clark/Morris-Goodall and Scott/André Pilette. Yet, three of the four body section mountings

using HRG components. The standard 1500 chassis was shortened by 5½ in to 8 ft 0½ in and a Standard Vanguard engine linered down to 1998 cc to conform to the 2-litre limit, power being transmitted via a three-speed gearbox. With a top speed of little more than 110 mph, the car was sadly outclassed, being

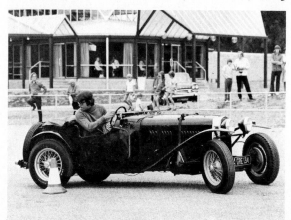

Left: Roger Newton driving his 1937 1½-litre HRG at the 1972 Beaulieu Lost Causes Rally; this vehicle is typical of the classic 'vintage-tradition' sports cars produced by the HRG Company

had sheared, the tail had come adrift and had been refixed with a clothes line and broom handle, the fuel tank attachment had broken and a headlamp had dropped off en route!

Rallying successes were also scored by the nimble 'Hurgs', among the successful drivers being Robin Richards, Jack Newton, John Gott, Nancy Mitchell, Betty Haig and Jack Richmond. There were class and team wins in the 1948 Alpine Rally plus a class victory and a coveted *Coupe des Alpes* for Gott in 1951. In the 1951 RAC Rally, John Brown and Nancy Mitchell took a 1–2 in the 1500 cc open car class. On the race track, class wins were scored in the 1949 and 1950 Production Touring-Car races at Silverstone.

In 1948, Peter Clark commissioned Marcus Chambers to build a Formula Two single-seater racing car

further handicapped by the lack of fully independent suspension. After a terrible 1949 season, it was abandoned, although it briefly reappeared with a Lea-Francis engine.

HRG continued to build their cars in small numbers with slight revisions year after year. Although Singer introduced the new SM1500 engine in 1949, HRG continued to rely on the older unit until 1953. Eventually, a change-over to the new engine was made, HRG modifications (which included reducing the stroke to bring the capacity below the 1500 cc division then common in racing) resulting in a power output of 66 bhp.

In 1955, a startling new model was introduced featuring advanced engineering. The old box-section frame was replaced by a tubular structure and indepen-

Above: the HRG proved ideal for trials and rallies, and also enjoyed some success in the field of racing; this is a 1938 HRG 1½-litre competing in the Lawrence Cup Trial

dent suspension was utilised front and rear with transverse leaf springs and wishbones. Wire spoked wheels gave way to cast magnesium 'spiders' bolted on to Dunlop rims, and disc brakes were specified. These were manufactured by HRG under licence from the Palmer Tyre Co and were also sold to the nearby Cooper racing-car factory for use on their 500 cc Formula Three machines. The bodywork, in light alloy, was a pleasing, aerodynamic two-seater, and a coupé version was planned. Dry weight was quoted at $14\frac{1}{2}$ cwt (1624 lb). The basis of its engine was the Singer SM1500 (or Hunter) block and bottom end with an HRG-designed and built twin-overhead-camshaft, light-alloy cylinder head. Singer produced special steel crankshafts and connecting rods to cope with the increase of power—108 instead of the 55 bhp being claimed.

The prototype made its first competition appearance in the 1955 Goodwood Nine-Hours race driven by Peter Calvert/R. C. Green, but was a lowly twentieth and last after an off-course excursion. Singer were interested in taking over the manufacture of the new model. Their seriousness was underlined by the fact that a Singer Hunter saloon was displayed at the Motor

Show in October 1955 with a cast-iron version of HRG's twin-cam cylinder head.

The death knell of HRG was sounded, however, when the Rootes Group acquired Singer shortly afterwards and decided neither to produce the new HRG sports car nor to pursue the HRG-Singer

Top: shortly after World War II, HRG introduced the Aerodynamic model; it was the first British sports car to feature full-width bodywork. This is Ray Barrington-Brock's Aerodynamic 1500 cc coupé of 1948

Above left: this is the cockpit of the 1947 HRG 1500

Above right: Ian Dussek in action in his 1948 HRG 1500

Left: the 1496 cc Singer power unit seen here in a 1947 HRG 1500 model. This engine was a single-overhead-camshaft unit developing 65 bhp at 4800 rpm

Opposite page: the delightful HRG 1500

Hunter project. The prototype Hunter was, in fact, used in hill-climbs by George Hartwell. Rootes eventually abandoned the Singer engine altogether, a move which upset followers of the marque.

Two of the new HRG sports cars were raced in 1956 by Calvert and Green, but they were outclassed by more potent machinery designed primarily for the race track—Listers, Coopers, Lotuses, Elvas, etc. This was also the year when the 'traditional' two-seater sports cars, little changed from their introduction in 1935, were discontinued.

HRG Engineering continued to exist until 1966. They specialised in light-engineering work such as mechanical handling equipment, cylinder-head conversions and aluminium rocker covers. Their final fling in the car world was an experimental sports car first seen in 1965. A space-framed, open two-seater, it initially used a Ford Cortina engine and later appeared with a Vauxhall VX4/90 power unit before being abandoned when the firm was wound-up.

Of the HRG personalities, H. R. 'Dan' Godfrey died in 1968 at the age of 81 following a long illness. In the latter years of the company's history, he lived in retirement and the day-to-day affairs of HRG were handled by the enthusiastic company secretary, Miss Grace Leather. She had started as a secretary in 1936, became a director and was eventually sole proprietor

before the company stopped trading. Other post-war directors were Stuart Procter (who evolved the twin-cam head for the Singer SM 1500 engine and is today, in 1974, at the age of 78, a senior RAC scrutineer at race meetings), T. A. S. O. Mathieson (who retired to take up writing) and Lord Selsdon.

Today, the name of HRG is preserved by the HRG Association whose secretary, Ian Dussek, lives in Sevenoaks, Kent. It is believed that over 150 models survive to be used on the road. MK

Below: a 1947 HRG 1500 in racing trim

Centre: the 1966 Vauxhall VX 4/90-engined prototype

Bottom: the 1949 HRG 1500 cc racing lightweights

THE STOREKEEPER AND THE ENGINEER

Although the Hudson was named after the owner of one of Detroit's largest department stores, the men behind it were some of the motor industry's finest brains

Right: 1909 Hudson Model 20. The roadster was an immediate success as the first public offering of the Hudson Motor Car Co, which was founded on 24 February 1909. The original price was 900 dollars and the original model was finished in maroon, trimmed in black

Below right: the 1910 Hudson Model 21, with four of the eight pioneers who founded the Hudson company. From left to right: R. B. Jackson, Frederick O. Bezner, Howard E. Coffin and Roy D. Chapin

IN A SENSE, the beginnings of the US motor industry had something in common with the Book of Genesis—the part where Adam and Eve start the ball rolling and all the subsequent begetting to get the show on the road. So it was in Europe, too, of course, with engineers dreaming up all sorts of ideas both weird and wonderful and then looking around for businessmen to provide the necessary finance. In Europe, there was much interchange of people as well as ideas across the national borders (for instance, Peugeot bought their first engines from Panhard, who made them in France under licence from Daimler in Germany) and involvement of families—fathers and sons, brothers and in-laws who worked together for a time before branching out independently.

In America, there was more money, and more businessmen were controlling it; and there was so much interbreeding in the begetting process, that the family tree of the motor world soon looked like a tropical jungle of intertwining branches under a dense foliage of thousand-dollar bills.

Top left: a meeting of two early motoring pioneers; on the left is a 1911 Hudson

Top right: the stark and sporting Hudson Roadster Mile-a-Minute model of 1912

Above: a 1922 Hudson Super Six. This was one of Hudson's most popular models. It was introduced in 1916 and remained almost unchanged until 1930

Who were the men behind the begetting of the Hudson Motor Car Company early in 1909? There was the president, Joseph L. Hudson, businessman, founder of a big Detroit department store, whose name was also used for the Motor Company presumably because his purse provided most of the initial capital; and there was Roy D. Chapin who had worked previously for Ransom E. Olds (who created the Oldsmobile and, later, the Reo) and gained personal fame some eight years before, in 1901, by driving a single-cylinder Curved Dash Runabout from Detroit to the New York Show as a reliability and endurance stunt. Between Olds and Hudson, he had helped to get the E. R. Thomas-Detroit Co off the ground, and its successor, the Chalmers-Detroit Co. However, the Hudson promotion was to monopolise his attentions until his death in 1936. Another begetter was Howard Earl Coffin from Ohio, who had built a gas engine in 1897, a steam car two years later, and joined

R. E. Olds in 1902. After becoming Chief Engineer there, he broke away to help Chapin launch the E. R. Thomas-Detroit and its Chalmers successor, and finally the Hudson. By 1910, when vice-president of Hudson, he was President of the Society of Automobile Engineers and, in that capacity, did much to establish the standardisation of items like material specifications, to the great benefit of the industry as a whole.

Hugh Chalmers, vice-president of the National Cash Register Co, came on the motoring scene in 1907 by joining E. R. Thomas-Detroit and, in next to no time, had bought half the stock—hence the Chalmers-Detroit. The begetting along this line later led to Maxwell and Chrysler. Looking forward to 1954, that was the year of amalgamation with Nash and the start of the American Motors Corporation, thereby linking Hudson retrospectively with other makes such as Rambler, Jeffery, Ajax and LaFayette.

In June 1909, the *Saturday Evening Post* carried the

first-ever advertisement for the new Hudson car and, on 3 July, the first example reached the end of the assembly line. It was called the Model 20, and conformed in every respect with the established US pattern for a low-to-medium-priced automobile in technical specification, appearance and body styles. Indeed, in retrospect, it may seem astonishing that so many engineers designed such similar products and yet were able to talk big business into backing them. However, history has proved time and again that the unorthodox is unlikely to sell well even if it works well, unless there is sufficient confidence and material support to keep it afloat until the buying public has been won over; the Volkswagen phenomenon exemplifies this. Slight variations around a familiar theme are generally a better bet for the 'Top Ten'.

Where the Hudson seems to have scored from the outset was in providing a healthy power output from a conventional engine and better than average performance through matching cylinder capacity to body style and weight. And, as we shall see, they tended more than most to stick to an established design, carrying forward outmoded features such as splash-lubricated big-end bearings and wet clutches long after these had been abandoned by other makers, but concealing them beneath visual ornament that changed to suit the times.

So, Howard Coffin's Model 20 had a 20 bhp, four-cylinder monobloc engine with side valves under an L-head. Bore and stroke was $3\frac{3}{4} \times 3\frac{1}{2}$ in, fired by an HT magneto, and it transmitted through a cone clutch and three-speed gearbox. It had half-elliptic springs at each end and rode on non-detachable wood-spoked wheels. The two-seat roadster, with the option of a single bucket-type rumble seat or an extra large oval petrol tank behind the front seats, was claimed to reach 50 mph with a 3.5 to 1 final drive, a 4 to 1 ratio being optional for the heavier bodies. Four thousand Model 20s were sold that first season and, by the end of 1910, Hudson were rated seventeenth in the league of American car makers.

For 1911, the 20 was succeeded by the more-powerful Model 33, for which there were three body styles—pony tonneau, roadster and touring four-seater, the latter having step-over sides for the front seat, and doors only for the rear tonneau. That year, sales reached 6486. 1912 witnessed the death of J. L. Hudson and the birth of the first six-cylinder Hudson, the Model Six-54, a big and handsome machine with 6 litres and 54 bhp to propel it. Advertisements

claimed a maximum speed of 65 mph for the car and the ability to reach 58 mph from rest in half a minute. Standard equipment for the Six and the four-cylinder Model 37 (now with a 4-inch cylinder bore) included electric lighting, 'self-cranking', and even a clock and speedometer. The larger car, with a 127 in wheelbase, was offered with a range of open and closed bodies to seat from two to seven, and the 118 in wheelbase four-cylinder had up to five seats. The sales line this year was that these cars were the work of no fewer than 48 design engineers, some coming from France, Italy, Germany, England, Belgium and Austria. They had worked in 97 factories and had a hand in building 200,000 cars. 'Experiment has been eliminated. The errors due to lack of experience and lack of knowledge have been left out of these cars.' A feature of the big Six was a four-speed transmission with geared-up or overdrive fourth, an arrangement that Rolls-Royce had tried with the first Silver Ghosts several years earlier, but soon abandoned because the plaintive whine of indirect gears in the normal cruising range was unacceptable.

By 1914, when the 4-cylinder had become the Model 40 (40 bhp) by virtue of having the crankshaft stretched

Top: a Hudson Super Six; to demonstrate the reliability of the car, the Super Six was driven from New York to San Francisco and back again, the first car ever to complete the journey. The outward journey took 5 days $3\frac{1}{2}$ hours while the return to New York took 5 days $17\frac{1}{2}$ hours—a remarkable feat by both men and machines in those days

Above: one of the many variations on the Super Six theme, this is the 1921 Landaulette, a model much favoured by President Hoover

with $5\frac{1}{4}$ in throws to bring it into line with the Six, Hudson considered themselves the world's largest manufacturer of six-cylinder cars, and total sales reached a record 10,261; by 1915, they were up again to close on 13,000, obviously unaffected by the war in Europe. The following year was even more successful, with production doubled (25,772) through the introduction of an instant winner, the Super-Six, and adoption of a one-model policy. Thereafter, there was never to be another four-cylinder engine behind the

Below: a 1922 Hudson Super Six Coach

Bottom: yet another of the Super Six range, this being the 1925 four-door sedan

famous red triangle badge, and the cylinder dimensions of the Super-Six were to remain unchanged right through to 1930, at $3\frac{1}{2} \times 5$ in (88.9×127 mm, 4739 cc). Right from its initiation, the Super-Six was marketed with either sedan, cabriolet, town car or limousine bodywork in addition to the touring versions, some having wire-spoked wheels. To demonstrate its staying power and performance over a long distance, a Super-Six became the first car to make the double crossing of the North American continent against the clock—outward from New York to San Francisco in 5 days $3\frac{1}{2}$ hours, and back again in 5 days $17\frac{1}{2}$ hours. A contemporary photograph shows a wire-wheeled touring car with four begoggled passengers looking (car and occupants) very travel-stained on a stony track in the Sierra Nevada. For a round trip of more than 7000 miles over every type of going—much of it unsurfaced and including mountain ranges and long tracts of desert—this was a very remarkable feat by both men and machine. Five years earlier the record for the single east-west journey, achieved by a Reo, had been only six hours less than the Super-Six's double crossing, but in the interim there had been a lot of road-building.

By 1917, the USA was embroiled directly in World War I and chief designer Howard Coffin's time was largely occupied with the US Board of Aeronautics, of which he was chairman. President Hoover had taken to a Super-Six landaulet and Hudson's output of almost 21,000 for the year included a large batch of military ambulances. Floyd Clymer's *Catalog of 1918 Cars* lists no fewer than ten body styles for the

Super-Six, each with identical specification apart from wheel and tyre dimensions, even the $125\frac{1}{2}$ in wheelbase being common to all. In America, the elegant nomenclature of the Horse Age persisted in the motor industry and, indeed, to this day there are broughams and landaus to be had. Simplest and cheapest of the Hudson range was a Seven-Passenger Phaeton (open tourer) for $1950, and you could have bought two of those with a bit of change left over for the price of the Full Folding Landau ($4250). Between these extremes were the Four-Passenger Phaeton (more costly than the Seven-Passenger for some reason) at $2050, a Runabout Landau at $2350, a Four-Door Sedan at $2750, a Touring Limousine at $3150, a Limousine at $3400 and Limousine Landau for $3500, or Town Car for $3400, and a Limousine Landau or Town Car Landau for $3500. In those days, the House colour for Hudsons was blue, but there was a choice of blues—Coach-painter's, Hungarian or India; other finishes were also available. Limousine equipment included a heater for the rear compartment, footrests and pillows, a vanity case and courtesy lights. Wood-spoked artillery wheels with detachable rims were the standard wear, with the option of centre-lock wire wheels and, in each case, the back wheels only were braked by contracting and expanding shoes sharing common drums, and actuated by the pedal and hand lever respectively.

At the Detroit Show for 1919 models, Hudson introduced a cheaper line under another name, as other major US companies were to do. This was the Essex, destined to turn full circle again in later years via the Essex Terraplane, then simply Terraplane and finally Hudson Terraplane. In the years 1919–32, some 1,331,000 Essex cars greatly expanded Hudson business and, in fact, their sales in the peak years 1925–29 greatly exceeded those of the parent company. Through to the end of 1923, it had a 2.9-litre, four-cylinder engine with overhead inlet valves and side exhausts. One source credits it with 55 bhp, giving the car a top speed around 60 mph, but this seems scarcely likely when related to the Model A Ford of some years later, which drew only 40 bhp from 3.3 litres and could also reach 60 mph. However, in the USA, there have always been discrepancies between the brake-horse-powers developed in boardrooms and those actually provided for the customer to transmit to the road. Cylinder dimensions were 85.7×127 mm, or $3\frac{3}{8} \times 5$ in, cooling was by thermo-syphon, the big-end bearings were lubricated by splash, and a three-speed gearbox was engaged through the customary Hudson multi-plate wet clutch. Initially, the Essex carried three body styles—four-door sedan, five-passenger phaeton and roadster with rumble seat. Advertisements extolled its light weight, durability, rich appointments, low cost and economy, and boasted it was a 'tremendous performer'. 'The Essex's motor would inspire a whole season's advertising campaign,' they wrote. 'A slogan might be written about its beauty.' Indeed it might, like: *'Even the right-angles are wrong angles'*. Not that it was any uglier than most US cars in that era of almost uniform sameness and drabness, before a brilliant nucleus of styling engineers, working first on their own account, had expanded their influence beyond the premises of the specialist coachbuilders. Even in its first year, however, the Essex outsold its costlier stablemate 21,879 to 18,175. In its second year, the Essex pioneered a very significant commodity, a two-door coach so inexpensive as to be within reach of humble buyers who hitherto had been denied closed coachwork. With its uncompromising boxy figure relieved only by a shapely posterior, it was not beautiful, but by

1925, 80% of Essex production was two-door coaches and other makers had had to follow suit. In 1920, a large fleet of Essex phaetons was ordered for rural deliveries of US mail and, to publicise this commercial jackpot, the company despatched four on transcontinental runs; one completed the classic San Francisco to New York marathon in 4 days 14 hours and 43 minutes. In that year, too, a specially equipped Essex phaeton was delivered to Edward, Prince of Wales. It quickly became a favourite in export markets and, in

1922, a Japanese hotel proprietor in Tokyo acquired a batch of 42. It is not known how many of these survived the great earthquake and devastating fires there in 1923, but a record of vehicles registered in that city soon after the disaster reveals that Essex were second only to the Model T Ford.

In 1924 came the first six-cylinder Essex which very soon supplanted the Rapid Four, as it was called. It had a side-valve engine of only 2.1 litres capacity, increased by three stages (in 1925, 1927 and 1929) to 2.6 litres, which final form carried it through to the end of the marque's existence three years later. After several lean years of post-war depression, the Hudson-Essex fortunes rose rapidly from 1923's 89,000-odd to almost 134,000 customers in 1924 and over 300,000 in 1929, of which about a third were Hudsons; after that, of course, the bricks of Wall Street suddenly crumbled away and things were never the same again for the Hudson Motor Car Company. During this period, the Essex was given balloon tyres (1925) and front brakes (optional from 1927 and standardised the following season), a plated radiator shell in place of a painted one from 1926 and also, for 1927, this item was changed in form from pseudo-Rolls-Royce angular with horizontal shutters to the arched style of the Hudson. As a guide to its place in the industry, the cheapest US car in 1929 was the Ford 'A' roadster at a rock-bottom $385, and the cheapest sedan, on the same chassis, cost $495; next in succession came the Whippet coach at $535, Chevrolet and Durant at $595, Plymouth at $690 and Essex at $695. In England, one could buy an Essex for as little as £185 in 1932.

Reverting to the true Hudson, the Super-Six was in full swing in 1919, but we should look back two years earlier to this model's first competition success, when R. Mulford drove a stripped and tuned version to victory in a 150-mile race on a track at Omaha at an average of 101 mph; in 1919, another finished in ninth place in the Indianapolis 500 with Ira Vail at the wheel.

Above: the Hudson Super Six, the model which formed the backbone of Hudson production for over thirty years. This is a 1929 model fitted with wire wheels and an elegant body coachbuilt by Grosvenor of London. The engine was a six-cylinder, 4739 cc unit

Then, in 1927, the famous cigar-smoking Barney Oldfield drove a two-door coach around the Culver City Speedway for a thousand miles at an overall average speed of 76 mph. It would have been powered by a new engine with the same cylinder dimensions ($3\frac{1}{2} \times 5$ in) but fitted with overhead inlet valves like the obsolete Essex Rapid Four. After a three-year run, the inlet-over-exhaust layout was again abandoned in favour of the simple L-head side-valve and, from that time on, no Hudson engines were made with valves in the head, although a few of the last cars to bear the name had ohv engines by Packard and American Motors.

In the peak year of 1929, Hudson-Essex combined rated third among America's best sellers, but this does not tell all the story because these cars were enjoying an exceptional popularity in overseas markets. For instance, more than 17% (about 40,000 cars) of the 1928 production went overseas, and this export prestige endured right through to the outbreak of war in 1939. The next landmark was in 1930 when a straight-eight engine was introduced to supplement the six-cylinder, but replaced it the following year as the sole Hudson

power plant. This was a neat piece of rationalisation in that it shared the cylinder bore and crankshaft stroke of the six-cylinder Essex, so that certain parts were interchangeable. This five-bearing unit received an increase in cylinder bore to 76 mm in 1932, bringing the swept volume to 4168 cc, and in that form it remained in production, still with its splash-fed big-ends, through to 1953, with successive increases in power output from 95 bhp at 3500 rpm to 128 at 4200.

Although there was no aesthetic pleasure to be had within the engine room of a Hudson Eight or its derivatives, which frankly looked a mess by comparison with its European counterparts, this strictly conventional unit was undoubtedly one of the finest of its time. It gave a very good power output, with lively response and a healthy torque curve from very low revs. It was also silky smooth, easy to maintain and reliable over long periods. Moreover, the Hudson chassis was comparatively light so that the power/weight ratio was favourable. The proof of this is evident in the retention of the same engine for over twenty years within body shells that were changed many times, fundamentally or in details of decor, in the

Below: 1932 Hudson eight-cylinder Phaeton

Right: from back to front, a 1932 Phaeton, a 1932 coupé and a 1927 coupé

Below right: a range of 1936 models with the 'world's first safety engineered chassis'

rat-race of the 1930s when Hudson were trying to recapture their earlier hold on the market now dominated by Ford, General Motors and Chrysler.

When the lighter Terraplane range had the option of the straight-eight from 1933, it inspired the first and most famous of a new breed of Anglo-American sporting concoctions which became quite a vogue in the 1930s. This was the Railton, which earned itself a reputation out of proportion to the small numbers sold—only 1460 including 81 with six-cylinder engines —during the years 1933–39, plus a handful after the war. The Railton was sponsored by Sir Noel Macklin, who had previously been the driving force behind the all-British Invicta, and was assembled in the old Invicta works at Cobham in Surrey. He engaged the services of Reid Railton, renowned designer of land-speed-record and track-racing cars who, in later years, emigrated to the USA and became a consultant engineer to Hudson. Railton modified the Terraplane chassis to improve its handling characteristics and bring it closer to the European concept of a sporting platform; he dropped the frame to lower the build, fitted Hartford friction dampers and raised the steering box ratio. A handsome radiator shell strongly remininiscent of the Invicta was complemented by a long bonnet with the earlier car's characteristic raised rivet heads along the hinges. Considering the car's

modest production output, the range of body styles offered was very ambitious. All were strictly British in appearance, emulating those of more expensive makes; for 1937, for instance, there were no fewer than three open tourers, three saloons, a coupé and convertible coupé on the shorter of alternative wheelbases, and a saloon, convertible and limousine on the long wheelbase. They were very lively performers with a maximum speed of around 90 mph, and a Light Sports Tourer with very spartan equipment, of which very few were made, was tested by a contemporary journal and recorded just over 100 mph, complemented by an acceleration time from zero to 60 mph of under 9 secs, which was sensational in those days. In 1938, one of these took the sports-car record at the famous Shelsley Walsh hill-climb.

For Hudson, the 1930s were a turbulent period of fluctuating fortunes, profits and losses, with annual production dropping from around 114,000 in 1930 to only 41,000 in 1933; thereafter, rising progressively to over 123,000 in 1936 and falling again to 51,000 in '38, in which year they suffered a trading loss of nearly

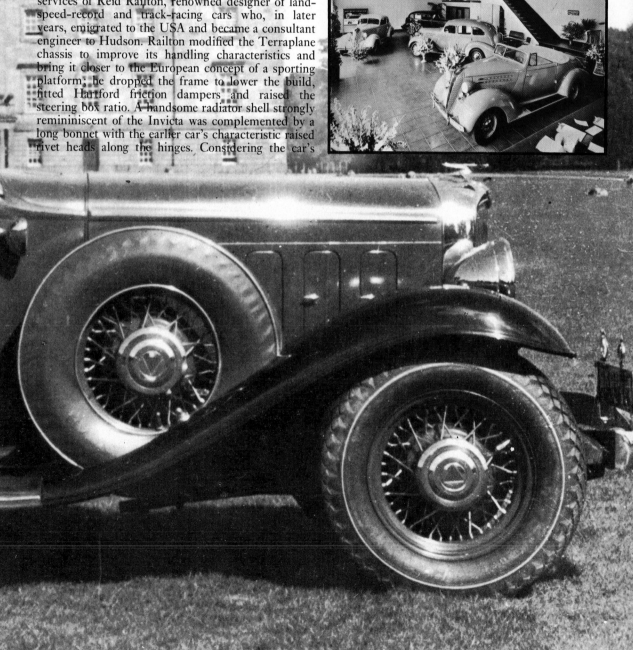

$4.7 million. While Europe was at war, the output was up once more to 87,000 in 1940, with a loss of $1.5 million but, the following year, they were in the black again with $3¾ million profit although fewer than 80,000 cars were sold.

In retrospect, the handsomest years from the styling viewpoint were perhaps 1930–33, before the arrival of valanced wings, ever more elaborate radiator shells and all the other gimmicky additives planned to date earlier models and attract new custom. In July 1932, the brave American aviatrix Amelia Earhart went to Detroit to christen the first-off Essex Terraplane in the presence of Orville Wright and, later that year, one of these cars broke the stock-car record for the classic Pike's Peak hill-climb in Colorado. Meanwhile, Hudson chief Roy D. Chapin was appointed Secretary of Commerce by President Hoover. Hudson fans also

remember 1932 as the year the company built the only really unconventional cars in its long history; these were six eight-wheeled specials commissioned by the Japanese Government and used in the Manchurian war. They had four wheels at the back, two steered front wheels and two idler wheels just behind these, raised clear of the ground by a few inches so that they only contacted the ground over very rough terrain. The bodies were typical staff-car open tourers.

In 1934, the Terraplane's 2.6-litre side-valve six, which developed about 75 bhp, was supplemented by a 3.5-litre six, which was later added to the Hudson range as an alternative to the eight. At about this time, there was a rather brief adoption of a curious form of independent front suspension named Axleflex. Each wheel was carried on a three-quarter length beam axle, giving it a swing-axle geometry, in conjunction with ordinary semi-elliptic springs. After a year or two, this was dropped in favour of a rigid beam axle located by radial torque arms, the springs being shackled at each end and relieved of all torque loads.

From 1934 to 1938, after the Essex name had been dropped, the Terraplane became almost indistinguishable from the top-line Hudson, sharing many of the body pressings as well as the 3½-litre, six-cylinder engine and, in 1939, the two 'makes' became one. For 1935, there was the option of an electric gear-shift—

Electric Hand—in conjunction with a conventional three-speed box having a constant-mesh middle gear, and vacuum-operated clutch. This was the single-plate type with cork inserts and running in oil, which Hudson had adopted in 1929 and retained even through to the early 1950s for the 145 bhp 6-cylinder Hornet.

In February 1936, Roy D. Chapin died; his place was taken by A. E. Barit, who had been with the company since its inception and carried it through to the merger with Nash and formation of American Motors in 1954, whereupon he became a director of that combine. Bendix hydraulic brakes were adopted in 1936, replacing the Bendix self-wrapping mechanicals which were so effective when in good order with all the adjustments correctly set, but could be so fiendishly wayward and unpredictable if anything was amiss. The new hydraulics were supported by a mechanical system which took over whenever they sprang a fluid leak.

In the war years, from 1941, Hudson ran a plant, near Detroit, manufacturing anti-aircraft machine guns and sub-assemblies for aircraft, and stopped car production in February 1942 to devote all their resources to these and other military hardware— Helldiver folding wings, Airacobra cabins, engines for landing boats and many other items. The car assembly

Top: the Hudson six-cylinder business coupé of 1939

Above: a 1946 Commodore Eight Sedan. The post-war Hudsons were basically 1942 models with minor front-end styling alterations

lines started rolling again in August 1945 with 1942 models, the front-end styling being rehashed for the following year's products. A shortage of steel kept production below demand for a time but, in 1947, they were able to celebrate completion of the three-millionth Hudson made since 1909.

For the 1948 model year, Hudson took their first really bold step forward into hitherto untrodden territory by bringing out an entirely new line with unitary construction of body and chassis, the innovation being that the frame enclosed the rear wheels. They called it their Step-Down Design, since the floor was considerably lower than the structural sills forming the side-members, and only the lower part of the back wheels was exposed to view. Independent coil-spring front suspension was introduced for the new range. The old straight-eight 4168 cc engine, now

and 3.8-litre, 112 bhp, six-cylinder engine. In the following year, the Hudson plant in Canada, set up in 1932, was again set in motion, and automatic transmission became optional for all the range.

However, once again, the company was in financial trouble: following a post-war peak in 1949–50, when production had comfortably exceeded 140,000, with the books showing over $10 million profit for 1949, there was a rapid decline to 93,000 in '51, 78,000 in '53 and a loss of over $10 million, and right down to 32,000 in '54. Unfortunately, the Hornet failed to retrieve the situation despite wide publicity for its virtual supremacy in stock-car racing, and extravagant styling with annual chromium-plated face-lifts to keep the fashions changing. The Hornet engine was just over 5 litres (96.8 × 114.3 mm) and gave 145 bhp at 3800 rpm, using a 7.2 compression ratio, and the

Below: Hudsons at the London Motor Show, Earl's Court in 1953. In the foreground, left, is the Italia, with coachwork by Touring; on the right is the Jet Liner; behind is the Hornet Special, one of the last Hudsons to be built in Detroit

claimed top speed of the sedan was 98–103 mph.

Early in 1953, yet another major effort to keep the company afloat materialised in the form of a compact light car, the Jet, with 3.3-litre six giving 104 bhp and wheelbase of only 105 in. There were Jets, Jet Liners and Super Jets, but they never really caught the public fancy. Meantime, the Pacemaker had given place to the Wasp and Super Wasp, the Hornet engine was boosted to 160 bhp and the faithful straight-eight was finally abandoned. A special leather-trimmed coupé called the Hudson Italia, to be built in limited numbers with bodywork by Touring of Milan and powered by a 114 bhp Jet engine, appeared at the international motor shows; all to no avail, though, and after 1954, no more Hudsons left the Detroit factory.

Resulting from the merger with Nash-Kelvinator, concluded in May 1954, Hudson production was transferred to Kenosha, Wisconsin, and the 1955 Wasps and Hornets were Nash-bodied with Hudson stings, apart from the Rambler compact which could sail under Hudson colours, if you wished, simply by a change of badges. As mentioned earlier, the last of the Hornets were powered by first Packard and then AM V8 motors and, after 1957, they were at last allowed to fade away after being progressively stripped of all the individualistic character and respectability invested in them by Roy D. Chapin and his associates. **RB**

Above: the last ever Hudson to be built, model 35787-2, which was completed on 25 June 1957

developing 128 bhp at 4200 rpm on a 6.5 to 1 compression ratio, was still the mainstay for the top quality models, but was now supplemented by a slightly larger, 4.3-litre, side-valve six giving 121 bhp at 4000 rpm. Appropriately, this was named the Super-Six. To take the place of the pre-war Terraplane, a lower-priced series, the Pacemaker, was added in 1949, with the same step-down body construction

The soft-hearted Old Bear

SOME RACING DRIVERS show an intuitive ability at the wheel of a racing car almost as soon as they step into their first racing machine. Others need to work away for many years, gradually honing their skills until they eventually reach the upper echelons of the profession. Examples of the former are Jimmy Clark and Jackie Stewart, but a prime example of the latter is Denny Hulme who had been a racing driver for nine years before he was given a drive in a Formula One car. However, after that, progress was rapid for he became World Champion within two years.

Born on 18 June 1936, Denis Clive Hulme (pronounced 'Hulm' rather than 'Hume') was the son of Clive Hulme, who gained distinction by winning the Victoria Cross during World War II, and his home town was Nelson in New Zealand. As with so many other racing drivers, schooling was suffered rather than enjoyed and much of his youth was spent on his grandparent's tobacco farm at Motueka on New Zealand's South Island. After the war, Hulme's family moved to Te Puke on the Bay of Plenty in the North Island, where his father started a small haulage business. After leaving school, Denny went to work in a garage where he soon showed an aptitude for engineering which he used to good effect when working on his father's fleet of trucks, tractors and cars. His father also paid him for delivering materials to farmers and Denny saved hard to buy his first car, a brand new MG TF.

The MG was kept for three years and, during that time, he joined a car club, taking part in his first event, a local hill-climb in 1956. He showed a liking for racing and often beat his rivals in events on the North Island. After three years with the TF, he graduated to a MGA, then to a 2-litre Cooper-Climax which was bought with the help of his parents. This was potentially one of the fastest cars in New Zealand at the time and, after he had rebuilt it, he began to win races in great numbers. So successful was his 1959/60 season that he was nominated by the New Zealand International Grand Prix Association for their 'Driver to Europe' scheme, which each year financed a promising young driver for a year's racing in Europe. The previous year, Bruce McLaren had been the winner, and for 1960 the NZIGPA picked both Hulme and George Lawton to go to Europe. Hulme chose a Cooper-BMC Formula Junior car and barnstormed around Europe, racing every weekend, gaining experience all the time. However, his friend Lawton was killed in Denmark and Hulme almost decided to give up racing, but he returned to New Zealand with a 2½-litre Cooper-Climax in 1961 and later that year he went back to Europe again to rejoin the Formula Junior circus. There was little money to be made in Formula

Above: Denny Hulme in a McLaren M8D, the car with which he won the Canadian-American Challenge Cup for the second time

Junior so, to make ends meet, he worked as a mechanic in Jack Brabham's garage in Chessington, Surrey. He was invited to drive a works Abarth at Le Mans in 1961, finishing an excellent fourteenth overall with countryman Angus Hyslop. In 1962, he was asked to drive Ken Tyrrell's FJ Cooper on occasions and then, later that year, he was invited to take over the works Formula Junior Brabham after Gavin Youl retired from racing. Brabham's manager, Phil Kerr, persuaded Jack Brabham to give Hulme a chance; Kerr and Hulme then worked together almost continuously until Hulme's retirement.

Hulme's first full season with the Brabham was in 1963, when he won seven races out of fourteen starts, but he was still not a full professional as he had to work in the garage and prepare his own car. By now, he was married to Greeta, a fellow New Zealander, who travelled with him to all the races around the World.

The successes of 1963 spurred Jack Brabham to invite Hulme to join him in the all-conquering Brabham Formula Two team for 1964, and between them they cleaned up most of the F2 races on the calendar, Brabham winning the Championship with Hulme second. For 1965, the F2 Brabhams were powered by Honda engines, which were far more powerful than the Cosworth engines used by most of the opposition, so both Brabham and Hulme picked up some easy wins over the 1965 and 1966 seasons. Jack Brabham gave Hulme occasional drives in non-Championship Formula One races during 1964, but Brabham himself—and Dan Gurney—did most of the F1 driving. However, Hulme

took Gurney's place at Monaco in 1965, finishing eighth, and later in the year he finished fourth in the French GP and fifth in the Dutch GP. He also won the Tourist Trophy in a Brabham BT8 sports car.

When Formula One changed to 3 litres in 1966, Gurney left the team to build his own cars and Hulme was given the second seat alongside Jack Brabham. The team ran what were considered underpowered Repco V8-engined Brabhams, but they proved ideal and, in 1966, Brabham won the World Championship. Hulme picked up a second place in the British GP and also took third places in France, Italy and Mexico to end up fourth in the Championship.

At long last, Hulme had reached the pinnacle of motor racing and, the following season, he outstripped his boss by taking the World Championship, winning the Grands Prix of Monaco and Germany, finishing second in the French and British GPs and third in Holland, the United States and Mexico. That season, he also finished fourth at Indianapolis in an Eagle and second in the Can-Am Championship where he drove a McLaren M8 to victory at Road America, Bridgehampton and Mosport.

For the 1968 season, Hulme was wooed away from the Brabham team by McLaren, where Phil Kerr was now general manager. He drove the M7A in Formula One and the M8A in Can-Am events, winning another three Can-Am races as well as the Italian GP, the Canadian GP and the International Trophy at Silverstone. With other good placings, he took third place in the World Championship. He also drove a Lola T70

for Sid Taylor in British sports-car events, winning the Tourist Trophy, the Players Trophy and the Martini race at Silverstone.

By 1969, the McLaren F1 car was less competitive and his only victory came right at the end of the season in the Mexican GP. However, he won no less than five Can-Am races in the works M8B McLaren-Chevrolet to finish second in the Championship to team mate Bruce McLaren.

Early in the 1970 season, Bruce McLaren was killed while testing a Can-Am car at Goodwood, but the remaining directors decided to carry on with the team. Hulme himself received badly burned hands when his car caught fire at Indianapolis, which put him out of racing for several weeks, but he won no less than six Can-Am races, to clinch the title again. He picked up a number of good placings in Formula One such as second in South Africa, third in England, Germany and Mexico, together with fourth places in Monte Carlo, France and Italy, but victory eluded him.

By now, he was a public figure in several continents, but, like his old boss Jack Brabham, he was basically shy and introverted; he hated giving speeches and was seldom good for a quote after a race. If anyone rubbed him up the wrong way he would give them his opinion in colourful language, a reputation which soon earned him the nickname of the 'old bear', because bears often have sore heads! However, with friends and colleagues, away from the spotlight of the circuits, he was invariably more relaxed and excellent amusing company.

The 1971 season was very disappointing, no doubt because the McLaren team was still feeling the reaction from the loss of Bruce McLaren and Hulme picked up a meagre nine points in the World Championship. He was

partnered in Can-Am races by Peter Revson and, although Hulme won at Mosport, Edmonton and Riverside, he had to take second place to his team mate, who won five races.

With the M19 McLaren, Denny Hulme had a much better 1972 season in Formula One, winning the South African GP, as well as finishing second in Austria and Argentina and third in Belgium, Italy and the USA. This gave him 39 points and a fine third place in the World Championship.

The new M23 Formula One McLaren was ready for most of the 1973 races, but Hulme had very little success with it, although he did win the Swedish Grand Prix. His best places apart from that win were a couple of third places in Brazil and England. He was overshadowed by his team mate Peter Revson who won the British and Canadian GPs. McLaren had, by now,

Denny's McLarens at Monaco: *top*, the M19A in 1972, and *above*, the M23 in 1974

withdrawn from Can-Am racing due to the overwhelming superiority of the Porsches, so Hulme contented himself with Formula One racing.

He was joined in the McLaren team for 1974 by Emerson Fittipaldi, the young Brazilian proving somewhat quicker than the 38-year-old New Zealander. However, Hulme showed that he was by no means finished by winning the Argentinian GP and taking a well earned second place in the Austrian GP. Nevertheless, with his team mate winning the World Championship, it was eventually announced that the taciturn Hulme would retire at the end of the 1974 season and return to the more peaceful life in New Zealand.   MT

979

HUMBER SCEPTRE

The Humber company once had its own individual range of cars in its own sector of the market and although, in 1974, it is still competing in that small sector, the cars are basically badge-variations of the more basic Hillman Hunters. Two Sceptre models are available: the saloon and an estate version.

Based on the Rootes Arrow body-shell, the Sceptre is powered by the Hunter GT engine producing 82 bhp, enabling the car to attain a top speed of 100 mph (saloon) and 98 mph (estate). A four-speed manual gearbox with overdrive on third and fourth gears is standard, while a four-speed Borg-Warner automatic transmission is available as an option on both models of the series.

The car has independent suspension on the front by means of coil spring/telescopic-damper struts, lower wishbones acting as trailing links and an anti-roll bar. The rear suspension is non-independent by a rigid axle, semi-elliptic leaf springs and telescopic dampers.

Standard equipment on the Sceptres includes a comprehensive range of instruments and a push-button radio set into the polished-wood fascia (which matches the centre console and door cappings), four individual cloth-covered seats, a 'leather'-grain vinyl roof covering and a vanity compartment for the rear passengers. The estate version has imitation-wood panels on the tailgate and door posts, a wiper/washer unit for the rear window and a factory-fitted roof rack as standard. All Sceptre models have Sundym glass to reduce glare.

ENGINE Front-mounted, water-cooled in-line four. 81.5 mm (3.21 in) bore × 82.5 mm (3.25 in) stroke = 1725 cc (105.3 cu in); maximum power 82 bhp at 5200 rpm; maximum torque 93 lb ft at 3300 rpm; maximum engine rpm 6000. Cast-iron cylinder block and light-alloy head; compression ratio 9.2:1. 5 main bearings. 2 valves per cylinder operated, via pushrods and rockers, by a single side-mounted camshaft. 2 Zenith-Stromberg 150 CD3 1½-inch semi-downdraught carburettors.

TRANSMISSION Single-dry-plate clutch and four-speed manual gearbox. Ratios 1st 3.352, 2nd 1.993, 3rd 1.296, Overdrive 3rd 1.13, 4th 1, Overdrive 4th 0.802, rev 3.323:1. Hypoid-bevel final drive. Ratio 3.890. Optional Borg-Warner 45 4-speed automatic transmission. Torque converter ratio at stall: 2.26. Ratios 1st 3.0, 2nd 1.937, 3rd 1.351, 4th 1, rev 4.692:1. Final-drive ratio 3.700.

CHASSIS Integral.

SUSPENSION Front—Independent by coil-spring/telescopic-damper struts, lower wishbones acting as trailing links and an anti-roll bar. Rear—non independent by a rigid axle, semi-elliptic leaf springs and telescopic dampers.

STEERING Recirculating ball; turns from lock to lock 3.36; adjustable steering column.

BRAKES Servo-assisted front discs and rear drums.

WHEELS 5 in × 13 in steel.

TYRES 155 × 13.

DIMENSIONS AND WEIGHT Wheelbase 98.50 in; track—front and rear 51.80 in; length 169.50 in; width 64.75 in; height 56 in; ground clearance 6.75 in; dry weight 2035 lb; turning circle between walls 36 ft; fuel tank capacity 10 gals.

BODY Saloon; 4-door, 5 seats.

PERFORMANCE Maximum speed 100 mph (manual saloon), 98 mph (manual estate), 97 mph (automatic saloon) or 95 mph (automatic estate); fuel consumption 29 mpg (manual cars) or 27 mpg (automatics).

Quality and comfort before performance

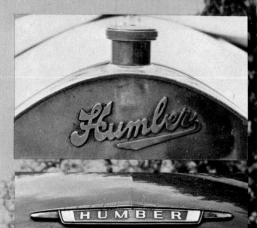

Above: the 1903 Humberette, a two-seater four-wheeler fitted with a five horsepower, water-cooled engine

THE HUMBER COMPANY always projected an image of quality and comfort for their products, which led inevitably to excess weight and consequently to lack of performance. Their one foray into the world of high performance was in 1914 when they spent £15,000 on a three-car team for the Tourist Trophy, run at the Brooklands track, and it would be fair to say that their effort was a dismal failure. Yet, ironically enough, designers who came from Humber had a big hand in the Bentley sports/racing cars and, later, the Jaguar concern.

Humber are usually credited with producing their first car in 1900, and even the 1974 owners of the name, Chrysler United Kingdom Ltd, put the date of the first car at 1899. In fact, the true date of the first model was 1896, when the three-horsepower Forecar was unleashed on a world avid for the newfangled mechanised transport.

The company itself began even earlier, when Mr Thomas Humber opened his pedal-cycle works in Great Alfred Street, Nottingham, in 1868, to produce a diamond-frame machine which was described at the time as a curious-looking contraption. In spite of this, Thomas Humber quickly made a name for a quality article and soon outgrew the capacity of his small works so moving to Beeston, near Nottingham, and turning himself into a limited liability company. The first move, to open the new works, came after only four years, in 1872, and it was five years later that Humber became a limited company (in 1877) with Thomas Humber as general manager.

Curiously enough, the rivalry between the Beeston works and the later Coventry factory lived on well into the motor-car era, and fans of the Beeston-Humber swore that the workmanship was better than that of its 'rival'—made by the same concern. Humber did well in the cycling boom of the nineties, but a destructive fire hit them in 1897, ten years after they had become a limited-liability company, and they were forced to move to Wolverhampton. This proved to be a temporary halt on the way to the Stoke area of Coventry, where they finally settled down. A signpost one mile outside Coventry on the Dunchurch road pointed the traveller to Humbertown, a self-contained community on twenty-two acres of ground. Even in the very early days, many people paid £30 for a Beeston-Humber pushbike when the 'common-or-garden bicycle' could be bought for £10.

Although Humber carried the quality image on from cycles to cars, they always aimed at the middle-man or middle-classes rather than the very bottom and cheapest segment of the market, or the rich man who wanted the very best. They pitched their aim at a sound quality article with enduring and endearing qualities at a reasonable middle-price. In spite of this, their first effort, the Forecar, owed much to the bicycle, with its spindly wheels and saddle for the driver, and a chair-type seat up front, ahead of the driver, in tricycle style; in fact, it looked like a tricycle with a fourth wheel added. Power was by way of a modest three-horsepower single-cylinder engine, with

Above: An 1899 Humber Phaeton. The car was powered by a 3 hp air-cooled motor in front, and was fitted with belt transmission and three speeds

Right: a 1903 Humberette 5 hp, fitted with two gear levers mounted on the steering column; one engaged high and low gears and the other forward and reverse

Louis Coatalen, a French designer now numbered among the greats, joined them and produced for the 1902 motor show, a much more ambitious machine, a 12-horsepower four-cylinder mated to a four-speed gearbox and fitted in a tubular frame. This was a very modern design, with both hot-tube and electric ignition, which was shown with a limousine body with curved plate-glass windows.

By 1903, the Humberette, still in production, had been modernised and was on offer with a choice of 5, 6 or 7.5-horsepower engines having the new four-speed gearbox and the chains replaced by shaft drive. These cars were made both at Beeston and at Coventry and they perpetuated the rivalry between the two factories. One of their daring innovations was a single-spoke steering wheel, as used—in not exactly the same form—on Citroëns in more recent times.

It was during this period that Humber entered a Beeston-Humber 24-horsepower model for the 1907 Tourist Trophy in the Isle of Man in the heavy class—and won. This was a production model, though, as TT entries were then required to be, rather than a racing machine. Meanwhile, Coatalen's 12 was so popular that the company ran out of space at their Coventry works and, as soon as their chassis had wheels on, they were pushed into the street where the 'assembly line'

Top: Humber's first effort, the Forecar, owed much to the bicycle, with its spindly wheel and saddle for the driver plus a passenger seat mounted in front

Above right: the Beeston-Humber 24 hp, winner of the 1907 Isle of Man Tourist Trophy heavy class; it was driven by S. P. Mills with J. Swift as mechanic

Above left: a 1908 Humber, fitted with a twin-cylinder, 1085 cc engine

pedals provided to help it up hills. This elementary and basic machine appeared at the first London Motor Show, held at the Imperial Institute in 1896. At this time, Humber came under the influence of the in-famous Mr J. H. Lawson, who formed the British Motor Syndicate in an attempt to gain monopoly control of the struggling British motor industry. Lawson tried to buy up everyone and everything in sight, and one of his tame inventors was E. J. Penning-ton of Chicago, whose Kane-Pennington engines powered the early Humbers, situated at the rear of course. The curious MD Voiturette shown by Humber at the Stanley Show of 1899 was powered by a $2\frac{1}{4}$-horsepower De Dion-Bouton engine, however, driving the front wheels, the rear wheels being steered. There was also, about this time, another device over which it is better perhaps to draw a veil, the Humber Phaeton, driven by a mixture of belts and gears to the rear axle. However, by the turn of the century, Lawson's empire was crumbling and on 27 March 1900 the Humber company became Humber Ltd, with capital of £500,000, and independent of Mr Lawson.

Humber then began making the Humberette, a two-seater four-wheeler with a five horsepower, water-cooled engine, and during the following year (1901)

continued and the major units were fitted.

Their later venture, in the 1914 TT, was with a true racing car designed by F. T. Burgess, who later move on to join W. O. Bentley and help with the successful three-litre Bentley. His Humber racer was astonishingly modern, with four valves per cylinder and twin overhead camshafts, claimed to develop nearly 100 horsepower at 3200 rpm from 3295 cc. The cars went well enough and very fast, but not one of them finished the race, and the war put a stop to any further development of the only Humber sports car.

During World War I, Humber made aeroplane engines and complete aircraft. They had, in fact, begun this work several years earlier, when they claimed to be the only British firm making complete aeroplanes. At the 1911 general meeting of the company, there was some criticism of the credit balance of £11,038, and the chairman, Mr Duncan F. Basden, referred to the setback caused by the placing on the market of a motor car which did a great deal of harm to the company, but unfortunately, did not specify which model.

After the war, in which they had made 25 aeroplane engines a week in addition to field kitchens, shells, bombs and fuse containers, Humber Ltd turned back to cars and cycles and in 1926 linked up with the

983

commercial-vehicle industry in the shape of Commer Cars Ltd of Luton. Then, in 1928, Humber bought the Hillman Motor Car Company, whose works were next door at Stoke. Humbers had shown profits of more than £100,000 yearly, up to 1926, when they fell to £93,000.

It was in the period from the end of World War I up to Humber's involvement with the Rootes family in 1928, that they made their most cherished models, apart from later successes like the Snipe and Pullman. But the 8/18 of 1923 and the 14/40 of 1928 are regarded by lovers of vintage cars as the apogee of Humber achievement, with their quiet, refined operation and construction of high-quality materials with a plethora of brass and leather. Performance was never their strong point, but they were smooth and long-lasting and pleasant to drive.

The first post-war model was the 15.9, although the pre-war side-valve 10 and 14 horsepower cars were continued up to 1923, when the 8/18 appeared with overhead-inlet and side-exhaust valves, which became a Humber practice right up to 1930.

The Humber company were always innovators but, having tried something, tended to stick to it even when it had been overtaken by events and become old-fashioned and superseded by later design knowledge or better ideas. Examples of this were the practice on their 1901 Humberette of using water-tight hinges on the side of the radiator so that it could be swung aside to work on the engine, and insistence that front-wheel brakes were dangerous. As a result of this belief, they retained their ineffective transmission brake up to 1928, without even supplementing it.

Humber's multiplicity of models is something of a numerologist's nightmare, and eventually led Humber into financial trouble. When the Humberettes were being made both at Beeston and Coventry, from 1905 onwards, there were also 8–18 and 16–20 cars in production in Beeston and 10–12, 12–14 and 20–25 models coming out of Coventry. Differences were slight and, in 1906, they chopped the range down to the Beeston 16–20 and the Coventry 12–14. The Beeston beast used a pressed-steel frame and a four-speed gearbox, and the Coventry one a tubular chassis with a three-speed box, but both had similar four-cylinder engines.

Rationalisation did not last long and by 1908 there was a twin-cylinder 8, a 30-horsepower six-cylinder and no less than five four-cylinder versions of 12, 15, 20, 22 and 28 horsepower.

Then, in 1909, the re-formed company dropped the 22 and 28 and replaced the 15 by a 16 with the new-fangled detachable wheels, which were also used on

Above: a 1914 Humber Tourist Trophy racer; the car was designed by F. T. Burgess, who later moved on to join W. O. Bentley. The car was extremely advanced for its time: it had four valves per cylinder, operated by twin overhead camshafts, and developed nearly 100 bhp at 3200 rpm from its 3295 cc

Left: a 1909 Humber two-seater runabout

Right: the 1923
8-18 hp Humber
'Chummy' four-seater
runabout

Far right: a 1927
9/20 hp Humber tourer

Above: a 1926 Humber
14/40; this was one of
the most popular
Humber models
produced. It was
typically vintage
Humber in appearance—
well built and dignified
rather than sporty

the 8-horsepower car. Only two years later, the 10–14 replaced the 8, another 28 appeared and the 12 changed its name to the 12–20, although it did have changes made to it like the addition of rear-wheel 'snubbers' or dampers, a torque tube and a different frame. Another two years, to 1912, brought yet another change, in the birth of the four-cylinder 11-horsepower, which Humber claimed was the first such car with a monobloc cylinder casting instead of the separate cylinders more usual at that time.

A somewhat non-standard version of the 11, with 'streamlining', was driven at Brooklands by W. G. Tuck, who was later one of the three TT drivers in 1914, and took three international class records under the name of 'The Golden Bug'. Matters were further complicated in 1913 when the Humberette of eight years earlier came back, in two different versions. One was a two-seater, with an air-cooled, twin-cylinder engine, which sold for only £125, complete with all equipment like a windscreen, hood, lights and horn—in that era usually extras. The alternative version had a water-cooled engine, but was still a twin. The air-cooled car was classed as a cycle-car as it weighed less than seven hundredweight, but it was really a scaled-down 'proper' car, with a three-speed gearbox, propeller shaft, quarter-elliptic springs at the rear and half-elliptics at the front, and rack-and-pinion steering.

This mass of differently named, but often similar,

models may be the reason that so few Humber designs have been given recognition, and why the 8/18 and 14/40 are the only ones widely known in the vintage movement. The only other well known car is one of the three 1914 TT racers which has survived in the hands of a member of the Vintage Sports Car Club, but it is not known if it is the actual car driven by the designer, Burgess, himself. All these three cars had their engines carried in sub-frames—another Humber trade mark—a transmission brake adjustable from the cockpit, and a separate gearbox. In the race, one car seized a piston and the other two had valve trouble.

Apart from the Beeston–Coventry rivalry, the most interesting cars from Humber were the two vintage models already mentioned, the 8/18 and 14/40, and the later Snipe and Super-Snipe, including the famous wartime Western Desert tourer Old Faithful used by Field Marshal Montgomery. There were many other models, including the 9/20 development of the 8/18, but they did not make history in quite the same way. Curiously enough, the Snipe was developed from the three-litre six-cylinder 20/55 of 1927, a car of an entirely different character.

In the 1920–1930 period, Humber made conservative family cars of quality and distinction but, unlike other makers of similar cars (Hillman, Rover and Wolseley, for instance), they did not go in for sporting or even pseudo-sporting versions to run at Brooklands, as was the fashion. It is generally conceded that they did not make any bad models, apart from the un-named villain of the 1911 general meeting, but they did not pretend to be trend-setters or perhaps, more appropriately, pace-makers; they were slow and solid: well made rather than flashy.

The successful 8/18 was typical. It had 985 cc to propel 12 cwt, and coil ignition, which was new in 1923 when most people would still be using magnetos for years on. It had the famous Humber inlet-over-exhaust valves, and was smooth and silent, if costly to make. Although not exciting to drive, it got there, and would cover 35 miles on a gallon of petrol. The production version was a four-seater open tourer which we might nowadays call a 2 plus 2.

The way the 8/18 evolved was typical of the decline in the small popular car between 1920 and 1930. In 1925, it changed its name to the 9/20 and was given a slightly larger engine and a much larger body, which killed what performance there was. In 1927, front brakes were added (at last) but, in 1929, people were tired of being out in the weather, and saloon bodies were the thing, so a saloon it became, hardly able to drag itself about even with a very low top gear of 5.5:1. In this form, it lasted only one year.

The multiplicity of model numbers/names makes it hard to follow their fortunes, but the post-war 10 became the 12/25 and the other model already mentioned, the 15.9, became, in turn, the popular 14/40. At the same time, the Snipe forerunner, the 20/55 appeared, and finally the light six-cylinder 16/50 completed the range in 1929. Middle-class people bought these middle-class models well until 1930 when the worldwide slump was in full swing, and Humber became part of the Rootes group.

From then onwards, a different style of car was made. The vintage-period Humbers had benefitted from the good exhaust-valve cooling of their inlet-over-exhaust system, which gave a poor power output but long life. A Humber expert has calculated that in the vintage years, more than 30,000 cars were made but fewer than 150 have survived, which is a pity. Lord Rootes and his brother Reginald were salesmen above all, and their first venture with their new company was the 1922 Humber Vogue, a stylish saloon designed to appeal to women drivers, still concentrating on the quality theme. It was still a heavy car with a small engine (12 horsepower) but with more performance than the earlier 60 mph-maximum Humbers.

In 1931, though, the chairman of Humber Ltd, Lt Col J. A. Cole, told the general meeting of shareholders that they had had the blackest year ever. Humber, he said, were healthier than Hillman or Commer and had increased exports, but there had been exchange difficulties as 'the world had become seriously impoverished'. There was talk of the £1,250,000 Humber–Hillman combine becoming a 'General Motors of Coventry' and taking over two other Coventry firms, but this remained in the realms of pure speculation rather than fact.

Nevertheless, the 1932 Vogue was followed, in 1933, by the Snipe, which carried a bird of that tribe as its mascot. It was a big luxury car with a big side-valve engine, later endowed with an aluminium cylinder head. Body-styles changed but the mechanical parts soldiered on, and made very good military vehicles in 1939, the aluminium head and light-weight wireless-truck bodies (open with a canvas tilt) endowing them with a rapid acceleration and a good top speed.

Top: part of the imposing fleet of Humbers used by HRH The Prince of Wales during a visit to Yorkshire in 1933

Centre: the elegant Humber Snipe Sports saloon of 1931

Bottom: a 1936 Humber 12 hp undergoing tests on the country roads of Devon

Above left: a Humber military staff car of 1941, used by Field Marshal Montgomery

Above right: the 1946 Humber Snipe saloon

In the last few years before World War II, the Rootes Group also took over the ailing Sunbeam/Talbot/Darracq combine, with its then-modern factory in Barlby Road, Bayswater, West London, and combined some products so that there was a so-called Sunbeam Talbot, which was mechanically a Humber Snipe but with an attractive new body style. There was also a smaller Sunbeam-Talbot, which was a Hillman Minx in disguise.

During those pre-war years, the name Humber was on a few models and, apart from the Vogue, the marque tended to belong to the chauffeur-driven segment of

Above: the four-cylinder, overhead-valve Humber Hawk VI saloon of 1954

the market, with Snipes widely used as hire and funeral cars. Eventually, the marque became lost in the badge engineering world of Hillman/Humber/Singer/Sunbeam/Talbot, and the Vogue model name came back as a Singer, after this amalgamation had taken place in the first half of the 1900's.

We are rushing ahead, though. World War II saw Rootes, including 'The Humber' in Coventry, back in the aircraft and armament business, although production of Humber cars, including the famous Snipe tourers and 4×4 wireless trucks (which had four-wheel drive and were used as command cars by armoured regiments and gunners) was stepped up to meet the military demands. Hercules, Pegasus and Mercury aero engines came out of the Coventry factories instead of limousines for British embassies in foreign countries.

After the war, the Snipes came back and were joined by the Hawk, a largish saloon with a smallish engine (2267 cc), rather in the old Humber tradition of comfort before performance. The original 1947 Hawk, an upright four-light saloon, gave way to the later version which was really a four-cylinder Humber

Snipe but, by this time, the Snipe was a much faster and better-looking car with an overhead-valve six-cylinder engine shared by the Humber Hawk model in four-cylinder form.

Reverting to the 1939/45 period for one moment, perhaps we should record that the Rootes factories made one of every seven British bombers, sixty per cent of armoured cars and thirty per cent of Scout cars, as well as 50,000 aero engines and assembly of 20,000 imported vehicles. How many came from The Humber has not been isolated from the total.

Although Humber had lost its separate identity as a company, it maintained its profile as a marque with the distinctive Pullman of 1952, the Imperial of 1964, and the Sceptre of 1967, although these shared components with other Rootes models. In 1964, Humber became an even smaller cog in an even bigger machine when Chrysler Corporation acquired 46 per cent of the ordinary shares of the Rootes Group and 65 per cent of the non-voting shares. Later, Chrysler, who had paid £27,000,000 for its initial stake in Rootes, invested a further £20,000,000 and, finally in 1973, Chrysler United Kingdom Ltd became a wholly owned subsidiary of the United States-based Chrysler corporation.

The thrusting personal style of the Rootes brothers gave way to multi-national management and the family members have mostly disappeared. All that remained in 1974 of the Humber tradition was one model, the Sceptre (saloon and estate) which is a badge-variation on Hillmans with 1725 cc ohv engines. It is pertinent to note historically that the 1974 Sceptre offered 100 mph with about 28 mpg from 1725 cc, whereas the much-loved 15/40 of 1923 produced only 40 horsepower from 2800 cc at 2000 rpm, giving probably not much more than half the speed for a much heavier fuel consumption.

Apart from the two classical vintage models, the 8/18 and 14/40, probably more affection has been generated for different reasons by the Snipe and Super-Snipe limousines, leaving out of account the open tourer military Snipes which also have their fans. Lord Montgomery's Old Faithful was given back to Rootes for their museum in 1954 after a million miles or some such astronomical figure.

The Snipes were the traditional embassy cars where something imposing but less costly than a Rolls was required, and there were many shouts of anger when they finally disappeared from the scene. The 14/40, however, must remain the star of the Humber constellation, as the 8/18 was criticised for its lack of performance, although praised for its economy.

To quote from an appreciation by Mr P. Bucknell in *The Guardian* of 1 April 1957, although it was not an April Fool joke: 'The Humber 14/40 of 1928 is perhaps the best car produced by the old Humber

Above: the 1961 Humber Hawk saloon

Below: a 1963 Humber Super Snipe saloon which had a 3-litre engine

Bottom: maintaining Humber's image of luxury and quality, the Super Snipe saloon

Company. It is a typical vintage Humber in its appearance—well built and dignified rather than sporting. It has the German silver radiator with its sloping sides and the complicated adjustable Auster windscreen which identify all cars of this make.

'The interior is roomy and comfortable. The seats are upholstered in the best hide which, after 29 years, is still in perfect condition. The doors are lined with leather, and close with a satisfying "clunk". When a door is opened, a brass plate is revealed stating "Coachwork by the Humber Motor Company, Coventry". The dashboard is of heavy mahogany and all

the instruments are perfect, including the eight-day clock.'

The article goes on for several hundred words in the same vein, and is quoted only to illustrate the fanaticism around the ancient Humbers with their quiet, unassuming character. The Humber company itself does not seem to have produced many notable characters among its people, unless their legends have become lost in the company's history of more than 100 years. Thomas Humber himself apparently disappeared without trace as far as personal legends go in the early days of the company, and did not generate a folk-lore like William Morris or Herbert Austin.

The Rootes Brothers were certainly formidable characters, but they were not strictly Humber men, as this was the only one of the marques and companies which they merged into their great car-making empire. Curiously enough, no one has ever written a book about the company, although practically every possible facet of the motoring scene has produced at least one volume.

If Humbers had pursued their one venture into competition after the 1914 TT race, the company history would have been a different story. As we have seen, the car's designer, F. T. Burgess, went on to join Walter Owen Bentley, and the three-litre Bentley emerged with four valves per cylinder, just like the Humber, but used a single overhead camshaft where Burgess had used two. There are said to have been other close differences and, according to one anonymous writer, the three-litre Bentley 'arose out of the ashes of the Humber failure'.

The other link which Humber have with the world of high-performance is that Bill Heynes, who was chief engineer of Jaguar in their hey-day, went to Jaguar from Humber so that, if things and people had moved a little differently, the staid old Humber might have been a Bentley/Jaguar high-performance machine, without any Auster screens at all.   GB

MASS-PRODUCTION PIONEER

The Hupmobiles were among the earliest of America's mass-produced cars

BOBBY HUPP, BORN IN 1861, was one of the pioneers of the mass-produced car in America, for he had helped Ransom Eli Olds develop the little Curved-Dash Oldsmobile, which was America's best-selling petrol car at the turn of the century. In 1908, just as a depression in the US motor trade was coming to an end, Hupp designed a little four-cylinder runabout which so impressed motoring enthusiast Charles D. Hastings that he put up $8500 in cash to enable Hupp to put the car into production. Eager dealers flocked to order the car, and their cash deposits brought the new Hupp Motor Corporation's capitalisation up to $25,000 (which was, at the time, the lowest figure of any of Detroit's eight motor companies).

The original Hupmobile, which had been developed by Hupp and his chief engineer, E. A. Nelson, was a $750 two-seater runabout with a 2.8-litre side-valve engine and a two-speed sliding gearbox. Its main

distinguishing feature was a tall filler neck to the radiator, rather like the old Napier 'water tower'.

The Hupmobile proved popular and by 1913 sales were running at 12,000 annually, which gave the Hupp Corporation 7.5 per cent of the $625–$1500 market sector. However, by this time, Bobby Hupp had left the company to build another light car, the RCH, which survived from 1911 to 1916 and was even exported to England, where the agents fitted it with British-built coachwork. A long-wheelbase touring version of the Hupmobile appeared in 1911; this had a three-speed transmission and cost just $900.

The four-cylinder Hupmobile survived until 1925, with progressive updatings: in 1916 an extra-long wheelbase version, which could carry seven-seat coachwork, appeared, and the radiator and bonnet were restyled in 1918. By 1923, sales had reached 38,000 and in the following year aluminium pistons were standardised.

A revolutionary new model, America's first popular-priced straight-eight, was announced in 1925; it made wide use of aluminium in its construction, and had external contracting Lockheed hydraulic brakes. A year later came a 3.2-litre six-cylinder, which had

mechanical brake operation; this replaced the four-cylinder in production.

By now, the company was in expansive mood and, in 1929, it took over the Chandler motor company in Cleveland, Ohio, using the Chandler factory to produce the lower-priced models. However, the Depression hit independent motor manufacturers, like Hupp, badly, and sales plummeted: from 50,374 in 1929 to 17,450 in 1931. Although sales were down so drasti-

Early Hupmobiles: 1909 runabout (*top*), 1911 two-seater (*centre*), 1909/10 four-cylinder tourer (*above left*) and a 1912 four-seater model (*bottom*)

cally, the 1923–33 Hupmobiles were perhaps the most handsome models to be produced by the company; 1934, on the other hand, saw the announcement of the aerodynamic range, with its ultra-modern form, including special wings, severely slanting radiator, D-shaped windscreen, extended tail and prolonged head-lamp fairings. This was, of course, the year of the Chrysler Airflow, so Hupmobile were well to the forefront of fashion, even though the streamlined bodywork cheapened the image of their cars.

The new aerodynamic models had been designed for lightness, and made wide use of high-tensile materials. Hydraulic dampers were fitted all round, augmented by an anti-roll bar at the rear; the front axle was tubular in section. For increased rigidity, the chassis was mounted in unit with the all-steel body-work, cross-braced and stiffened towards the front by a special truss, which extended from the scuttle forwards under the bonnet.

Although some 1931 Hupmobiles had been fitted with four-speed transmissions, the new models were of the three-speed all-synchromesh type; a freewheel could be fitted. A proposed front-wheel-drive variant never reached production. The eight-cylinder model had a five-bearing crankshaft, fully counter-balanced.

Equipment was comprehensive, and a radio was a standard fitting. The three-panel windscreen was cleaned by twin wipers sweeping in towards the centre to give the maximum number of blind spots. This new model gave Hupmobile the opportunity to launch a vigorous sales and export programme: 'We have spanned the Western Ocean by establishing our depot at the free port of Antwerp with one million dollars of spares delivered before we shipped our beautiful Aerodynamic Automobile to Europe'. Here, it was claimed, the importing agents could draw on a large float of new cars to supply their customers, giving guaranteed delivery. The agent who took over in

Above left: a 1913 Hupmobile tourer; note the ornate horn

Above right: a 1914 Hupmobile two-seater tourer

Britain in 1935 waxed lyrical: 'Today, the would-be motorist is beset with difficulties. So many claims crowd and confuse his choice . . . in sorting the wheat from the chaff it is obvious and logical that "air-moulding" must win his favour. And if he carries his logic to finality, he must buy a Hupmobile. Not only because it is streamlined—yet not self-consciously so—but because of its inspiriting performance—its comfort, speed and docile power'.

A new 4-litre six was announced in the spring of 1935, bringing the Hupmobile range to probably its

Top: a 1914 Hupmobile four-cylinder tourer in action during a vintage and veteran car meeting

Right: the front-end view of a 1915 15/18 hp Hupmobile sports tourer. The four-cylinder engine fitted to these vehicles survived until 1925

Bottom: in 1925, Hupmobile introduced America's first popular-priced vehicle fitted with a straight-eight engine. This is a 1930 straight-eight Hupmobile sedan

Opposite page
Top: a 1923 Hupmobile tourer

Centre left: Stan Laurel poses with wife, daughter and 1928 Hupmobile

Centre right: a 1929 Hupmobile two-door sedan

Bottom: a 1932 eight-cylinder Hupmobile cabriolet

greatest strength, with the old 3.6-litre six and the 5-litre eight (which was available in two wheelbase lengths) giving a price spread from £325 to £895.

At the end of the year, the company announced 'astounding price reductions', which seemed to leave the figures exactly the same, save that the wireless was now a 16 guinea extra but, of course, there must have been some difference, for did Hupmobile not boast that '28 years of integrity claim your respect'? Certainly, the range had been trimmed, leaving only the straight-eight and the larger six; the long-wheelbase eight had English coachwork of aerodynamic aspect, and many luxurious items of equipment, including a cocktail cabinet for the passengers. Among the standard features of the cars were cast-aluminium wheels, which reduced unsprung weight considerably, but such devices were really aimed at reviving flagging sales, in which important respect they were a complete

failure, for in mid 1936, Hupmobile suspended production for several months.

There was a revival, during which the eights gained automatic overdrive, and then Hupmobile produced one last effort. In common with Graham, they utilised the body dies of the recently defunct Cord 810/812 sedan, with the coffin-nose modified to give the effect of a more conventional grille, and rear-wheel drive using standard Hupp mechanicals. However, this venture proved totally abortive, and Hupmobile abandoned car production altogether.

This, however, was not the end of the story for, like many other American car manufacturers who had suffered in the Depression, Hupmobile had learned the necessity of having several strings to their bow. Exit the Hupp Corporation, manufacturers of motor cars. Enter the Hupp Corporation, makers of car spares, kitchen equipment and electronics.   DBW

PUTTING PRESSURE ON LIQUID

The term 'hydro' means water. These days, however, much more efficient liquids are being used in the car's hydraulic systems

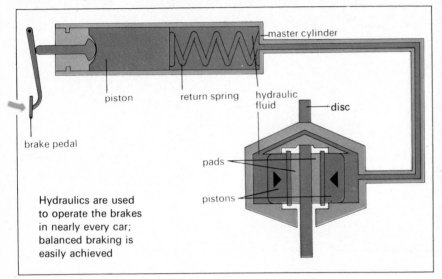

piston — return spring — hydraulic fluid — disc — master cylinder — pads — pistons — brake pedal

Hydraulics are used to operate the brakes in nearly every car; balanced braking is easily achieved

Above right: a hydraulically operated car lift, as used in many service stations; an electric motor drives a high-pressure pump, which forces fluid into a cylinder the piston of which is connected to the lift. By having a large cylinder and piston a great deal of weight can be raised by the lift

PEOPLE WHO ARE MORE AMUSED than bored by modern technology relish the story of a Russian linguistics computer which, set to translate the term 'hydraulic ram', rendered it in the Russian equivalent of 'water goat'. Almost completely irrelevant, this little anecdote has the saving grace of reminding us that hydraulics is really concerned with water, and hydraulics engineers are concerned with such things as reservoirs, dams, barrages and the like. Indeed, the earliest effective hydraulic brakes on cars, fashioned by Duesenberg and Bugatti in the early 1920s, used water as the working fluid; this called for some exquisitely accurate machining and fitting for, in those days, it seemed safest to introduce the fluid to the front brakes through the hollow king-pins at the extremities of the axle and, not unexpectedly, the frequent leaks were considered more troublesome than the advantages of the system could justify. Within a few years, it became clear that some kind of oil would serve better as the working fluid (especially in winter!) and that a foot or two of armoured flexible pipe was worth yards of precision engineering. Since then, hydraulics have thankfully never looked back, and they continue to grow more complex, more sophisticated, and more universally applicable to car-borne mechanisms.

Hydraulic systems rely on the fact that a liquid is virtually incompressible. The fact has been expensively verified from time to time: if, as a result of some mishap, a quantity of oil, petrol, or water leaks into the cylinder of an engine, until the volume accumulated is greater than the volume of the combustion space then, when the piston rises on its compression stroke, you will find that it cannot complete the journey. This is called hydraulic lock, and has proved quite capable of bending a connecting rod. In hydraulic dampers, the principle is sometimes applied in a controlled way to furnish limit stops for the suspension at one or both ends of the designed spring travel.

The other feature of hydraulic systems to remember,

in conjunction with the incompressibility of the liquid, is that pressure applied anywhere in a fluid is transmitted equally throughout it in all directions. Thus, if a piston is moved in a cylinder full of fluid, and that cylinder be connected by piping to another similar one, the fluid pressure will move the other piston simultaneously. If the second piston has a larger area than the first, then the force it exerts will be proportionally greater than that applied to the first piston. It is common parlance for the cylinder at which the force is applied (by pedal, for example) to be called the master, while the one to which the effort is transmitted is called the slave; and, because of the equal transmission of pressure throughout the fluid, any number of slave cylinders can be connected to one master cylinder. Thus, foot pressure on the brake pedal may be communicated from the master cylinder on which it bears to slave cylinders at the brakes on all four wheels and, by judicious selection of piston diameters, the amount of effort applied to front and rear brakes may be apportioned according to the demands of the car's weight distribution, etc.

Compared with the mechanical systems that it superseded, the hydraulic system—as applied to brakes in particular—has several advantages. Perhaps the greatest is that braking effort on both sides of the car is automatically balanced and equalised, but scarcely less in practical value is the ease with which the system can be installed: the small-bore connecting pipes can be led almost anywhere, around corners and through small gaps in a way that mechanical systems could only reproduce with the aid of pulleys, wires, chains, bellcranks and a host of other jointed subsystems, each of which would introduce an undesirable and unpredictable amount of friction into the control system. Hydraulics are as near to frictionless as the mechanical engineer can get, and are self-lubricating into the bargain. In addition to their flexibility, they are also silent; and they can also be lighter than an equivalent mechanical control system, although the need for accurate machining of the piston's cylinder bores, and the importance of using high-grade material for the pipework, may prevent them from being any cheaper than the mechanical set-up.

A further advantage of hydraulics is the ease with which they can be servo-assisted, relieving the driver

diaphragm to move and force is communicated by a push rod to the hydraulic circuit, multiplying the pressure in it considerably. By a clever arrangement of the valves, it is possible for the amount of servo assistance to be made proportional to the force applied by the driver to the pedal.

A quite different means of servo assistance is

Below left: a hydraulically operated clutch is used, together with a torque converter, in the Wankel-engined NSU Ro80, making this an easy car to drive

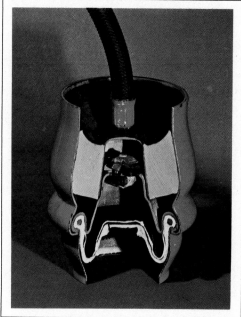

of the need to exert considerable effort for a suitable operating force to be applied at the slave ends of the system. Mechanical servos have been associated with mechanical brake operation, but only with the virtually frictionless hydraulic system could appreciable artificial multiplication of pedal effort be combined with the required delicacy and sensitivity of operation.

Most brake servo mechanisms are operated by a vacuum tapped from the engine inlet manifold, although diesel-engined cars have to rely on a mechanically driven extractor pump, and one or two particularly sophisticated petrol-engined cars (such as the Fiat Dino 2.4) employ both methods in parallel. Operation of the brake pedal makes the master cylinder function in the usual way, and would in itself be sufficient to apply the brakes, but the hydraulic pressure developed in the master cylinder is communicated to a valve in the servo which opens, to flood with air, a chamber hitherto subjected to vacuum. On one side of the chamber is a flexible diaphragm, on the other side of which is a similar chamber that retains the vacuum, so the air pressure differential forces the

embodied in systems of powered hydraulics, pioneered in production cars by Citroën in their DS series and found in other cars (including Maserati) and some commercial vehicles. (Some racing cars tried it even earlier: the Le Mans Jaguar D-type had it in 1954, and the GP Alfa Romeo in 1935.) Here, an engine-driven pump maintains a very high pressure in an hydraulic reservoir, which pressure can be introduced to the brake lines by the opening of a valve controlled by the brake pedal; and the necessary progressiveness and sensitivity of operation is ensured by making this valve pressure-sensitive. The greater the force applied to the pedal, the more does the valve (which is of the pressure-limiting type) open, and thus permit proportionally higher pressurisation of the fluid in the brake lines and slave cylinders. An interesting and valuable attribute of such a system is that the pedal, being sensitive to pressure rather than to movement, has no perceptible motion and needs much less space than the conventional variety.

Given a high-pressure hydraulic system of sufficient capacity, it is obviously possible to adopt a kind of

Top right: a Hydrolastic displacer, as used in several BLMC cars; the unit is cut away to show the diaphragm (bottom), which, when raised or lowered, forces fluid through the pipe to another unit

Above: as one wheel rises over a bump, fluid is transmitted from its displacer to that at the other end of the car, keeping it approximately level

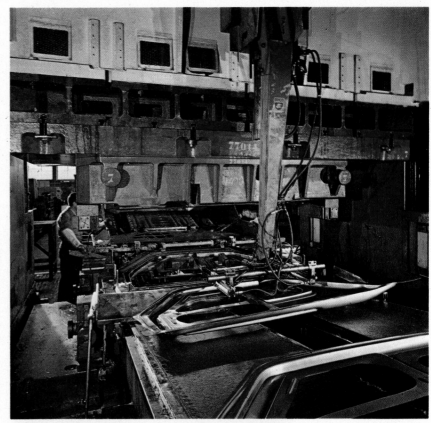

ring-main circuitry, with pressure being tapped off at suitable points for the operation of other things as well as the brakes. The most obvious such application is the steering, for all power-assisted steering mechanisms are, in effect, miniature powered-hydraulic arrangements of the kind already described. The pressure generated by the engine-driven pump is communicated to slave pistons that assist the movement of the steering linkage or sometimes of a steering rack and, indeed, sometimes the rack itself serves as the slave piston. There is, however, nothing to stop a powered hydraulic system from being exploited in the operation of clutch, screenwipers, throttle, jack, doors, or seat adjustment and even window winding—all these having at some time or other been hydraulically actuated in cars, although seldom by powered systems and never all in the one car.

One of the most valuable uses of powered hydraulics, and one in which considerable development work has been done, is in vehicle suspension. The ability of a column of fluid in a pipe to act as a flexible but incompressible pushrod allows the spring elements of the suspension to be located in the car remotely from the link mechanisms that determine the geometrical motion of the wheels. Whether the spring be metal or compressed gas or rubber or any other elastic medium is immaterial; the hydraulic pipeline can link it to the wheel motion as unerringly as it can link a brake pedal to all four brakes. A beauty of powered hydraulics is that they can force extra fluid into the system, or allow some to be withdrawn, and thus, in effect, vary the length of the 'fluid connecting rod'; and this is the essence of hydraulic self-levelling of the suspension. Displacement of the wheels from the positions they would occupy when the car is at its correct ride height, simply operates a valve to bleed off or introduce extra high-pressure fluid into the system, until the ride height is restored to its correct level when the valve closes again. If, as is normally the case, self-levelling is only needed in order to compensate for variations in the

Above left and right: in car manufacture, hydraulics are used to power a great many tools, especially the giant presses which stamp out body panels from flat sheets of steel

Left: the use of hydraulic transmission precludes the necessity for mechanical linkage between engine and wheels; the engine drives a pump which forces fluid along a pipe to a hydraulic motor (probably a turbine) which then returns the fluid to the pump. The hydraulic motor shown in the picture, upper left, is of the radial piston type

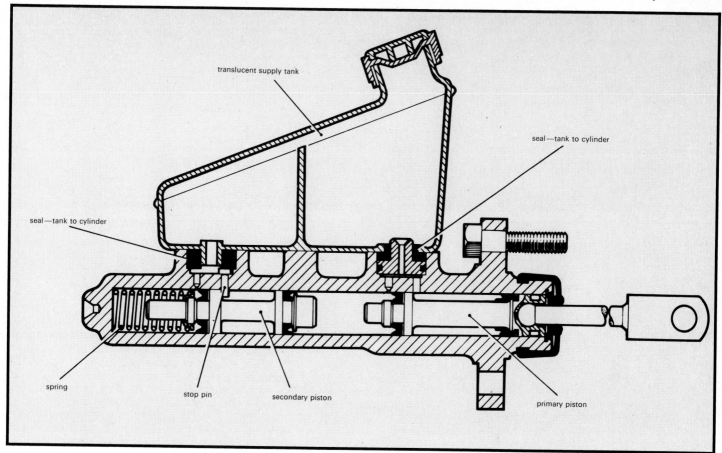

translucent supply tank

seal—tank to cylinder

seal—tank to cylinder

spring

stop pin

secondary piston

primary piston

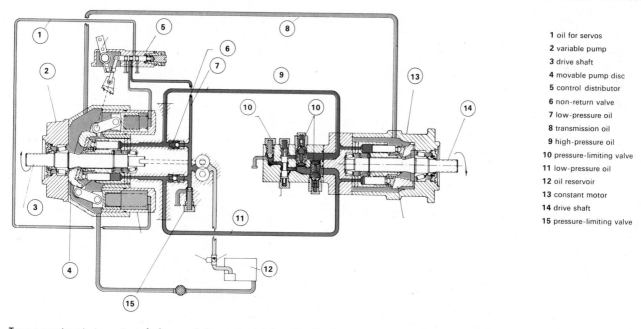

1 oil for servos
2 variable pump
3 drive shaft
4 movable pump disc
5 control distributor
6 non-return valve
7 low-pressure oil
8 transmission oil
9 high-pressure oil
10 pressure-limiting valve
11 low-pressure oil
12 oil reservoir
13 constant motor
14 drive shaft
15 pressure-limiting valve

Top: a sectional view of a hydraulic brake master cylinder; this incorporates twin pistons for separate circuits front and rear

Above: a diagram showing the layout of a hydraulic or hydrostatic transmission system similar to that pictured on the opposite page

laden weight and weight distribution of a car (for example when passengers mount or alight, and as the fuel tank is filled or exhausted), then it is quite easy to build a little delay into the operating valve so that the self-levelling system does not interfere with the normal of the suspension over each little bump or hollow on the road. The value of self-levelling lies in the assurance it gives that the integrity of the suspension and steering geometry, headlamp alignment, and so forth, can be maintained; and, by dispelling the difficulties associated with load variations, it allows the adoption of softer springing, which in itself contributes not only to ride comfort, but also to the roadholding qualities of the car.

The disadvantage of such a system is its susceptibility to squat in acceleration, nose-dive in braking,

and roll in cornering. Various methods of interconnection, whether hydraulically or by torsion anti-roll bars, constitute a palliative, but are not entirely satisfactory, whether because they inhibit the working of the suspension, or because they produce spurious oscillations (particularly noticeable in the case of strong anti-roll torsion bars) that are difficult to damp effectively. It has, however, been demonstrated by Automotive Products that it is possible to go a stage further by the adoption of what they call 'active suspension'—one that is capable of doing work with a fast response rate rather than simply absorbing energy as do conventional springs and dampers. In this arrangement, the modulation of suspension height by pumping high-pressure fluid into the hydraulic struts is controlled by a rapid-acting valve mechanism,

The diagrams above show the operation of BLMC's Hydragas suspension system. As in the Hydrolastic set-up, fluid is transferred from front to rear or *vice-versa* in order to keep the car level; the difference is that the springs are gas-filled balls rather than rubber cones

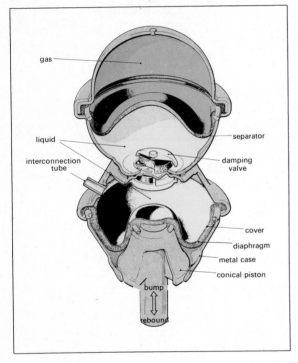

gas
liquid
interconnection tube
separator
damping valve
cover
diaphragm
metal case
conical piston
bump
rebound

Left: a sectional view of one Hydragas unit, as employed on the Austin Allegro; damping is achieved by limiting the movement of fluid from one chamber to another

Below: if two pistons, placed in openings at the top of a liquid-filled container, are the same size and the same weight, the liquid levels will be equal, as they will be if one weight is four times as heavy as the other, but also four times as large. In this way, mechanical advantage or 'gearing can be obtained in a hydraulic system

actuated by a pendulous mass that is, in effect, a model of the entire car on its suspension. Since this valve is responsive to all load changes, correction of squat, dive and roll are automatic, and the car remains on an even keel and at a constant ride height, regardless of transient longitudinal or lateral accelerations. The result is a very comfortable ride, an improvement in road/tyre adhesion (since the tyre is at all times perpendicular to the road—which implies longer tyre life and allows the simplest of suspension geometries), consistent handling because of the constant ratio of roll resistance at the front and rear, and all the normal advantages of self-levelling suspension such as correct headlamp alignment and full wheel movement under all load conditions.

It is a characteristic of hydraulically operated suspensions that the relatively small bore of the pipes connecting the major elements provides a consistent and controllable measure of damping of the system. Considerable energy can be absorbed in forcing a quantity of fluid through a small orifice, and this is the essence of dampers on virtually all cars today. The fluid employed has to have special properties, and much the same applies to the fluids used in the hydraulic systems discussed here. Usually of an oily nature, it must not change materially in viscosity with changes in temperature, and it must be free from frothing tendencies. Usually synthesised from mineral oil base stocks with substantial and complex additives, it has to be chemically stable at high temperatures, have a high boiling point, and be harmless to any natural or synthetic rubber part (such as a piston seal) or any other material used in the system. It must be free of water, too, but it is a characteristic of most such fluids that they are inclined to attract it—that is, they are strongly hygroscopic—and it is therefore important to change it at regular intervals. A car manufacturer's handbook always specifies the fluids that should be used in the braking system and any other hydraulic apparatus, and it is absolutely imperative that the specified fluid and no other be used. Even in the case of the Moulton Hydrolastic and Hydragas suspensions which feature on certain British Leyland cars, it is important to ensure the use of the correct fluid; basically it is water, making these systems truly hydraulic, but trouble will ensue unless it contains the correct proportion of the right alcohol-based anti-freeze additive. The ride of a car could be very uncomfortable, not to mention dangerous, should the hydraulic fluid freeze, but on the other hand it would be disastrous for the fluid to boil. LJKS

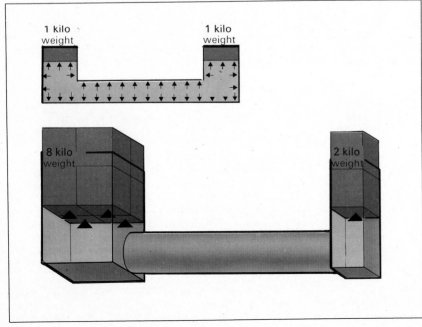

1 kilo weight
1 kilo weight
8 kilo weight
2 kilo weight

LIFTING BRITISH RACING'S POST-WAR GLOOM

Following World War II, the British racing scene was in a state of severe depression. The arrival of the HWM, however, helped to brighten the gloom

Above: an HWM two-seater pictured at a race meeting held at Crystal Palace. Suspension was independent all round, by transverse springing at the front. Power was supplied by a 2-litre Alta engine developing 125 bhp

THE HWM—the initials stood for Hersham and Walton Motors—was one of the more successful British racing cars of the immediate post-World War II period, and the marque's successes did much to offset the gloom caused by the poor showing of the much-publicised BRM.

The HWM was sponsored by George Abecassis and John Heath, who ran the HW Motors business at Walton-on-Thames, Surrey. Abecassis had been the leading Alta driver before the war, and had continued to race this car in 1946 and 1947, alongside his Bugatti and ERA. His partner, John Heath, who started racing in 1946, was also a competent Alta pilot, and had taken second place in the 1947 Grand Prix des Frontières. So, when the two planned a racing car, it was natural that it should be Alta-powered. The engine of that original HW-Alta was an unblown 2-litre Alta, fitted in a new chassis-frame clothed in full-width aerodynamic bodywork. It was, if not immediately successful, a car of considerable potential: Heath took fourth place in the 1948 Stockholm Formula Two Grand Prix, and he and Abecassis were class leaders in that year's Spa 24-hour race until a crash on the 55th lap put the car out of the running.

In 1949, the aerodynamic body was replaced by more conventional, two-seater racing coachwork, and Heath won the Manx Cup Race and took second place in the French sports-car GP at Comminges. That same year, the archetypal HWM chassis, with twin tubular main members, was evolved, and a team of three cars, with two-seater bodies that were eligible for either Formula Two races or sports-car events. Suspension was independent all round, by transverse springing at the front. The power output was around 125 bhp from 2 litres.

The main victory of the year was gained by Belgian jazz musician Johnny Claes (he led a band with the unlikely title of the Clay Pigeons), who came first in the Grand Prix des Frontières at Chimay, Belgium, a splendid event held on closed roads near the Franco-Belgian border.

The designs were completely revised for 1951, with coil suspension replacing the front transverse leaf while, at the rear, the axle was now laid out on the de Dion system.

That year's works drivers included Lance Macklin and two young unknowns who were just breaking into Formula Two—Stirling Moss and Peter Collins. Moss

Above: Peter Collins in action in his HWM at Silverstone The HWM assisted Collins eventually to become a works Ferrari driver and was also responsible for the grooming of yet another promising young British star: Stirling Moss

Above right: a 1952 HWM Formula Two machine showing the car's four-cylinder Alta engine

Bottom: Rivers Fletcher's 1955 HWM fitted with six-cylinder Jaguar engine

won the Lavant Cup and Madgwick Cup at Goodwood, and the Wakefield Trophy at Dublin; these victories contributed to his remarkable achievement of becoming British Champion at the age of 20.

An extra 25 bhp was wrung from the engine for the 1952 season, which saw the marque's most spectacular victory, a 1–2–3 win in the Silverstone International Trophy, led home by Lance Macklin, as well as another first in the GP des Frontières, this time by Belgian driver/journalist Paul Frère.

The process of extracting more power from the Alta engine reached its climax in 1953, when twin Weber carburettors and a Weslake cylinder head boosted the output to 183 bhp, at which point it became difficult to persuade the unit to stay together. In any case, the Alta-engined HWM was rapidly becoming outclassed by the Italians, who had the money that the Walton company lacked.

A couple of HWMs were built with the new 2.5-litre Alta engine, but the company turned to Jaguar for their supply of power units after that, though other engines—even a 5.4-litre Cadillac unit—were essayed.

The first Jaguar-engined HWM appeared in 1953, using the old 1949-type chassis; from 1954 to 1956, George Abecassis won many events in the HWM-Jaguar sports cars, winning at Castle Combe, Oulton Park and Snetterton.

In 1956, after some time away from racing, John Heath decided to drive an HWM-Jaguar in the Mille Miglia (in which, Abecassis had taken eleventh place with an Austin–Healey the previous year); the event was made particularly hazardous by torrential rain and undisciplined crowds and, at Ravenna, Heath crashed, receiving fatal injuries.

Production of the HWM ceased after that, and George Abecassis, who had just married the daughter of Sir David Brown, head of the Aston Martin/Lagonda combine, retired from racing to devote himself to the running of the motor-agency side of the business, which was still flourishing in 1974.　　DBW

The almost World Champion

Below: Jacky Ickx in action in the John Player Special Lotus 72 during the 1974 French Grand Prix. 1974, however, proved to be a very frustrating season for the talented Belgian

JACKY ICKX became recognised as one of the world's outstanding drivers when he joined the Grand Prix circus in 1968. On occasions, he would show the sort of skill that marked him down as an almost certain World Champion, but he would often be let down by his cars and, like one or two other drivers, he would change teams just when the team he was leaving produced a race-winning car.

Born on 1 January 1945 in Brussels, Jacques Bernard Ickx was the son of a well known motoring journalist, and the younger brother of Pascal Ickx who began a promising career as a motor-cycle racer. However, this close involvement with cars left no great impression on young Jacky, and he confessed to having been thoroughly bored by racing cars when taken to meetings by his father. Nevertheless, he soon learned to ride a motor cycle and began to show a natural flair for competitions. By the age of sixteen, he was showing up well in local trials, and the Belgian concessionaire for Zundap offered him works rides on trials and road-racing machines. Then Ickx was snapped up by the Japanese Suzuki firm who entered him in 50 cc racing events. The young Ickx won race after race and became a

public figure in Belgium before he was eighteen. He was offered a BMW 700 car for hill-climb events and, once again, he showed great skill and speed in such a tiny car, although his main claim to fame came when he rolled it spectacularly in front of TV cameras. He was offered a drive in a works-entered Ford Cortina as a result of his BMW exploits, but the intervention of National Service prevented any serious development of his potential for a couple of years, although he was often given time off from being a tank instructor to race at Belgian meetings.

Returning from the army in 1965, he once again began racing saloon cars, but after two years of local success with BMWs and Lotus Cortinas, which included successive wins in the Spa 24-hour race, he was spotted by Ken Tyrrell who gave him a drive in one of his Formula Three Matras. Ickx was fast, but the car often broke; however, he impressed Tyrrell enough to gain a few drives in his Matra-BRM Formula Two car. Although the Brabham-Hondas were winning everything in sight, Ickx put up fastest lap at Reims and finished fourth in the Albi GP, towards the end of the 1966 season. This persuaded Tyrrell to give the young Ickx a full-time

F2 drive in the Matra, for 1967; he showed that this confidence was not misplaced by winning three races, including the Crystal Palace event in England, and taking the European Championship for non-graded drivers.

Ickx really came to the fore during the German Grand Prix of 1967 when his tiny F2 Matra qualified third fastest, behind two of the new 3-litre F1 cars. The F2 cars had to start behind the F1 cars, but Ickx shot through the field and reached an incredible fourth place before retiring with a broken front suspension. This single drive ensured that he would soon be among the ranks of Formula One drivers, for team managers were clamouring for his signature at the end of the race. He drove an F1 Cooper into sixth place in the Italian GP, but he signed with Ferrari for 1968. During 1967, he had driven the Mirage-Fords to four wins and he stayed with the Gulf-John Wyer team for 1968.

In Formula One, he soon showed his prowess by winning the French Grand Prix which, together with a string of third and fourth places, earned him fourth place in the World Championship. In the Gulf-Fords, he won the BOAC 500 at Brands Hatch, the Watkins Glen 6 hrs and the

Most of Jacky Ickx's greatest successes have been in the works Ferrari team cars. He is pictured, *above*, in the 312P sports prototype and, *below*, in the 1970 GP single-seater

Spa 1000 Km race, which he had also won in the previous season. He broke his leg whilst practising for the Canadian Grand Prix, but he was soon back in action and, for 1969, he decided to drive for the Brabham team. The Brabham was very fast in Ickx's hands and only the brilliance of Jackie Stewart kept him in second place in the World Championship. He won the German and Canadian GPs, as well as taking second places in the British and Mexican races. He also won the Oulton Park Gold Cup race and took a thrilling last lap victory at Le Mans in the technically outclassed Ford GT40, against Hans Herrman's faster Porsche.

In 1970, Ickx returned to Ferrari for Formula One with the new 312B but, although he won the Grands Prix of Austria, Canada and Mexico, he once again had to take second place, this time to the late Jochen Rindt. He also drove the 5-litre Ferrari in sports-car races, but fared poorly, his only good finishes being second place in the Spa

1000 Km and third in the Daytona Continental. During 1970, Ickx became disenchanted with the Grand Prix Drivers Association, because he disagreed with their policy on circuit safety which led to the loss of his home circuit at Spa as a Championship track.

He stayed with Ferrari during 1971, but his only victory was in the Dutch Grand Prix, although he was placed fourth in the World Championship. In sports-car racing, Ferrari tested their new 3-litre car against the 5-litre machines and Ickx picked up only one place of note—second in the BOAC 1000 Km. In 1972, the well tested Ferrari 312P swept everything before it and Ickx won the Daytona Continental, Sebring 12 Hours, BOAC 1000 Km, Monza 1000 Km, Austrian 1000 Km and the Watkins Glen 6hrs, as well as taking second place in the Spa 1000 Km, to give Ferrari a runaway win in the World Sports-Car Championship. In Formula One, he was less fortunate, winning only the

German Grand Prix and dropping out of other races while leading, because of mechanical troubles.

Once again, Ickx opted to stay with Ferrari for 1973, but the team deteriorated even further because of the great load of work in running both sports-car and Formula One teams. A series of poor results forced Jacky to make a withdrawal from the F1 teams and he drove a McLaren at the German Grand Prix, finishing a comfortable third. Later in the season, he also drove an Iso-Marlboro without success. In the sports Ferrari, he was more successful, winning the Monza 1000 Km and the Nürburgring 1000 Km, as well as taking second place in the Dijon 1000 Km and Watkins Glen 6hr races.

Ickx was thoroughly disenchanted with the Ferrari team and gladly signed for Lotus in 1974, but Ferrari made a brilliant come-back and Lotus went into decline as their new 76 car failed to come up to expectations, forcing them to revert to their old Lotus 72s. Whilst the Ferraris were winning, Ickx retired from many races, his best GP placings being a couple of thirds at the Brazilian and British GPs. Jacky did, however, win the non-championship Race of Champions at Brands Hatch when his wet-weather driving technique (something he is renowned for) was enough to show the other cars, including the Ferraris, the way home in torrential conditions.

Still only 29 in 1974, Jacky Ickx had been among the top five Grand Prix drivers since 1968, having won eight Championship Grande Epreuves, although the World Championship still eluded him. So far, he had given no hint of impending retirement, but his reticent character and lack of interest in the glamorous side of motor racing seemed to indicate that he would not find it difficult to make the break with motor racing. After each race, he quickly flitted back to Brussels and did not appear again until the next race. With his extensive property interests in Brussels, he said that when he did retire he would spend just one season following the Grand Prix circus as a spectator and would then disappear from the scene. MT

SETTING FIRE TO THE CHARGE

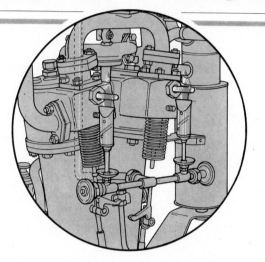

Right: In the early days of the internal-combustion engine, the fuel/air mixture was ignited by a platinum tube which passed through the cylinder wall and was heated on the outside by a petrol-burning flame; illustrated is a Daimler engine of 1887

Far right: the distributor was first introduced around 1925, thus allowing one set of contact breakers to feed any number of cylinders; the Avions Voisin C11 of 1927 was one of the first cars to use this system

Below: a high-tension magneto, mounted on a Chenard Walcker of 1910; (this type of unit was popular until World War II); a glow plug used on the Fiat 621 diesel of 1937; a French sparking plug of 1902 with two sets of electrodes for connection to two different ignition systems—one with a battery and vibrator, the other with a low-tension magneto; a Champion spark plug, of the type popular until World War II—it has an 18 mm thread and can be dismantled for cleaning purposes

SETTING FIRE to the compressed charge of fuel and air, in the combustion space of a car engine, has, for a long time, been a matter of fairly simple electrical and mechanical engineering. It may not be as crude as the early hot platinum tube which kept the most primitive engines banging away so long as a spirit lamp was played upon its exposed end; nor is it as costly and mechanically intransigent as the magneto which thereafter served most cars until the late 1920s or early 1930s, and whose performance and reliability kept it supreme for aero engines and racing engines for another 30 years. Since then, the usual equipment has been what is comprised in a coil set: a battery to supply electricity, a coil to transform that low voltage supply to a much higher electrical pressure, with the assistance of a contact breaker which triggers it to provide a very high voltage pulse, which is then led, via a distributor, to the appropriate spark plug where the pulse comes across the gap between the electrodes, igniting the charge in the process. The only other essential is a condenser, wired to the contact breaker to prevent excessive arcing or sparking across the points as they open to trigger the pulse from the coil. It is a simple arrangement, cheap to make, and easy to maintain; but it may seem excessively patronising to describe it as rudimentary, considering that even in the engine of an ordinary family car, the system provides 200 sparks a second, each timed to an

accuracy of 1/7000th of a second. However, in relation to the engine's needs—especially if it is to comply with the most modern requirements of environmental legislation governing exhaust emissions and the like—the conventional coil-ignition apparatus makes a rather poor job of ensuring that the spark occurs at exactly the right moment with exactly the right characteristics, particularly in view of the fact that the timing needs to be different for every combination of speed and load within the engine's operational envelope.

Even disregarding these new requirements, satisfactory ignition is often overlooked as an essential prerequisite to good engine performance. How often do we find people doing all sorts of mechanical work on their engines, raising compression ratios, altering valve timing, improving induction and exhaust breathing, revising carburation, and so on, only to find that they have not achieved the improvement they sought and reasonably expected. Sometimes, it is even worse and they have holed a piston. Almost always, the explanation proves to be that they have made no alteration to the ignition system, despite the fact that any one of these modifications to the mechanical specification of the engine is almost certain to require ignition re-timing, if not a change in the shape of the advance curve or something even more fundamental. In some cases, especially when engines have very large cylinders

Far right: one type of breakerless distributor; the rotor arm is at the top, as usual, but underneath is a rotor which has as many magnetic projections on its circumference as there are cylinders in the engine; as each pole passes a coil, a current is generated in that coil and is then stepped up to cause a spark. The advantages of this system are that the timing stays exactly where it was set, as there are no points to slip out of adjustment, and the absence of points means that they cannot bounce at high speed

Right: this series of diagrams shows the various systems which can be used to light the charge in a cylinder

Left: the cockpit of a Ferrari 312P sports-racing car, containing the yellow box for the electronic-ignition system. This system, which uses capacitive discharge to cause a spark, is fitted to many racing engines, as it is capable of providing more sparks per unit time than a standard layout

or are running at exceptionally high speeds, severe variations in performance of a given cylinder from one operating cycle to the next, may result in a much poorer performance overall than theory or snap measurements may suggest, and will almost certainly produce rough running into the bargain. In such a case, even more drastic alteration to the ignition system may be necessary, such as the provision of multiple spark plugs, or a change of spark-generation system so as to produce sparks of a different character.

Basically, the study of engine ignition requirements may be broken down into three divisions: the timing of the spark, the qualities of the spark, and the means of generating it. Needless to say, these three are closely related, sometimes to the point where we have to sacrifice a little in one direction in order to avoid jeopardising another.

Before we consider how to get our spark and when, we must examine the kind of spark we want to produce. How long should it last, for example, and how long should it take to build up to its peak voltage? For that matter, what should that peak voltage be?

Although we are concerned at this stage with ends rather than with means, it is worth remembering the old basic distinction between coil and magneto ignition; the former gave its healthiest spark at low speeds, and grew progressively weaker as the spark rate increased, because there was less time between each triggered pulse for the coil to 'soak'—to build up a magnetic field in its secondary windings as the current from the battery flooded its primary windings.

The magneto, by contrast, gave a stronger spark as the rate increased, the voltage in its windings increasing as they were rotated faster in the instrument's magnetic field. So, there is another thing to bear in mind; do we want the best spark at high speeds in order to get optimum power from the engine, or would we rather have a good spark at low speed so that we can actually get it started? Clearly, it is desirable to have both the chicken and the egg present, and many of the most modern ignition systems, notably those employing electronic circuitry, achieve this by producing a substantially constant spark voltage over the full range of operating speeds.

Consider a typical voltage available from ignition systems in general current use. The output characteristics of a conventional coil ignition system, under simulated fouling conditions with a one megohm load, gives a voltage output of perhaps 15 kilovolts from say 1000 to 3000 rpm. Under the same conditions, a typical transistor-controlled system will have a voltage output somewhat less whereas, in the case of a capacitor discharge system, even with a shunt resistance of only 50,000 ohms, the output is a good 7 or 8 kilovolts higher over this speed range. At higher speeds, however, we notice a most important contrast: the coil output drops steadily for reasons already explained, the others do not, and may even increase. Nevertheless, it must be remembered that in the lower speed range, the contact or magnetically triggered transistor systems under fouling conditions, actually have less output available to fire the spark plugs than is available from perfectly ordinary bread-and-butter coil systems.

It is evident from this that the capacitor-discharge system, widely used in two-stroke engines and beginning to be applied to others, has certain very definite advantages. It also has certain very definite characteristics that may not be so advantageous, and this is where the question of arc duration and rise time intrudes. The CD (Capacitor Discharge) system produces a spark of very short duration, as little as ten or twelve microseconds. Often, this is grossly inadequate, for arc duration has a marked influence on the ability of the spark plug to ignite lean mixtures. Broadly speaking, on lean mixtures, the longer the arc duration, the better spark advance the engine will accept and the better will be the specific fuel consumption. Nor is it any use arguing that your engine is not set to run on lean mixtures because, apart from the fact that all the latest engines are (for emission control purposes), there are certain conditions of part-throttle or idle running in any engine when the mixture is often anything but homogeneous, and the region around the spark plug may very well be lean, although elsewhere in the combustion chamber it may be extravagantly rich. If, in these conditions, which prevail during starting and in traffic, the spark is of

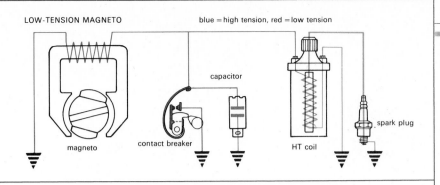

LOW-TENSION MAGNETO

blue = high tension, red = low tension

magneto | capacitor | contact breaker | HT coil | spark plug

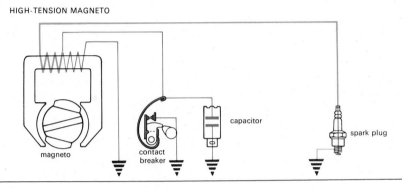

HIGH-TENSION MAGNETO

magneto | contact breaker | capacitor | spark plug

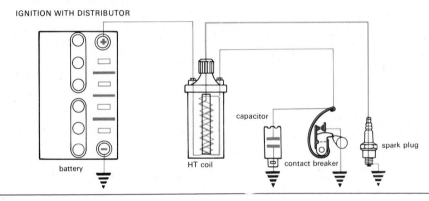

IGNITION WITH DISTRIBUTOR

battery | HT coil | capacitor | contact breaker | spark plug

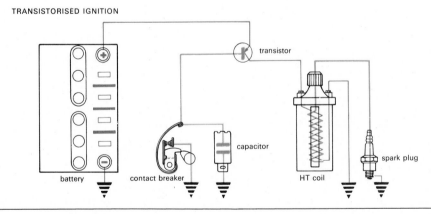

TRANSISTORISED IGNITION

battery | transistor | contact breaker | capacitor | HT coil | spark plug

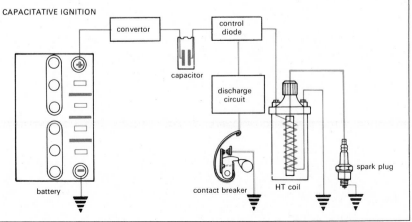

CAPACITATIVE IGNITION

battery | convertor | capacitor | control diode | discharge circuit | contact breaker | HT coil | spark plug

very short duration, the probability of appropriate and optimum ignition is very poor. Lengthening the duration of the spark improves things enormously, and improves the cleanliness of the exhaust, the longer arc reducing emissions of hydrocarbons and of carbon monoxide. When the mixture is homogeneous, as is more likely to be the case at high operating speed, the arc duration does not exercise this same influence.

Only the most refined CD systems have been adapted to provide a spark of adequate duration, the most notable being the Mobelec which gives a spark of 250 microseconds, and doubles this at lower engine speeds. Such refinements are inevitably costly, but are essential if the other advantages of the CD system are to be enjoyed without handicaps. These advantages are that it produces a very rapid rise of voltage to the peak level, and this has a profound influence on spark plug tracking — what happens when the spark is dissipated and run to earth through conductive deposits on its surface (e.g. carbon, water, or lead salts) instead of arcing across the spark plug gap. The faster the voltage rise time — which is usually defined as the time needed for the voltage to reach 90 per cent of its maximum — the longer the plug can run without the usual tracking in fouling conditions, and the better the chance of the fouling being broken down and normal conditions resumed. An ordinary coil system might give a rise time of perhaps 80 microseconds, and most of the so-called 'electronic' ignition systems (which are basically coil systems with transistor-assisted contacts to reduce current through the contact breaker and prevent arcing there) take even longer, perhaps 125 microseconds. With the CD System, the voltage rise time is seldom more than 6 microseconds.

So we want a spark of consistently high voltage at all engine speeds (at least 30,000 kilovolts), reaching its peak very very quickly and lasting a fairly long time. Not too long, however, lest the electrode temperature at the spark plug grow too high, and erosion of the gap between the electrodes be accelerated as a result, leading to an even higher voltage requirement — for the greater the gap, the greater is the voltage needed to jump it.

In most European engines, although not in many American ones, the spark plug temperature curve over the speed range is appreciably steeper nowadays than it used to be, and smaller engines are used more extensively at the extremes of this rather steeper curve. This is why spark plug choice has become so critical today, with the danger of the fouling of too 'hard' or cool-running a plug in part-throttle or idling conditions having to be offset against the much more

Near right: a distributor, for a four-cylinder engine, with its cap screwed on

Centre right: a four-cylinder distributor with its cap fixed by elastic

Far right: a cutaway view of a four-cylinder engine's distributor with vacuum advance unit

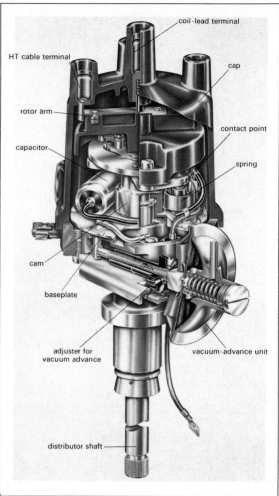

coil-lead terminal

HT cable terminal

cap

rotor arm

contact point

capacitor

spring

cam

baseplate

adjuster for vacuum advance

vacuum-advance unit

distributor shaft

serious danger of wrecking the engine through the overheating of too 'soft' or hot-running a plug when going hard or at full throttle. Of the two, the former risk is the better one to run.

Sometimes, the build-up of deposits on plug points is due to the low voltage available—perhaps just a matter of bad maintenance of the ignition system, or of its basic unsuitability. There is also the possibility that too much suppression or the wrong kind of suppression could be responsible. Radio suppression is an important thing to remember, for it is not something left to the individual's choice or conscience. It is now a matter of law, not only in Britain but in most other countries as well, although the standards do vary somewhat, being notably stringent in France.

The need for radio suppression is due to the fact that the complete ignition circuit, including the spark plug gap, resembles quite closely the circuitry of spark-gap radio transmitters such as were used in the early days of wireless transmission. In effect, the ignition system is a radio transmitter, and its broadcasts (at frequencies that may be several megacycles per second) will be detected by radio receivers in the vicinity. Picking up these signals results in spurious noise in the output of a radio receiver.

The amount of noise is related to the amount of energy that is transmitted during each train of the damped waves that the resonating element of the ignition circuit has in use, one train occurring at the time of each firing of a spark plug. The problem is a straightforward one of damping the oscillations in the circuit, sometimes by means of a resistor actually within the spark plug. Another resistor may be used in the high-voltage lead from the coil, or in the distributor rotor. Some manufacturers use instead high-tension cables with built-in suppression characteristics, but these often give trouble, for they are not consistent with temperature and they deteriorate rapidly with age, final failure usually occurring when starting in cold weather or in damp conditions.

Undoubtedly, the most difficult aspect of ignition is the timing of the spark. When the engine is running at full throttle, it is not difficult to establish the amount of spark advance at any given speed, and it is likely to be found that the ideal advance curve will rise steadily with speed and then level off as the influence of turbulence—which may be thought of as a wind fanning the flames—increases the velocity of the combustion front. However, if the throttle be closed, the weight of each incoming charge will be smaller, and the ratio of weight of residuals to fresh mixture

larger, while the compression pressure will be lower, and, because of these things, the speed of burning is a lot less rapid. Accordingly, the spark advance angle needs to be greater in part-throttle/part-load conditions; but it is very difficult to determine how much greater. On a level road at less than maximum speed, when the car is not being accelerated, the optimum spark advance could be anything up to double what it should be at full speed and full load. Running downhill it could be greater still, even at maximum speed. This is the function of the vacuum control of ignition advance built into the majority of modern distributors. The depression in the induction system is used as a measure of engine load; by operating on the aneroid capsule attached to the distributor, it can override the speed-sensitive centrifugal advance mechanism in order to increase the spark advance at part load. It is a device that cannot be relied on not to over-advance the spark in certain transient conditions, and, because of the danger of pre-ignition or detonation thus created, it is best deleted from the ignition system of a highly tuned engine. Even when the engine is idling and induction vacuum is high, the compression pressures are low, the ratio of burned residuals to fresh gases is high, turbulence is slight, and the speed of burning is low and erratic. In these circumstances, the engine runs better when the spark advance angle is reduced. Likewise, the advance must be reduced in any circumstances where detonation might occur.

While an over-advanced ignition is to be avoided at all costs, unnecessarily retarded ignition is nothing but a burden. It can cause misfiring because retarding the spark increases the voltage requirement across the plug gap for a satisfactory spark to occur. On the other

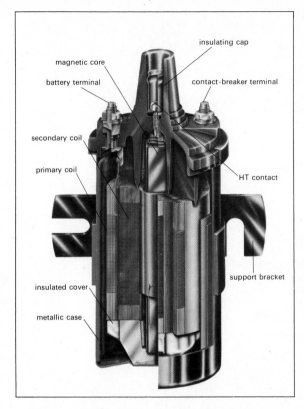

insulating cap

magnetic core

battery terminal

contact-breaker terminal

secondary coil

primary coil

HT contact

insulated cover

support bracket

metallic case

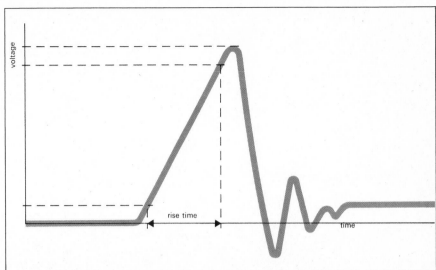

hand, retarding the ignition reduces the temperature of the plug tip, much more so at full load than at part load, and this could either save the engine from pre-ignition or encourage plug fouling, according to the heat-range suitability of the particular plug in use.

Hitherto, it has not been possible to make an ignition system so perfect that at any load level it could ensure optimum ignition performance throughout the operating speed range. Today, it is theoretically not impossible, but to achieve it would be so forbiddingly expensive that it is still practically impossible. The art of devising a suitable ignition advance curve has to stay subservient to the mechanical limitations of most advance mechanisms, which are surprisingly crude affairs of weights and springs, spinning in the nether regions of the distributor. In fact, the majority of engines already have retarded ignition settings in the lower speed ranges. If you were to examine their centrifugal advance curves you would find that they are running down at 1000 rpm at something like 5 per cent torque loss. There are so many conflicting requirements that have to be taken into account: engine starting, regular idling, and the absence of hot stalling, are some of them, and the situation is now being further complicated by legislative requirements about exhaust emissions that postulate the ability to burn leaner mixtures than used to be considered normal in such conditions.

There is little to be done about it; the average amateur and most professionals will have to be content with the curve determined by the engine manufacturer, but they still have control over the actual degree of advance. How this is set depends on a lot of things, notably on how gullible you are in believing what manufacturers tell you. Strobe lights and flywheel marks are merely a means to an approximation that takes no account of the production variations between one engine and the next off the same production line, and it is widely thought that the most reliable method is to use a vacuum gauge or revolution counter, setting the engine at a very fast idle, and then swinging the entire distributor until the maximum induction

vacuum or highest rev-counter reading is indicated at that particular throttle setting. The distributor is then clamped at that point, the timing being just about as good as you can hope to get it.

It is unlikely to remain where you put it. The distributor may not shift, but steady erosion and pitting of the contact points in the mechanical breaker of the conventional ignition system will gradually alter the timing and, incidentally, alter the coil performance as well by varying the dwell angle during which the primary windings of the coil are allowed to soak, as already described. Some engines with a large number of cylinders and a high rate of revolutions have distributors incorporating two sets of contacts, reducing the further dangers of contact float or bounce at high speeds; but, although one contact breaker can be adjusted in just a few minutes, synchronising two can take half a day. There is no doubt that the conventional simple mechanical contact breaker works amazingly well when it is new; neither is there any doubt that its performance displays severe degradation in quite a short time thereafter. Several modern electronic ignition systems substitute a contactless form of electrical trigger to replace the mechanical circuit-breaker; most commonly, it takes the form of a magnetic detector, which notes the passage of a projection or a recess on the rim of a rotor in close proximity, but there are some versions (the first was the Lumenition apparatus) which rely on a photo-electric cell responding to interruptions by a shaped rotor of a beam of light directed at it.

The most advanced electronic ignition systems now function with notable accuracy and consistency over a tremendously wide range of operating speeds, and the majority of them are immune to most troubles provided they are located in a suitably cool place. Increasingly stringent emission laws have forced many manufacturers, notably the Americans, to adopt electronic ignition for all their production engines, in place of the older breaker systems, simply in order to achieve consistent results over long periods of running. Further developments can be expected, the first probably being electronic rather than mechanical control of ignition advance (already developed by Mobelec and by a number of specialists in ignition systems for racing motor cycles), after which the next great challenge will be the evolution of a miniature computer aimed to provide the spark timing variations demanded by the approaching generation of stratified-charge engines. The whole problematic business was foreseen by Job: *Man is born unto trouble as the sparks fly. . . .* LJKS

Above left: a cutaway view of a high-tension coil as used in nearly every car

Above: a graph showing how the high-tension current builds up in the ignition circuit, and how it decays after the contact points have opened to allow the plug to spark. The time taken for the voltage to rise from 10 per cent of maximum to 90 per cent of maximum is known as the 'rise time'

A BELGIAN COMPANY WITH AN INTERNATIONAL MARKET

The makers of the Imperia were relatively late starters in the Belgian motor industry.
Nevertheless, it did not take them long to make their mark on the motoring scene

Above: although the Belgian motor industry has faded away, it was once represented by famous makes like FN, Minerva and Imperia. The Imperia company came into being in 1906 and survived until the mid 1940s. Pictured is a 1911 Imperia model

Right: the luxurious and elegant 15.9 hp of 1914

THE ATELIERS PIEDBOEUF OF LIÈGE were relatively late starters in the Belgian motor industry—they did not begin production until 1906; six years after Minerva, eight years after Métallurgique and nine years after Germain. Designed by the German Paul Henze, the Piedboeuf-Imperia range consisted of an 18 hp 3-litre, a 24/30 hp 4.9-litre and a 50/60 hp of 9.9 litres.

Henze drove a Piedboeuf-Imperia in the 1907 Kaiserpreis; it dropped out on the third lap, and the kindest thing that *The Autocar* could find to say about it was that the name Piedboeuf means 'calf's foot' in English. In any case, the 'Piedboeuf' part of the name was dropped the same year, when the company moved into a factory at Nessonvaux that had formerly been used for the manufacture of the Pieper voiturette.

By 1908, the marque was available on the British market. At Olympia that year, the London agents showed the 18 hp, marketed in England as the 16/20, noting that its engine had a crankshaft running on ball-bearings. Perhaps, because of this, the Imperia had a minor competition record, with class successes at Château-Thierry and Mont Ventoux hill-climbs, and outright victory in the Circuit of Ostende, an obscure and badly organised light-car race. There were also the 'obligatory' appearances at Brooklands.

The year 1909 saw the introduction of a new light Imperia, the 12 hp, which had its four cylinders cast *en bloc*; as on the 16/20, the gearbox was in unit with

the engine. It sold on the British market for £270 in chassis form. In 1910, came a merger with another Liège firm, Springuel; for a short time, Springuel-Imperias were marketed, with the 16/20 hp engine and a 28 hp engine also used on Imperias from 1910 on but, by 1912, they had become simply 'Imperia'. Although, surprisingly, Jules Springuel was manager of the combine at the time.

On the scene now came Spanish super-salesman

Francisco Abadal, who had introduced His Most Catholic Majesty King Alfonso XIII to the Hispano-Suiza, and now intended to produce a sporting car of equal quality to the Alfonso Hispano. It was, perhaps, somewhat more than coincidence that the Abadal had identical cylinder dimensions to the Hispano (there was also a 40/45 hp six-cylinder version) and, as Señor Abadal happened also to be the Spanish agent for Imperia, it was natural that the new cars were soon being sold in Belgium as Imperia-Abadals, although pre-World War I production of this marque within a marque seems to have been entirely Barcelona-based. The chassis frames and cylinder blocks, it is said, were imported from Belgium—but not from Imperia.

In 1916, Francisco Abadal acquired a General Motors agency, and started selling modified Buicks as Abadal-Buicks, and that ended the Spanish end of the story; Imperia-Abadals went on however, being produced at Nessonvaux after the war.

Imperia had now come under the control of M. A. Van Roggen and, at first, limited production of the Abadal four and six-cylinder cars was undertaken. At the 1921 Brussels Show, Imperia announced a 5.6-litre straight-eight with an overhead camshaft and Perrot four-wheel braking. This, however, proved to be short-lived and was replaced after only three examples had been built by a new sporting Imperia-Abadal, with a 3-litre long-stroke engine of identical dimensions to the Bentley, in common with which it also had an overhead camshaft and four valves per cylinder. Maximum speed was around 90 mph, and the Baron de Tornaco drove one of these cars to victory in the first Belgian Grand Prix at Spa, averaging 55 mph over the event's 375 miles. This car, too, was doomed to a short life, and did not see out 1923. Replacing it was Imperia's most famous model, the slide-valve four-cylinder designed by the 'eminent engineer' Couchard, who was the technical head of the company. The slide valve was an attempt to replace the poppet valve with a more positive and silent means of allowing the combustion gases to enter and leave the cylinder. Couchard's system had neither simplicity of production nor ease of maintenance on its side for, unlike the sleeve valve, which completely encircled the piston, the slide valves moved up and down in slits in the cylinder walls, into which they were dovetailed like the lid of a pencil box.

'It will be impossible,' claimed Couchard's critics, 'to maintain sufficient gas-tightness between cylinder and slide. Nor can you mass-produce such an engine'. However, Couchard was equal to the challenge. The cylinder blocks, having been rough-bored, were placed on a special Lapointe machine which cut the dovetailed grooves in their walls. Then the slide valves, cut out four at a time, were machined and fitted in their grooves; a special hone gave cylinders and valves their final surface finish. The camshaft, machined from a solid billet of forged steel, moved the valves up and down desmodromically; it should have been an exceptionally silent power unit, but it was not. *The Autocar*, who tested an 11/24 hp Imperia in 1926, remarked pettishly: 'The engine . . . is not as quiet as

Above: the Imperia stand at the 1928 Brussels Motor Show; in the foreground is the Imperia two-door coupé which featured a six-cylinder, 1800 cc, 40 bhp engine. The car had a top speed of around 75 mph

Left: an Imperia 11/24 hp model; the engine was an 1100 cc, four-cylinder unit and the car was fitted with a four-speed gearbox. Top speed of the car was around 50 mph. This was probably Imperia's most famous model

would be expected, nor altogether free from roughness at low speed, and it is very difficult to discover exactly what causes the noise. At higher speeds, and particularly when the engine is warm, the running is smoother and the engine happier'.

The tester was, however, sufficiently impressed with the performance of this four-speed 1100 cc car (the original slide-valve model had only 1000 cc, soon enlarged for extra power) to remark that: 'Even driving into the teeth of a gale does not extend the engine to its utmost, and the performance on top gear is quite up to modern standards, the lowest limit of speed being in the nature of 4 mph'. An interesting sidelight on driving habits in the 1920s, that. Top speed, carrying a four-seater fabric saloon body, was 50 mph. And, incidentally, that bodywork was one of the first to be fitted with a sliding sunshine roof which, commented *The Autocar* profoundly, 'enables an occupant to look out at the sky if he so desires'—it also leaked, unfortunately.

The catalogue of the 11/24 Imperia's unorthodoxies did not end there: apart from the fact that the engine revolved anticlockwise viewed from the starting handle end, the car was also fitted with a braking system which incorporated an early form of that computer-age phenomenon, feedback. The front-wheel brakes and transmission brake were interconnected in such a way that the transmission drum acted as a servo for the front brakes, so that the harder you put your foot on the brake, the greater was the inclination for the car to fold in the middle. From 40 mph, the car could stop in 95 feet and a cloud of fried Ferodo.

Surprisingly, the little Imperia had quite a sporting record: it took the first three places in its class in the 1925 Spa 24-Hour Grand Prix and, driven by Van Roggen, took the light-car award in the 1926 Monte Carlo Rally.

There were even plans to produce the Imperia in Britain, at the Cordwalles Works, Maidenhead, home of the GWK (Van Roggen and Grice of GWK had been business associates before the War); although a few cars were assembled, circa 1926, the project came to nothing.

On the home market, however, Imperia, whose sales in 1927 were only 504, was gobbling up the ailing Belgian motor industry with avidity. Imperia

production was now said to be running at 2500 a year, and a six-cylinder variant of 1624 cc had been introduced in 1927. At the end of 1930, a Supersport variant of the six appeared. This had an engine '*nettement plus pousé*' with triple carburettors, and was said to be capable of over 80 mph with 'suitably profiled coachwork', as the makers put it.

The day of the slide valve was, however, virtually over. In 1934, the Nessonvaux management signed an agreement with Adler of Frankfürt, and the subsequent Imperias were no more than Belgian-bodied Adler Trumpf and Trumpf-Junior front-wheel-drive chassis. A merger with Minerva in 1936 did neither marque much good, although the Imperia survived until 1948, its last fling being a curious amalgam of the Adler Trumpf and the stillborn 1340 cc Hotchkiss-Amilcar designed in 1940.

After that, all was anticlimax, for the Imperia badge was finally stuck on the front of Standard Vanguards assembled in Belgium at Nessonvaux. DBW

Above: another view of the Imperia 11/24 hp model, this being a 1927 version. One of these machines won the small-car class of the Monte Carlo Rally 1926

Below left: the TA II Jupiter Imperia of 1939

Bottom left: the 1.3-litre sports Imperia TA8 of 1948; features of this car included gravity feed, hydraulic brakes, a three-speed gearbox with dashboard change, and composite wood and metal coachwork

The richest race in the world

Left: part of the huge crowd that flocks to Indianapolis

Below: to the victor, the spoils—this is the huge trophy for the winner

Bottom: winner of the first Indy 500 in 1911 was Ray Harroun's yellow six-cylinder Marmon Wasp

THE INDIANAPOLIS 500-MILE RACE has long been one of the major sporting attractions in the world. In the United States, it is *the* motor race of the year. It is a race of glory, with a record prize fund in excess of $1,000,000 (£416,500), and a race of attrition, the toll in human lives and mechanical misfortune over the years sometimes having precipitated public outcries. Up to 1974, no less than thirty-four drivers have been killed at the Indianapolis Motor Speedway.

The Indianapolis 500 is unique. Although in modern times its duration is a little over three hours, it consumes the entire month of May. This is the month during which the Indiana state capital, a city with a population of over 750,000, regularly features in newspapers throughout the United States. Early in the month, the 2½-mile Indianapolis Motor Speedway is opened for testing; new drivers undergo the ritual of 'rookie' tests at predetermined speeds under the eagle eyes of seasoned veterans, and new cars are developed by their teams to reach peak performance for the two weekends of qualification runs which

Top Row, left: Joe Dawson, winner of the 1912 event in his giant 8-litre National at an average speed of 78.72 mph

Top row, right: Ralph Hepburn in his 1935 Miller Special. Winner that year was Kelly Petillo in his Gilmore-Miller

Bottom row, left: Jimmy Murphy's 1922 winning Duesenberg-Miller

Bottom row, right: Ralph Hepburn again, this time in the 1946 Novi Governor Special. Victory that year went to the Thorne-Sparks machine of George Robson at an average speed of 114.820 mph

Opposite page, top: while clouds of smoke, steam and dust rise skywards, competitors for the first Indianapolis 500 event, held in 1911, prepare for the start

Opposite page, centre: Pat O'Connor poses in his Sumar Special prior to the 1957 event, won by Sam Hanks at 135.601 mph

Opposite page, bottom: Troy Ruttman, winner of the 1952 500, poses in his John Zink Special before the start of the 1957 race. Unlike European cars, most Indianapolis machines are named after their sponsors, rather than their manufacturers, thus it is possible for an entry list to include such unlikely sounding names as Blue Crown Spark Plug Special, Wynns Friction Proofing Special and Sugaripe Prune Special

determine the starting field of 33 cars for the classic Memorial Day event.

The history of the Indianapolis Motor Speedway can be traced back to the turn of the century. Then Indianapolis, not Detroit, was the centre of the United States automobile industry, with several car and accessory manufacturers. In 1908, one Carl G. Fisher of the Prest-O-Lite Company (which manufactured carbide lamps for cars) decided that the motor industry needed a race and test track upon which to develop its somewhat fragile products—indeed, his decision was confirmed after his Stoddard-Dayton machine had three times encountered tyre trouble and twice required water replenishment on the return from a business trip to Ohio. Fisher had seen the benefits of motor racing during a visit to the Gordon Bennett Cup race in Europe in 1905 and, being a businessman, he saw the possibility of making money from his scheme.

Fisher's colleague, Lem Trotter, located an old farm west of Indianapolis, a mere 15 minutes' drive from Fisher's office. This was it. For $72,000 (£30,000), Fisher and his new-found business partners—Jim

P. T. Andrews, the New York engineer commissioned to supervise the construction, said Fisher had no chance of finishing the track by July and, moreover, also thought the August motor-cycle fixture a trifle optimistic. Fisher, a determined self-made man, shouted, 'We have to be ready. We have already signed contracts for the balloon race and the motor-cycle events. Hire as many men as you need. Go to Chicago and get more machinery. But we have got to be ready in time—if I have to build the track myself'.

Andrews retaliated, claiming it was not a matter of men and machinery. The grandstands, buildings and most of the track *could* be completed. The chief problem was a creek which meandered across the south-west corner of the grounds: ordinary culverts could not cope with the volume of water should there be a heavy rainstorm. Eventually, it was agreed that the car races should be postponed, but the balloon and motor-cycle fixtures had to be run.

Andrews also suggested shortening the length of the circuit to $2\frac{1}{2}$ miles and his idea of having four quarter-mile corners separated by two straights of five-eighths of a mile and two of one-eighth of a mile

Joe Dawson, Winner 1912

RALPH HEPBURN IN NOVI GOVER...
FASTEST LAP EVER MADE
Indianapolis Motor Speedw...

Allison of the Allison Engineering Co, Arthur C. Newby of the National Motor Vehicle Co, Frank H. Wheeler of the Wheeler-Schebler Carburettor Co and Stoughton Fletcher, an Indianapolis banker (who later withdrew from the scheme)—purchased the 320-acre site. The Indianapolis Motor Speedway Co was incorporated on 8 February 1909.

The original plan was to construct a three-mile oval circuit and a two-mile infield road section. Shunning the idea of a dirt track, the founders agreed to use a clay base and lay an amalgam of crushed stone and asphalt. The grand opening for racing was set for 2 July for a series of car races from five to 300 miles, while a balloon race was planned for 5 June (to earn money while the track was still being completed) and motor-cycle races scheduled for mid August. These were ambitious plans indeed, especially as work did not commence until 15 March.

was also adopted. The corners were to be banked. Work commenced with 450 men, 300 mules, 150 road scrapers, four six-ton rollers and three 10-ton rollers striving to meet the tough deadlines.

The balloon race (in which Fisher competed himself) attracted a paying crowd of 3500—but 40,000 more jammed the roads outside the Speedway to view the occasion free of charge. As the date for the inaugural motor-cycle meeting drew nearer, Fisher had to arrange for day and night shifts to prepare the track. Practice had to be delayed for a day while the track was still receiving the finishing touches, but there were soon complaints that the surface was too abrasive. The meeting was a fiasco. Rain delayed the start of the proceedings and the majority of the riders refused to participate, claiming the turns were too treacherous for their machines. Eventually, the meeting was abandoned half-run, and interest fortunately soon be-

came focused on the car-race meeting the next week.

During practice, the track started to deteriorate, with pot holes and ruts appearing. However, interest was at fever pitch with Barney Oldfield having lapped at 1m 58s, an average speed of 76.27mph. On the first day of racing, huge crowds packed the Speedway, all 15,000 grandstand seats being sold out. The first race, a two-lap, five-mile sprint, was won by Louis Schwitzer's Stoddard-Dayton at 57.43mph. Feature race was the 250-mile Prest-O-Lite Trophy and, as feared, the track began to crumble again. Early leader Art Chevrolet (Buick) was hit by flying débris which smashed his goggles and injured an eye. Then, William Bourque lost control of his Knox which hit a pot-hole, veered into a ditch and landed upside-down. Both Bourque and his riding mechanic, Harry Holcomb, were fatally injured. The winner was Bob Burman (Buick), who averaged 53.77mph in the fearful conditions.

Anxious officials attempted to cancel the following day's programme, but Fisher retaliated by patching up the track overnight, and a crowd of 25,000 watched a full day's programme. This was boosted to over 35,000 for the third and final day when 17 powerful machines were run in the 300-mile Wheeler-Schebler Trophy race. It was more than the new track could withstand and soon the surface broke up again under the pounding. Charley Merz, driving a National, had a tyre burst and his car flew over the track embankment into the spectator area. The National landed upsidedown in the soft mud of the creek; Merz was able to crawl out slightly hurt, but his riding mechanic, Claude Kellum, was thrown out and killed. Two spectators also perished. When news filtered through to the start-line officials—this after another serious accident—the race was brought to a premature halt with 26 laps left to run. Lee Lynch (Jackson) was the winner at 55.61mph.

Quick on the ball as ever, Fisher decided that the track should be resurfaced, and he chose bricks. Three-million-two-hundred-thousand of them were laid at a cost of $155,000, and a concrete retaining wall 2ft 9in high was built along the outer edges of the corners; plans for the infield road section, however, were scrapped. The work took 63 days and, in an effort to recoup some of the money, a race meeting was planned for December. Because of freezing conditions, though, only a handful of hardy souls braved the elements and the programme had to be cut short. To whet people's appetites for 1910, however, Lewis Strang's 200hp Fiat registered an unofficial American 5-mile closed-course record of 91.813mph and also unofficially clocked a record quarter-mile speed of 111.86mph on the main straight.

Sixty thousand people turned up over three days for the first meeting of 1910 during the Memorial Day holiday period. Ray Harroun was the hero, winning the 200-mile Wheeler-Schebler Trophy race in his new six-cylinder Marmon.

However, the crowd figures dwindled as the 1910 season progressed. For 1911, Fisher and his colleagues decided to promote just one race, planning 'the biggest race in the world'. Initial ideas of a 24-hour or 1000-mile race were dropped and the outcome was a 500-mile event for Memorial Day (May 30). A terrific prize fund of $25,000 (£10,400) ensured this was to be the greatest race the world had ever seen.

A crowd of over 80,000 lined the track for the first Indianapolis 500. Forty competitors qualified to take part, among them drivers who had imported European machinery especially for the event. All cars had to have engines of less than 600cu in (9832cc) and to

Above: one of the greatest problems facing drivers at Indianapolis is surviving the rolling start; many a race has been marred by a start-line incident, with one car getting out of line and causing a chain reaction of accidents. Here, officials attempt to clear the track following just such an incident at the start of the 1961 event

qualify, they had to average at least 75 mph over a measured 440 yards on the main straight. They started in rows of five, the order determined by the filing of their official entry forms. It was Harroun who triumphed, being relieved briefly in the middle stages of the race by Cyrus Patschke.

For 1912, the prize money was doubled, a reflection of the enormous profit made from the 1911 500. Other rule changes included the mandatory carrying of a riding mechanic and a maximum of 33 starters. This year, it seemed as though Ralph de Palma's Mercedes must win but, with 10 miles to run, its engine went sick and lapsed on to three of the four cylinders. De Palma struggled on, but with a lap and a half to complete, the game Mercedes cried its last and Joe Dawson came through in his massive 8-litre National to win at 78.72 mph.

Then the Europeans stole the show. With the engine capacity limit lowered to 450 cu in (7374 cc), there was nothing to stop Frenchman Jules Goux from stealing the thunder in his Peugeot in 1913. The following year, it was a question of which European would win, a third of the total entries being made up by the competitors from the other side of the Atlantic. It was French again with René Thomas (Delage) conquering Arthur Duray's 'Baby' Peugeot. World War I spoilt an anticipated European onslaught for the 1915 race, when a 300 cu in (4916 cc) maximum engine capacity limit was imposed and the starting line-up was based on official one-lap qualification attempts; however, de Palma was able to ship home a Mercedes before the hostilities commenced and beat Dario Resta's Peugeot.

With war concluded late in 1918, Fisher lost no time in making arrangements for the Indianapolis 500 the following year and arranged for European participation. The winner was Howdy Wilcox in a Speedway-owned Peugeot with a similar car, driven by Jules Goux, third; second was Eddie Hearne's Durant machine.

Over the next eleven years, there was a move to smaller capacity engines—183 cu in (3000 cc) from 1920–22, 122 cu in (2000 cc) from 1923–25 and 9.5 cu in (1500 cc) from 1926–29. It coincided very much with European ideas, although there were few European entries apart from Ballot, Peugeot, Grégoire and Sunbeam under the 3-litre rules and later 2-litre entries from Mercedes-Benz and Bugatti.

In the 3-litre years, Gaston Chevrolet in one of his brother's Frontenacs scored in 1920, Tommy Milton won in 1921 (his Frontenac equipped with an eight-cylinder engine, the first '8' to win the 500) and Jimmy Murphy ran a Miller-engined Duesenberg to a record 94.48 mph victory in 1922. In the 2-litre reign, Tommy Milton's Miller-engined HCS Special triumphed in 1923, while Duesenberg Specials won the following two years, Peter de Paolo's car averaging an incredible 101.13 mph in 1925.

In 1926, the first year under the 1½-litre formula, Frank Lockhart's winning drive in his Miller Special had to be halted at the 400-mile mark owing to rain. A Duesenberg won in 1927, but Miller engines powered the winners for the following two years.

By this time, Fisher and Allison were losing interest in operating the Indianapolis Motor Speedway, tired of fighting legislature and being involved in other projects. They were offered a fortune by a real estate company who proposed to develop the site, but held out for someone who wished to continue to operate the Speedway. Ex-racing driver and World War I flying ace Eddie Rickenbacker found the necessary financial backing to purchase the assets for an undisclosed sum in 1927. Of the founders of the project, Fisher died of a gastric haemorrhage in 1939, a much poorer man after the 1929 market collapse; Allison died of pneumonia in 1928, his Allison Engineering Co being absorbed by the General Motor complex, and Arthur Newby died in 1933 after a long illness. Frank Wheeler had already died in 1921, taking his life because of his diabetic condition.

Rickenbacker added a golf course to the site and then sought to change the formula for the race in an effort to entice the big manufacturers back to the 2½-mile 'oval'. He banned superchargers—introduced to the Speedway in the 1920s with the first victory being recorded in 1924—and raised the maximum engine capacity limit to 366 cu in (5981 cc). Riding

mechanics, a breed of brave men who had been banned since 1923, were also re-introduced. The result was direct factory support by Ford and Studebaker with 'stock-block' engines, but none powered a winner. The eight-cylinder Miller engines and four-cylinder Offenhauser engines ruled supreme.

Billy Arnold's Miller-engined Hartz won in 1930, the second car to average over 100 mph for the 500 miles—his official speed was 100.448 mph. In 1931—when Lou Schneider's Miller-engined Bowes Seal Fast won—history was made by Dave Evans, his Cummins Diesel Special running the entire race without a pit stop. Miller-engined machines won in 1932, 1933, 1934, 1935 and 1936 and, in 1937, the Offenhauser scored its first victory. For some years, petrol restrictions had been applied—in 1934, no more than 45 US gallons (37.5 UK gallons) could be consumed; for 1935, this was changed to 42.5 US gallons (35.4 UK gallons) while it was further lowered by 37.5 US gallons (31.25 UK gallons) in 1936. This led to several top competitors running out of fuel in the closing stages so, for 1937, an unlimited amount of petrol was permitted, which had to be commercial fuel.

With the Japanese bombing of Pearl Harbour in December 1941, all thoughts of a 1942 Indianapolis 500 evaporated. For the second time in its history, the track was minus the sound of racing exhausts owing to a World War. The government declined an invitation to use the Speedway for any purpose and it lay dormant until, during the winter of 1944–45, Wilbur Shaw was given government permission to test a new synthetic rubber tyre on the track. To Shaw's dismay, the weed-covered grandstands and buildings were in a poor state.

Shaw took it upon himself to ensure competition returned to Indianapolis after the war. He saw Rickenbacker who could not afford the repairs but agreed to sell the track 'for exactly what I have put into it'. Shaw eventually concluded a deal with Tony Hulman, a sportsman and a top Indiana businessman. On 14 November 1945, Hulman bought the Speedway. He was content to remain chairman, leaving Shaw the active responsibilities of president and general man-

ager. All profits were to be ploughed back into improving track facilities and increasing the already substantial prize fund.

The first post-World War II Indianapolis 500 was run in 1946; seven wooden grandstands had been repaired, while the paddock and another grandstand had to be replaced. A full field of 33 cars qualified, but only seven survived to run the full 200 laps. The winner was George Robson's nine-year-old, six-cylinder Thorne Engineering Special which defeated strong Offenhauser and Maserati opposition. Even an attempted professional drivers' 'strike' in 1947 failed to stop the spectacle, this race providing the first of three victories in a row for Lou Moore's front-wheel-drive Blue Crown Spark Plug Specials. Mauri Rose was the winner in 1947 and 1948 and Bill Holland (who was second to Rose on both occasions) triumphed in the 1949 event.

The chief limitation on cars—3-litre supercharged or 4½-litre unsupercharged engines—remained until 1956, by which time both the 110 mph and 120 mph 'barriers' for the 500-mile race had been cracked. The four-cylinder Offenhauser engine continued to rule the roost, although the very powerful, supercharged Novi (ex-Winfield) V8s showed immense speed from time to time, but were never lucky or reliable enough to last the distance. Accidents were becoming all too common. In 1955, the winner for the previous two years, Bill Vukovich—'The Mad Russian' —was attempting the first hat-trick in the history of the Speedway when he became involved in a three-car accident ahead of him. His car flew over the outer wall and crashed in flames; Vukovich, pinned in his

Below: the 1974 Vels Parnelli Viceroy Special of Mario Andretti. The team was run by Parnelli Jones who, in his time, was one of Indy's greatest ever drivers. Jones won the race outright in 1963 and was always a contender until his retirement in 1968

Left: a view of the main straight at Indianapolis. The two straights are joined by banked curves and speeds of over 200 mph have been recorded on the circuit. Oval-track racing is peculiar to the United States and attracts enormous crowds and large prize-money purses

Above: yet another rolling-start catastrophe; this was the scene at the start of the 1973 event. Several spectators and drivers were injured and the race was stopped and postponed until the following day. However, it rained the next day and once again the race was postponed. When the race was eventually run the following day, victory finally went to Gordon Johncock, but only after the race was stopped after 133 miles because of rain

machine, died of a fractured skull.

For 1957, the engine capacity was reduced to 4200 cc for unsupercharged engines and 2800 cc for supercharged units. The hope was that speeds would fall slightly, but improved chassis design more than cancelled this out. The winner, Sam Hanks, driving a low-line car with its Offenhauser engine mounted on its side, set a new record of 135.601 mph!

Speeds continued to rise. In 1962, Parnelli Jones qualified at over 150 mph and the winner, Rodger Ward, averaged a record 140.293 mph. But in 1961, there were the beginnings of a revolution: World Champion Jack Brabham ran a rear-engined, 2.7-litre Cooper-Climax in the race, a tiny 'toy' compared with the 4.2-litre front-engined 'roadsters'. Brabham proved roadholding could be as important as power and, despite losing time in the pits, finished a gallant ninth. The writing was on the wall and soon American constructors realised they had to catch up with the Europeans in chassis development. Although for a while there were moves to ban rear-engined cars, it was soon a case of 'if you can't beat 'em, join 'em'. In 1963 there was further consternation among the 'establishment' when Jim Clark, another top European driver, drove a Ford V8-engined Lotus to a strong second place behind Parnelli Jones' 'roadster.' Two years later, Clark won, notching the first Indianapolis victory for a rear-engined car and the first for a Ford engine. Graham Hill's Lola-Ford won in 1966, heading Clark home in a confused finish, and this was a bitter result indeed for the Americans to accept.

Speeds rose and accidents occurred with frightening regularity. Clark's 1965 victory was at 150.686 mph and, by 1968, the 170 mph lap was being achieved in qualifications. There was a change on the engine front, too. Offenhauser reacted to the Ford challenge by coaxing even more power out of their trusty old four-cylinder engines, reducing them to 2.8 litres and turbocharging them. Turbine-powered cars were seen in the late 1960s—in fact, leading the 1967 and 1968 races until problems intervened—but they were quickly outlawed by the rule-makers. By this time,

the engine formula was vastly complicated.

In 1964, a fiery second-lap pile-up claimed the lives of Dave MacDonald and Eddie Sachs; in 1966, a horrific multiple pile-up seconds after the start, somehow resulted in no injuries, but the message was plainly there. By the 1973 race there had been some attempts at reducing speeds, but these were more than offset by advanced chassis and tyre designs. Johnny Rutherford's McLaren, powered by a turbocharged Offenhauser engine developing a lusty 900 bhp, achieved a record 198.413 mph in qualifying (when veteran Art Pollard was killed in a 190 mph accident), which meant that cars were achieving well over 220 mph down the straights. After the start, there was a pile-up in which Salt Walther was badly hurt, and spectators were sprayed by burning fuel, over a dozen being injured. Presently, Swede Savage lost control of his Eagle and crashed at high speed; he died several weeks later. The public was sickened by the 1973 Indianapolis 500, which was mercifully curtailed by rain. So, for 1974, the United States Auto Club (the controlling body of Indianapolis-style track racing) had to alter the rules. The cars were made slower by a stiff fuel consumption limit and by 'trimming' the aerodynamic wings; additionally, the Speedway itself was made safer. Johnny Rutherford's McLaren won an exciting and thankfully safe 1974 race, ensuring a future for the world-famous classic that a year before had almost choked itself to death.

Over the post-war years, the facilities at the track have been improved, tunnels replacing footbridges, elegant multi-storey grandstands replacing early ramshackle wooden affairs, a smooth asphalt surface replacing the famous bricks—although the Speedway remains affectionately known as 'The Brickyard'—and younger, modern-thinking officials replacing old, dyed-in-the-wool types. It remains the world's richest motor race and vies with the Le Mans 24-hours and Monaco Grand Prix as the most glamorous. In 1974, the total prize fund was \$1,015,686 (£423,200) of which the winner claimed \$245,031 (£102,100)—or \$22.50 (£9.35) per second of racing!   MK

SHOWING THE WAY

Flashing lights are the standard wear of modern cars, being safer than semaphore arms

DIRECTION INDICATORS ON CARS have had a somewhat chequered history as a result of the law being changed a number of times over the years. The law regarding them today is both complicated and confusing.

If you drive a car built before 1936, direction indicators are not legally necessary at all. If your car is older than 1 September 1965, several systems are permitted, including semaphore arms, roof blinkers and flashing lights combined with a side and rear lamp system.

Cars first registered after that date must have all-amber flashing light indicators, visible from the side and fitted between 17 in and $7\frac{1}{2}$ ft from the ground. They must be optically separate, flash between 60 and 120 times a minute and have either an audible or visual indication to the driver. All the indicators on the same side of the car must be worked by a single switch.

The older type of direction indicator, still seen in use on our roads sometimes is the semaphore arm. This is usually recessed into the centre door pillar of the body and consists of an illuminated arm, raised by means of an internal solenoid when the indicator switch is operated. A festoon bulb in the arm is wired in parallel with the solenoid winding.

Modern vehicles are all fitted with flashing indicators. Four lamps with amber lenses are used, two at the front and two at the rear. Nowadays, they are separate lamps, ie they do not share their lens unit with any other, and twin-filament bulbs are not used. A movement of the indicator switch to the right will operate the lamps on that side, both front and rear, and synchronised with them will be the dash panel indicator bulb. All of them must flash on and off together. Moving the switch to the left operates the bulbs on the left side, fore and aft.

One of the most important components in this circuit is the flasher unit, a little metal can, usually with three terminals on it. These will be marked L, P and B. This is how it works: moving the indicator switch completes a circuit from the battery through the flasher unit, two of the indicator lamps, and back to the battery via the earth return. Inside the flasher unit, current flows from the B terminal, through the actuating wire and ballast resistor, the coil on the armature, the L terminal and thus to the indicator lamps. Because this current flows by way of the ballast resistor, it is insufficient to light the lamps, and it heats up the actuating wire which expands. When the wire is fully expanded, it causes the main contacts to close and effectively short out the ballast resistor. Then, immediately, full current can flow via the main contacts through the armature coil and indicator lamps which are then lit. The magnetic field produced around the armature at the same time pulls the moving contact of the secondary armature, closing the pilot contacts and lighting the panel indicator bulb.

Now, while the bulbs are lit, no current is flowing through the actuating wire and its cools down. As it cools, it contracts to its original length and both sets of contacts again open. Current flows by way of the ballast resistor and the lamps go out. The sequence will go on repeating itself until the indicator switch goes off (is cancelled).

It is interesting to note that if one of the indicator lamp bulbs fail, the current passing through the armature coil is halved. The flasher will go on working but there will not be enough current to attract the secondary armature and the panel indicator bulb will not work. Often in these conditions, the remaining good bulb indicates at very much increased speed, and sometimes the circuit is arranged so that the panel indicator bulb does the same. Direction indicator

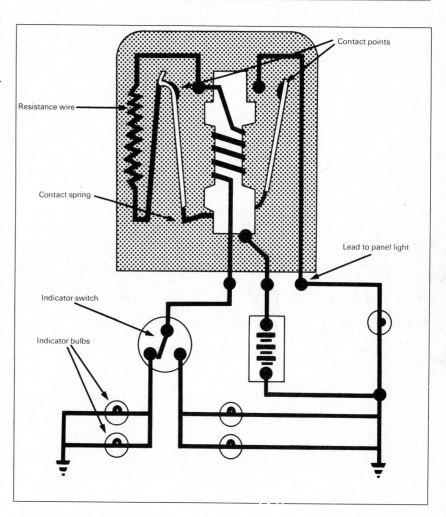

bulbs are usually rated at 21 watts.

There are possible complications to the basic circuit and one often found is the addition of repeater flashers. These are put on for extra safety. When alongside a vehicle which is already indicating a direction change, it is not always possible to see the front and rear lights because of the angle involved.

Another possible complication now being increasingly used in modern cars is two-level signalling. The reason is that in bright sunlight, high intensity lights are needed in order to show up. At night, these same lights would be far too bright, so something has to be done to dim them. Two-level signalling is achieved by using special lamps to give higher illumination without increasing the bulb wattage rating. At night, a special relay device is switched into circuit. This imposes resistors on the rear indicator light circuits, bringing a reduction in intensity of illumination. The switching is usually linked to the sidelight switch and the reduction operates on both flashers and stop lights. JJ

Above: indicators are required by law on all cars built after 1936. The main variety is of the flashing-lamp-type, which is shown here

Labels on diagram: Contact points · Resistance wire · Contact spring · Lead to panel light · Indicator switch · Indicator bulbs

BRITISH LEYLAND'S ITALIAN OUTPOST

For some time, Innocenti have built cars based on BMC models, but now they are starting to build their own-design vehicles

GIANT MANUFACTURING MACHINES, produced in Italy and used in all the major industrial centres of the world, a steel works on a 540-acre site hewn out of the Venezuelan jungle on the banks of the Orinoco river and car and scooter production are all activities resulting from the drive and imagination of one man, Ferdinando Innocenti.

Innocenti started his climb to the top of Italy's industrial ladder early in life—at sixteen; when he was not studying, he was employed in a small workshop.

By the age of eighteen, he had his own small work-shop and in 1922 he moved to Rome and began to experiment with the production and improvement of steel tubing. In later years, when the huge Innocenti industrial complex was growing, it was to be steel tube and its manufacture which was to play a great part in the development of the company.

In 1931, the Rome workshops gave way to premises in Milan, already the capital of Italian industry. For the next ten years, Innocenti prospered, only to have his handiwork destroyed by World War II.

Undeterred by the fortunes of war, Innocenti began to rebuild his company by basing his formula for success on a car and scooter-production plant. Coupled to the manufacturing side would be his own production of the heavy mills and presses required to build the cars and scooters. At the same time, this heavy machinery would be for sale to outside concerns.

Post-war Italy, suffering from shortages of fuel and vehicles, was ripe to receive a method of transport as simple as the scooter. The scooter's value as economic transport in those early years continued into more prosperous times, for it had opened up basic inexpensive mobility to millions. When the Innocenti company controlled Lambretta (sole manufacturing rights have now been sold to an Indian company), they had the majority share of the scooter market in Italy, forty per cent of production going for export. Besides the home market, countries in South America, and the Far East held concessions to assemble Lambrettas.

Seven models were produced, with engine capacities ranging from 50 cc to 200 cc, these scooters being designed for basic transport, competition and commerce. A particularly useful variation of the scooter is often seen in Latin countries in three-wheeled form with either platform or tilt body. Ideally suited for local delivery and often staying inside the lowest engine tax levies, it made ideal cheap commercial transport. Scooter design reached such sophisticated heights at one stage that one of Italy's top car designers, Bertone, designed scooters in co-operation with Innocenti.

Some interesting innovations came from the industrial-manufacturing side of the business, stemming mainly from the development of steel tube. One of the most notable was the world-wide use of Innocenti scaffolding-connection joints. Following the research, came the manufacture of auxiliary machinery to turn

out welded and seamless tubing. Innocenti also designed and manufactured many types of rolling mill and special machinery for steel-producing concerns.

Contracts with some of the world's largest industrial names gave Innocenti an open door to international markets; this led to eighty per cent exports for the heavy machinery.

Innocenti designed and built single, double and triple-acting presses used by Fiat, Alfa Romeo, Lancia, Pininfarina, Volkswagen, the Ford Motor Company and the Fisher Body Company. All assembly-line presses for the factory built to Fiat specifications at Torgliattigrad, in the Soviet Union, which produces the Lada 1200, were from Innocenti. This order comprised more than 170 units and represented the largest group of its kind ever bought from a single manufacturer.

Although in the immediate post-war period it was Ferdinando Innocenti's idea to produce cars, it was not until 1960 that the first cars bearing his name appeared on the market. The first two cars built by the Innocenti were the A40s and the Roadster, both

Top: a prototype Innocenti, based on Ferrari mechanical parts, that was shown in 1964. The body was designed by Bertone

Above: inside the Innocenti factory. Here can be seen some of the company's other products, such as the three-wheel utility vehicle and the ever-popular Lambretta

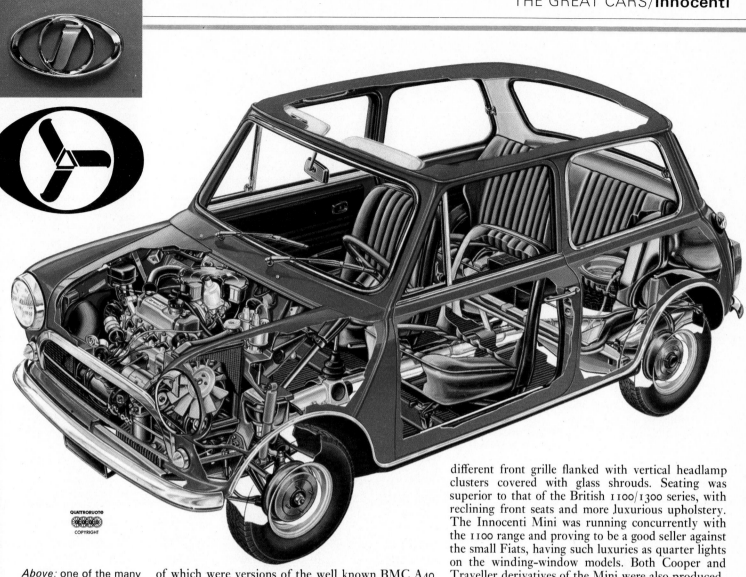

QUATTRORUOTE
COPYRIGHT

Above: one of the many Mini variations that was made by the Italian company, this being a 1000 cc version. The Innocenti company built a reputation for making Minis somewhat better than the parent factory in England. Most notably, the Innocenti Mini interiors were far better equipped than their British counterparts

Right: the Italian-built Austin A40, with bodywork by Pininfarina

of which were versions of the well known BMC A40 Farina of the same period. In the early days of Innocenti car production, the models produced arrived as 'knocked-down' vehicles which were then assembled locally by the company.

Next came the Innocenti C sports car, which was really an Austin-Healey Sprite with a redesigned body; the chassis was the same as that of its British counterpart. The redesigned body proved expensive to produce, but was certainly attractive.

The front-wheel-drive market was entered with the IM-3S, a slightly restyled BMC 1100 with Hydrolastic suspension. Externally, the IM-S3 was treated to a

different front grille flanked with vertical headlamp clusters covered with glass shrouds. Seating was superior to that of the British 1100/1300 series, with reclining front seats and more luxurious upholstery. The Innocenti Mini was running concurrently with the 1100 range and proving to be a good seller against the small Fiats, having such luxuries as quarter lights on the winding-window models. Both Cooper and Traveller derivatives of the Mini were also produced.

In 1966, after more than fifty years in industry, Ferdinando Innocenti died. He was superseded by his son, Luigi, who had worked for years with his father, and had begun at the bottom of the company. After nine years of production, the factory had produced over 300,000 cars.

In June 1972, the Innocenti company split up, but the name was retained for the British Leyland-controlled car-manufacturing company.

A greater proportion of the 1974 models used local parts, but the majority of the components, some 55–60 per cent, came from Great Britain. These included

Left: the 950 Spider
was based on the
Austin-Healey Sprite, as
Healey enthusiasts can
see from the style of the
wheels

Below: the Allegro-
based Regent was
available with either
1300 or 1500 cc engines
for the Italian market

Bottom: the IM 3 was
one of many variations
on the 1100/1300
series

all the running gear and most of the body panels. The remainder, some of the minor panels, electrical components, tyres and the materials to trim the vehicles were purchased locally. The Mini had a good following in Italy where the subtle changes appealed to Italian eyes.

The 1974 models were the Mini 1000, the Mini Cooper and the Mini Traveller. A further model of the Mini, called the 1001 Mini, was a more luxurious version and, beside selling on the home (Italian) market, it was exported to other EEC countries such as France, Holland and Germany. The acquisition of the Innocenti company was a major part of British Leylands plan to take a much larger part share of the European sales market. The marketing of other British Leyland cars, principally Triumph, Rover and Jaguar, previously controlled by British Leyland Italia, was taken over by the Innocenti organisation.

With British Leyland in sole control of marketing and assembly facilities in Italy, the Corporation aimed for a larger slice of the Italian market, 1974 sales figures being around 60,000 units per year. Production in the present factory could easily be increased to 100,000 with a little adjustment of plant.

The last model, in 1974, to join the Innocenti range was the Regent, which was an Allegro in 1300 and 1500 versions, again with subtle styling changes from the British car.

Innocenti were gradually branching out by themselves, though, for, in 1974, they were planning to produce a new Mini exclusive to themselves.　　RP

Announced at the 1974
Turin Motor Show was
this Mini Innocenti with
bodywork by Bertone;
this car replaced the
Mini, with the same
body shell as the
British car

A contrast in styles: the 1975 Citroën CX, *left*, presents even the most concerned motorist with all the information he could need, while the 1908 Itala, *right*, offers the bare minimum; the driver probably used his senses of smell and hearing to detect any problems, anyway!

Jody Scheckter's Tyrrell, *left*, has as few dials as possible for weight saving and simplification, while the Fiat 124 Spider in rally trim, *right*, has many instruments; of course, in a rally car, there is a co-driver to help out

The *avant garde* Audi dashboard as seen in the 'Ace of Spades', *left*, compares with the British standard walnut facia of this 1960 Rolls-Royce, *right*,

Bottom: the brilliant Jaguar XJS has an equally brilliant instrument layout; the complex dashboard, *left*, of the car, *right*, is self explanatory

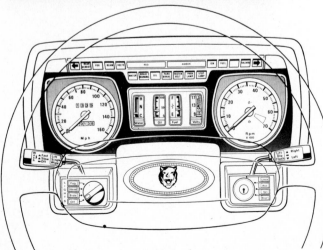

INFORMATION AT A GLANCE

Instruments relate not only engine condition,
but also whether the driver is within the law

Left, from top to bottom: the Delaĝe Torpille of 1922 has its instruments obscured by the steering wheel; however, the driving conditions of that period meant that the driver had plenty of time to seek out the dials and read them;

the Ferrari California Cabriolet Special has a fairly common GT instrument layout, with the speedometer and tachometer right in the driver's line of vision and the other dials angled towards the driver and situated in the centre of the dashboard, where they can be easily read at a glance;

in recent years, stylists have paid more attention to the car's instruments, although in this case the various dials and warning lights are grouped so close together that it might be difficult to get a quick reading for the oil pressure, for example;

the instrument layout of the 1973 Formula One Ferrari; the dials of a racing car are usually arranged so that when all readings are normal, the needles point straight up, making it easy for the driver to see what is happening, without having to scan the dials thoroughly; with the racing engine running at such high stress, the dials can mean all the difference between a competitive race and up to £20,000 worth of scrap machinery behind the driver

MODERN DASHBOARDS ARE SO WELL EQUIPPED with instruments which accurately record the car's speed and the behaviour of its engine, that it is difficult to realise that the first generation of motorists got by without any instruments at all. Their engines which, in the words of one critic, 'barked like a dog and stank like a cat', advertised their presence audibly enough in sickness and in health and, as long as the driver remembered to raise the motor-bonnet at the specified intervals (usually every 50 miles) to check that the oil cups which fed the engine bearings were still operational, there was little point in providing more detailed information.

Indeed, the first 'instrument' fitted to a motor car seems to have been the pointer fitted to the steering handle of Benz cars in the 1890s to show the driver which way he was going.

Not that there was anything new about instrumentation for wheeled vehicles: the 1813 steam locomotive *Puffing Billy* had a spring-loaded indicator which showed the blow-off pressure of the safety valve on a calibrated scale, but the breakthrough which made the production of compact and accurate instruments possible came in 1849, with the invention of the Bourdon gauge.

Bourdon discovered that if pressure was applied to the interior of a curved tube, closed at one end, the tube would tend to straighten out; by linking the end of the tube to a pointer, the pressure could be measured with extreme accuracy.

Bourdon gauges were used to measure boiler pressure on steam engines, and from the steam engine came another device which was to be used in car instruments, the centrifugal governor, in which the speed of the engine forced bobweights mounted on a parallelogram linkage to move outwards against spring pressure.

Perhaps the first true car instrument was the speed indicator for tricycles, price 12s 6d, indicating up to 32 miles an hour, shown at the 1899 National Cycle and Motor Show at the Crystal Palace by the Southern Motor Car Company of Brixton; an advanced feature was the fact that the scale of the instrument was engraved with both miles and kilometres per hour.

By the early part of 1902, the first company seriously to specialise in the manufacture of car instruments had placed its wares on the market. This was S. Smith and Son Limited, a firm of clock makers which had been established in London's Strand since 1851. Their first offerings to the motorist were 'Automobile Timepieces' and 'Chronographic Speed Indicators'. By 1903, they had progressed to 'Motor Watches with Electric Light' and 'Combined Motor Watch and Speed Indicators', as well.

The introduction of the Motor Car Act at the beginning of 1904 must have been a major boost to speedometer manufacturers: in place of a somewhat arbitrarily enforced 12 mph limit, motorists now had a rigidly policed 20 mph maximum allowed them, and

Right: two pages taken from a Smiths catalogue just prior to World War I. These motor watches could be purchased in materials and colours to suit the interior of most limousines. The communicators, however, could be rather dangerous if James the chauffeur was a loyal chap and the master in the rear quarters was an enthusiastic back-seat driver; the master might, for example, give a combination of faster' and 'turn round', which could cause problems if James obeyed his instructions to the letter !

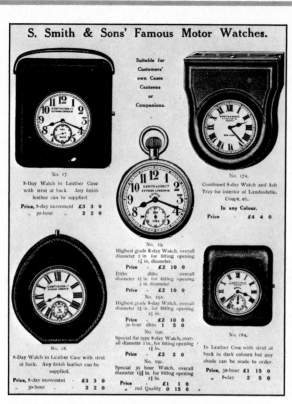

Dunhills, the accessory company, offered Bobby Finders—combined goggles and binoculars—to motorists worried about falling foul of the law.

In such a climate, speedometer makes flourished. One of the most ingenious of the new 1904 designs was the Vulcan Speed Indicator, built by Geipel and Lange of South London. This had a small magneto generator driven off one of the road wheels, supplying current to a hot-wire voltmeter calibrated in miles per hour: the theory was simple—as the car went faster, so more current was generated, directly related to the car's speed. Of course, an electric speedometer could not incorporate an odometer, like the mechanically-driven Smiths centrifugal unit, so Vulcan supplied an odometer which fitted on to the front hub cap of the car, recording distances of up to 10,000 miles in half-furlong increments.

Other types of instrument were now making their appearance. In those pre-dynamo days, a voltmeter was a useful accessory for the owner of a car with coil ignition. These were often pocket instruments, but in 1903 Charles Peacock of Clerkenwell, maker of the Carpeviam car, announced a dash-fitting voltmeter. Toledo steam cars had a gradient meter, to indicate the steepness of the hill they had just climbed (or failed to); steam cars, of course, carried pressure and water-level gauges for their boilers, the Locomobile having a 'rear-view mirror' so that the driver could keep an eye on the gauge glass, which was beneath his seat.

The boiler gauge idea was used on the 1904 Cossor Densimeter Petrol Gauge, which not only showed the level of petrol in the tank, but also incorporated a densimeter float to show the specific gravity of the fuel. Simple gauge glasses of this type were used to show the petrol level on low-priced cars into the 1920s.

A speedometer novelty of 1905 was the Cowey Recording Speed Indicator, which not only showed the

Above: opulence with an air of practicality; although this car is fitted out with such luxury appointments as a crystal glass ash tray and mother-of-pearl door cappings, the instruments are laid out in fairly accessible positions

glowed if the oil level was too high, and a red light if it was too low. If the level was correct, neither bulb lit up. Although this Edwardian aid to easy motoring was not long in production, it is interesting to note that more recently a similar device was made by Smiths Industries, whose 1974 Oil Check performs an almost identical function to that of the Lubrimeter.

By 1910, motor instruments were proliferating thick and fast: Smiths listed such esoteric delights as the All-English Communicator for limousines, by which the sybarite in the rear compartment could make his wishes known to the chauffeur by just pressing the appropriate button on a push box hanging beside his seat. This rang a bell and caused a bulb to light beneath the appropriate instruction—Faster, Slower, Home, Left, Right, Stop Left, Stop Right and Turn—on a display panel in front of the driver. For those who distrusted the electric fluid, there was a mechanical communicator, working like a tiny engine-room telegraph.

Another example of a 1910 instrument with no modern equivalent was the Consumeter, which measured the total petrol consumption, the varying rate of consumption under different running conditions and the amount of petrol used on each trip. Then there were Aneroid Barometers, Gradometers, air and oil pressure gauges, ammeters . . . even combinations of clock, speedometer and communicator, with duplicate instruments for the rear seats.

A minor styling revolution occurred around 1912 with the introduction of flush-fitting instruments— hitherto, they had been mounted proud of the dash— and the combination lighting and ignition panel incorporating an ammeter for use with the newly available electric lighting outfits. Some switchboards even incorporated a tell-tale lamp to indicate whether the tail-lamp bulb had failed, as this was a favourite cause for prosecution.

At about this time, too, came the radiator thermometer mounted in the filler cap. There were two types —the Boyce MotoMeter, which measured the temperature of the steam above the water, and the Wilmot Calormeter, which dipped into the water, whose heat caused a bi-metallic strip to bend and move a pointer round the dial.

These two useful instruments, which unfortunately fell victim to styling changes in the 1920s and '30s, pioneered the modern concept that an instrument should be instantly visible to the driver without him having to glance down. The Calormeter, especially, had the added virtue of being as easy to read by day as by night, as the reflected glow from the headlamps silhouetted the pointer.

Another sign of the future was the Lucas switch panel of the 1920s which, instead of complex wiring internally, used flat metal stampings to link the various positive and negative terminals in exactly the same way that printed circuits are now laid out. Such a switch panel, plus a speedometer and, perhaps, a clock, were all the instrumentation fitted to most cheap cars of the decade.

By the 1920s, speedometers had settled into three distinct types: firstly, there was the original centrifugal type, containing a spring-loaded governor. This was used on the majority of cars. Secondly, there was a cheaper sort, fitted to most American cars, in which a spring-loaded ribbon-type dial was activated by a spinning magnetic disc and, finally, for sports and racing cars where extreme accuracy was required, there was the chronometric speedometer, which moved to each successive reading with a jerk. Until the early 1920s, many cars still had the speedometer driven by a

speed that the car was moving at, but also the speeds reached over the preceding quarter mile. Thus, when the motorist was caught in a police speed trap, his speedometer would (hopefully) prove his innocence.

Oil pressure gauges had not yet made their appearance, since the majority of engines were lubricated by splash, but most cars had a drip feed unit on the dash, containing oil which was fed through sight glasses to pipes leading to the various engine bearings. The rate of drip could be controlled, and it was thus easy to see that enough oil was reaching the power unit.

In those days before the introduction of that simple device, the dipstick, it was a matter of some difficulty for the motorist to ascertain the actual depth of oil in the sump. So, in 1908, J. E. Garrett of Southwark, introduced the Lubrimeter, the first of the many idiot lights which have graced car dashboards. The Lubrimeter consisted of a float chamber connected to the drain plugs of the sump; on top of the float were two contact strips of different length, one completing a circuit when there was too much oil in the sump, the other when there was too little. An indicator unit mounted on the dashboard was fitted with a push button: when the driver pressed this, a white light

cable from a gear on the front hub; by the end of the decade, the take-off point was nearly always incorporated in the gearbox or final drive.

Up to the end of the 1920s, the instruments were usually round on European cars (although MG used octagonal bezels to echo their trademark), but the ribbon speedo gave the Americans, who had just discovered the Art of the Stylist, the chance to run riot across the dashboard with instruments of the most bizarre shapes, surrounded by baroque swags and curlicues of metal, usually cast in a cheap zinc-like alloy which soon assumed a leprous appearance.

The first sign that the rot was spreading to Europe came in the first years of the 1930s, when there was a craze for 'big instruments'. Speedometers became twice the size, and quasi-sporting vehicles acquired soup-plate tachometers to match. Often, these instruments were so big that they could incorporate a secondary instrument—the speedometer would have a tiny clock in the dead area between zero and maximum, while the tachometer might have a fuel gauge.

The era of the idiot light was just dawning. In the 1920s, it had been assumed that the motorist had enough sense to check that his engine contained sufficient oil before a run and, thus, lower-priced cars were generally devoid of any form of oil pressure indicator (although the Austin Seven had a little button that popped out of the dash, so long as there was sufficient oil pressure). An ammeter, however, was regarded as essential.

In a 1933 description of the Essex Terraplane we read: 'There are also two tell-tale lights which indicate, respectively, the sufficiency or otherwise of oil and whether the dynamo is charging or not. But then, as now, there was no tell-tale to indicate whether the tell-tales were working or not. Some British cars of the mid 1930s had a different kind of tell-tale—a warning light which came on when they exceeded the newly instituted 30 mph speed limit.

By then, improved magnetic materials had made it possible for manufacturers largely to replace the old centrifugal and chronometric speedos with the induction type; clocks, too, were almost exclusively electrically driven, and instruments, which in the beginning had almost exclusively had black figures on a white or silver background, were now virtually without exception made with white on black.

The post-war period saw some car manufacturers attempt to alter the status quo with instruments which were styled for the showroom rather than the road; speedometers acquired dials which were arcuate or rectangular, calibrations were made in the worst of typographical taste, and instruments even appeared with white figures on a beige background. But such irrelevancies have, fortunately, largely gone the way of the tailfin and the dollar grin grille, and modern instruments are as handsome as you please.

Save for internal refinements, they operate on much the same lines as they have for many years, although the instrument cluster fitted to the Mk III Ford Cortina was noteworthy for making use of modular 'building block' construction, so that a number of different instrumentation packs could be assembled to suit the various models of the car from the most basic to the most luxuriously specified using a minimum of units. This feature, plus the clear calibration, won this instrument panel a Design Council Award in 1974.

A speedometer which does not need a circular dial, but gives a straight-line reading like a thermometer, was introduced in 1960 by AC-Delco. In this, a cylinder behind the dial is divided helically into a red half and a black half. As the car's speed is increased, the cylinder is twisted, giving the effect of an advancing coloured line to indicate the velocity. From the driver's point of view, it is doubtful whether this form of speedometer had any other merit save that of novelty.

Recent years have shown an increasing awareness of the importance of correct instrumentation among

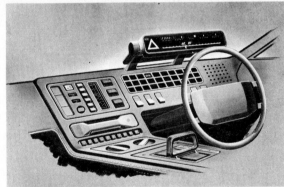

Above: the layout of a modern car—the 1974 Ford Cortina 2000E. By 1974, instruments had become clearer and easier to read; note the lack of confusing calibrations on the fuel and water temperature gauges, the slightly oval steering wheel also helping to make the dials visible

Right: two examples of what Smiths Industries have thought we might be facing in the future: head-up displays, myriad warning lights, buzzers and bleepers. It all seems a long way from the pioneering days of motoring when all one needed was a keen ear and a sharp eye to note the condition of the motor car

motorists, and many family cars have been equipped as standard with tachometers (electrically operated by induction from the ignition system), oil-pressure gauges, battery-condition indicators (an improved form of voltmeter), as well as the normal speedometer, ammeter, fuel gauge and water-temperature gauge.

As for extra instruments, Smiths industries list vacuum gauges for measuring the depression in the inlet manifold, and thus monitoring engine perfor-

mance and condition, remote-reading outside thermometers which warn of possible road icing in winter, warning lights which remind motorists to fasten their seat belts when the ignition is switched on, an oil check device and clocks with conventional or digital faces.

Another modern trend is the grouping of warning tell-tales into one information panel. Now, lights are fitted to some cars which inform the driver that his handbrake is still on, that the brake fluid level is dangerously low, that one of the lamps has failed; it is all rather like the classic Duesenberg, which gave a light-up warning at the appropriate service intervals.

In 1974, experiments were already being made with head-up displays, which project a distant focussed image into the windscreen, so that the driver can read his speed or be warned of any mechanical malfunction without taking his eyes off the road.

Other possibilities included liquid crystal and similar solid-state instruments, which needed only simple electrical connections to the car's power unit, eliminating all mechanical linkages. Smiths Industries also invented ECSTASY.

ECSTASY, let it be added, stands for nothing more lustful than Electronic Control for Switching and Telemetering Automobile SYstems, which did away with the conventional wiring loom, substituting a ringmain with a power cable and a control wire. Every electrical accessory was connected to this by the shortest possible route, and each one was scanned at millisecond intervals by the control wire to make sure that it was working properly. The advantage of the system was the number of different functions which could be handled simultaneously, and the simplification of the vehicle's wiring system. The only drawback was that ECSTASY required expensive transistors, but this could be overcome by mass production.

It might also be easy to add an interrogation/memory system to ECSTASY's control unit, so that the driver can ask his car what is wrong with it! DBW

ITALIAN CARS WITH AMERICAN ENTHUSIASM

The Intermeccanica company was founded from the ashes of a succession of American-engined GT cars, and became a maker of pure GTs

AN AMERICAN, FRANK REISNER, since the early 1960s, has been involved with several sports cars that have been built, or whose bodies have been built, in Turin. The first of the Reisner projects was the little IMP, which stood for Intermeccanica-Puch, a rear-engined car that looked like a scaled down Porsche 365. The IMP, which first appeared in 1960 was powered by an Austrian Steyr-Puch 645cc twin-cylinder engine, which produced just 40 bhp. Only 21 cars were built before production finished in 1961.

Reisner then turned his attention to the TVR Griffith, an American-engined sports car powered by a Ford Fairlane V8 engine. With 271 bhp on tap, the Griffith had a top speed of about 145 mph and could accelerate from 0-60 mph in 5.5 secs. Soon, TVR decided to drop the car, and Reisner took over the production of the cars' bodies in the Turin workshops. The car was subsequently renamed the Griffith GT. With the change in manufacture of the body and the new name, came a change in power unit from Ford to Chrysler. Few examples of the car were made and the project was handed over to Steve Wilder in the United States of America.

Once again, the source of power for the car was changed, again to Ford, and Wilder assembled the cars, with bodies still made across the Atlantic in Turin, at the Holman & Moody works at Charlotte, North Carolina. The Omega, as the car was now called, had the proven 4.7-litre V8 engine, which could take the car to 160 mph and accelerate it to 60 mph from rest in under 5 seconds. Production of the car trickled on until 1967, when, yet again, the whole works was transferred back to Turin, where the car was renamed the Torino. Little had changed since the model first appeared as the Griffith GT.

The Torino was a sports two-seater that was developed into the IMX Italia, a glassfibre coupé with a choice of 5.4-litre or 5.7-litre engines, the latter producing a healthy 310 bhp at 5500 rpm.

After the myriad variations on the Griffith theme, things settled down, and it looked as though Reisner would concentrate on building the cars completely by himself. This is, in fact, what did happen. It is interesting to note another Intermeccanica project, the Murena, which was a luxury 7-litre station wagon.

1972 saw the arrival of the car that was still in production in 1974, the Bob Cumberford-designed Indra. It was available with a choice of three Opel power units: the 2.8-litre Commodore and two Chevrolet-based V8s of 5.4 and 5.7-litres. Three body styles were offered, being a coupé, a spider and a fastback. The 5.7-litre version was available only as a fastback, whereas permutations of all the others were available.

When the Griffith GT was acquired from TVR and, subsequently, passed like a hot brick across the Atlantic, it seemed as if there were more name changes and power changes than there were cars built. However, in 1974, with twenty workers turning cars out of the Turin workshops, it seemed as if things would settle down and make the Indra the first of a long line of luxury GTs in the De Tomaso and Iso tradition.   LJC

Below: the IMX Italia 5.7-litre V8 in hardtop form

Right, above and below: two versions of the Italia convertible at the Turin motor show

Opposite page: the Intermeccanica Indra 5.7-litre fastback. The car bears a resemblance at the front to the Chevrolet Corvette, as well as some Maserati models

INTERMECCANICA INDRA

The Intermeccanica Indra, introduced in 1972, is a small-production sports car built in Turin, Italy. The Indra is available in three body styles: coupé, spider and fastback. There are three power units available: Opel Commodore 2.8-litre straight six and Opel Diplomat V8s of 5.4 and 5.7 litres. A four-speed manual gearbox is standard, while a GM automatic three-speed unit is available as an option.

The Indra is based on a massive box-section chassis which would do justice to a heavy lorry. The suspension is independent at the front by means of wishbones, coil springs, an anti-roll bar and telescopic dampers. The rear suspension is of the semi-independent type with a de Dion rear axle, twin swinging longitudinal trailing arms, transverse radius arms, coil springs, an anti-roll bar and telescopic dampers to absorb the bounces.

The coupé and spider are both two-seaters, while the fastback is a 2+2.

Top speed of the car is between 115 mph for the automatic 2.8-litre and 140 mph for the 5.7-litre fastback. To stop the car, servo-assisted ventilated disc brakes are used at both ends of the car.

ENGINE Front-mounted, water-cooled straight six or V8. 92 mm (3.62 in) bore × 69.8 mm (2.75 in) stroke = 2784 cc (169.9 cu in) (2.8), 101.6 mm (4 in) bore × 82.6 mm (3.25 in) stroke = 5354 cc (326.7 cu in) (5.4), or 101.6 mm (4 in) bore × 88.4 mm (3.48 in) stroke = 5733 cc (349.8 cu in) (5.7). Maximum power 165 bhp at 5600 rpm (2.8), 230 bhp at 5000 rpm (5.4), or 280 bhp at 5600 rpm (5.7); maximum torque 169 lb ft at 4100 rpm (2.8), 322 lb ft at 3400 rpm (5.4), or 301 lb ft at 4000 rpm (5.7). Cast-iron cylinder block and head(s); compression ratio: 9.5:1 (2.8), 10.5:1 (5.4), or 9:1 (5.7); 7 main bearings (2.8), or 5 main bearings (V8s); 2 valves per cylinder operated by a single overhead camshaft (2.8), or via pushrods and rockers by a single side camshaft (V8s). Bosch fuel injection (2.8), 1 Rochester 4-barrel carburettor (5.4), or 1 Holley 4-barrel carburettor (5.7).

TRANSMISSION Single-dry-plate clutch and four-speed manual transmission, or torque converter and three-speed automatic transmission. Manual ratios: 1st 2.200, 2nd 1.640, 3rd 1.270, 4th 1, rev 2.260:1. Hypoid-bevel final drive; ratio 3.890 (2.8) or 3.000 (V8s). Optional GM automatic transmission with torque converter. Maximum ratio of converter at stall: 2. Gear ratios 1st 2.480, 2nd 1.480, 3rd 1, rev 2.080:1. Final-drive ratio 3.670 or 3.00. Limited-slip differentials optional.

CHASSIS Box-section frame.

SUSPENSION Front independent by wishbones, coil springs, an anti-roll bar and telescopic dampers. The rear is non-independent by a de Dion axle, twin longitudinal swinging trailing arms, transverse radius arms, an anti-roll bar, coil springs and telescopic dampers.

STEERING Recirculating ball; turns from lock to lock 4. Optional ZF power-assisted system.

BRAKES Servo-assisted ventilated discs all round.

WHEELS Light-alloy 14 in.

TYRES 195/70 VR × 14.

DIMENSIONS AND WEIGHT Wheelbase 98.43 in (coupé and spider) or 102.36 in (fastback); track front and rear 61.02 in; length 174.41 in (coupé and spider) or 178.35 in (fastback); width 70.47 in; height 46.46 in; ground clearance 4.92 in; dry weight 2800 lb (2.8 coupé and spider), 3021 lb (2.8 fastback), 3153 lb (V8 coupé and spiders), or 3374 lb (V8 fastbacks); turning circle 42.6 ft; fuel tank capacity 17.6 gals.

BODY 2-door 2 or 2+2 seats in either coupé, spider or fastback forms.

PERFORMANCE Maximum speed between 115 mph for the automatic 2.8 and 140 mph for the manual 5.7 fastback. Fuel consumption (overall) between 24 mpg for the manual 2.8 and 14 mpg for the 5.7-litre automatic car.

TRANSPORT FOR THE DISABLED

For many years now, the disabled have travelled in purpose-built vehicles, but specially adapted production cars are becoming ever more popular

THE MOTORISATION OF INVALID VEHICLES was first seen in 1920, when the British Red Cross Society made available a few motor-cycle engines for fitting to wheelchairs supplied to disabled soldiers and sailors.

Before World War I, invalid vehicles had been no more than wheelchairs which offered little mechanical advance on the original wickerwork Bath chair. These vehicles came into the public province in 1917 with the formation of the Ministry of Pensions, when some wheelchairs were provided out of the Lord Kitchener Memorial Fund. The Ministry assumed direct responsibility in 1918, supplying wheelchairs to paraplegic cases confined to bed, and to double-leg-amputation patients, or where the physical condition of the pensioner made the supply of a chair necessary.

Hand-propelled tricycles were provided for those of the above who needed them to get to and from work. Others were considered on their merits. From 1934, those qualifying were slightly extended.

It was not until 1945 that the first powered units for invalid tricycles were supplied as a Ministry responsibility. From July 1948, the Minister of Health had the duty under the Health Act to promote the establishment of a comprehensive health service including the provision of surgical, medical and other appliances. The Ministry of Pensions undertook to act for the Ministry of Health in the supply of wheelchairs and tricycles, the Ministry of Health assuming direct responsibility in 1953, a responsibility which the Department of Health and Social Security, in 1974, still discharged.

The development of motorised tricycles after World War II fell to two small firms, each working initially in isolation—Invacar of South Benfleet, Essex, and AC Cars of Thames Ditton, Surrey.

Invacar's involvement began after a director, Mr D. Preston-Cobb, who was handicapped, had designed for him by his friend, Bert Greeves (of Greeves motor cycles), a three-wheeled vehicle which could be driven by a one-armed driver. It was powered by a small side-mounted engine.

This layout was developed, and a New Era tricycle, an Invacar vehicle based on the Preston-Cobb one-off was shown at the 1947 Motor Cycle Show. This, a square open box, allowed a person confined to a wheelchair to drop the tailboard and wheel himself in, locking his chair in position.

In 1950, Invacar won a Government contract to supply vehicles to the war disabled. Their Mk 6 was powered by an offside-mounted 1.25 hp Villiers two-stroke motor-cycle engine (later increased to 2 hp) driving the offside wheel. There was no electric start, a hand lever acted as the equivalent of a kick-starter. The vehicle was initially fitted with three forward speeds, and reversing was achieved by manoeuvring manually, using the 'free' nearside wheel. The bodywork was of steel panels on a steel frame. It was open, and wheels were of the motor-cycle type. Suspension was non-

Top: the heavyweight motor-propelled tricycle which was for use only by patients over 16 stones and living in hill districts'

Above: this machine has a specially widened left-hand door so that a wheel chair can be accommodated

Left: driving compartment of the Harper Mk IV

existent. A later version had four forward speeds and a six-volt electric starter system.

In 1952, the vehicle acquired a soft top, windscreen and side-screens, and a rear luggage carrier. The Mk 8a of 1954 had improved weatherproofing and metalastik rear suspension. In 1956, the Mk 9 was fitted with a Villiers four-stroke engine with a centrifugal clutch, and was governed to do 20 mph.

The Mk 10 and 10a of the following year saw considerable advance with aluminium 4.00 by 12 wheels, purpose-built by Invacar, a pressed-steel body (still with the soft top which could be rolled back) with a hinged door, and a dark-blue finish (the previous paintwork had been black).

The vehicle's suspension was independent by rubber-mounted coil springs and dampers. The power was provided by a Villiers 197 cc two-stroke engine with Siba electric dynastart, as fitted to the Bond and Berkeley cars. There were four forward gears with a straight-through lever change, and the vehicle was capable of 55 mph. A hand-operated Girling hydraulic clutch was fitted. Reverse progress was achieved with this system by stopping the engine and engaging a separate drive, with a safety device to prevent 55 mph reversing! There was a Lockheed hydraulic braking system on the rear wheels.

The Mk 11 adopted Girling brakes, a rearward-sliding door and pressed-steel Dunlop wheels. The 1959 Mk 12 brought a glassfibre body of hard-top design, although the sliding door was still of steel. The rear screen became glass instead of perspex, and variations in controls, to suit the many dif-

Below: the sliding door of the 1974 AC type 70

Bottom left: this tiller mechanism has a left-hand throttle and clutch lever. On the right of the cabin is the gear-change lever and the parking brake

Bottom right: the Invacar Mk 10A with a 197 cc Villiers engine

ferent sorts of disabilities, were made available.

In 1961, the 12a brought glass to the side windows, the 12B which followed allowed the seat to slide sideways to the door, the 12C of 1966 added an hydraulic brake on the front wheel, and the body colour was changed to 'ice-blue'. The door became glassfibre in the 12D, and the 12E of 1968 saw the first significant borrowing from AC, their leading-arm front suspension replacing the previous Invacar C-tube.

AC had entered the scene in 1950 when they produced an all-weather tricycle in response to Ministry pressure for motorised transport for the disabled. AC's answer had a 250 cc air-cooled BSA power unit, driving through an Albion transmission and driving both the rear wheels. This was behind the driver. The vehicle had a soft top, and suspension, differential and driveshafts were all produced by AC at Thames Ditton, Surrey.

After a couple of years, AC went out of the invalid-car side and produced a similar vehicle commercially, calling it the Petite. Their invalid-car function was taken over by Stanely Engineering, of Egham, Surrey, a member of the Exeter-based Harper Aircraft company.

The Harper vehicle had Villiers 197 cc power with a Siba starter—a similar animal to the Invacar of the day, although suspension was Bramber rubber in torsion with Armstrong dampers, and the body was in glassfibre—the first invalid vehicle to have it.

Harper faded from the scene in 1957, and AC tendered for, and won, the vacant Government contract, producing a vehicle similar to the Harper, but

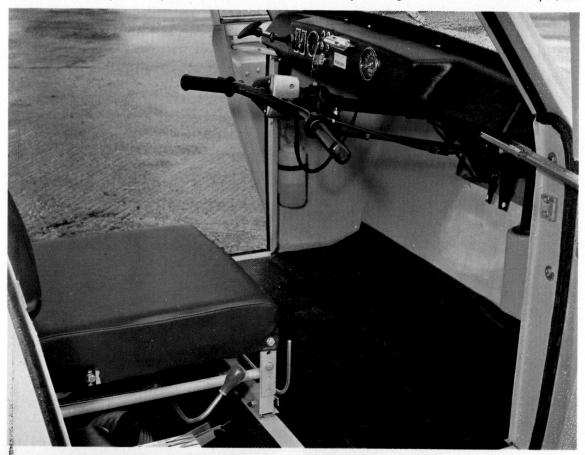

Left: the controls of the AC type 70

Below left: the DAF-type transmission and Salisbury torque converter of the AC type 70. This AC has a twin-cylinder, four-stroke Steyr-Puch engine

Bottom right: the 1974 Invacar

Right: the AC 70 and other invalid vehicles of this type were severely criticised in 1974 for, among other things, their instabilities in cross winds. Measures were taken to disprove this when a selection of vehicles were taken to Southend Airport for trials. Cars were driven down runways and given handling tests around bollards. Also, they were driven across the wind generated by the propellors of a line of stationary aircraft at full thrust. Although the cars proved sufficiently stable, it was still felt that ordinary production cars with hand controls were a better proposition for the disabled

with an aluminium body on a steel frame and chassis. This vehicle lasted for some years until AC developed a new automatic transmission. Needing a more powerful engine, they failed to find one in Britain and, with Ministry approval, negotiated with Fiat for a 500 cc unit. Having settled on this and produced a prototype, they were told that it was to be superseded, and were advised to negotiate with Steyr-Puch.

It was from these negotiations that the Government-specification P70 invalid tricycle emerged, drawing the two British strands of development and manufacture of these vehicles.

The P70 appeared in November 1971 and was still being produced in 1974. Powered by a 500 cc two-cylinder, four-stroke, air-cooled Steyr-Puch engine made in Austria, the vehicle had a DAF-type belt-drive transmission and a Salisbury torque converter. The rear suspension was by trailing arms with coil springs and dampers. The body was pale blue glass-fibre with two sliding doors. The heater, seat belts and fire-extinguisher were standard. There were 56 variations in the controls, including 14 variations in steering, to enable the car to be adapted to individual needs.

Later, the P70 was severely criticised on safety grounds by the Disabled Drivers' Action Group, supported by certain public figures, and by a report from a government committee under Baroness Sharp. A report by the Cranfield Institute of Technology also criticised the stability of the vehicle, and an unpublished MIRA report was said to have done the same, although there were official denials, and Invacar and AC manufacturing licences were renewed in May 1974.

The DDAG wanted P70 production to cease and disabled drivers to be issued with conventional cars adapted to their needs. The Mini was one of a line of small production cars (including also the Morris Minor 1000, and DAF) which specialist firms adapted to the needs of the disabled.
 EF

Above: the front suspension of the AC 70, also seen *left.* The one-wheel-front and two-wheel-rear layout was one of the main points of criticism of this type of vehicle

A FLYER FOR SCOTLAND YARD

The true British Invicta was originally to be a combination of American flexibility and British quality

CAPTAIN NOEL CAMPBELL MACKLIN, the man behind the Invicta car, loved the lazy, effortless torque of the steam engine, which could take a vehicle from a standstill to maximum speed without gearchanging. That sort of performance was what he looked for in his motor cars, whatever their motive power.

Barely out of his teens, he had raced big Mercedes and Fiats at Brooklands from 1909; during World War I, he served with the Royal Horse Artillery.

In 1919, he decided to go into car production, so Macklin and Hugh Eric Orr-Ewing took over part of the Handley-Page aircraft factory at Cricklewood, where they built a sporting light car called the Eric-Campbell; its specially tuned 1.5-litre Coventry Climax engine gave a maximum speed of 65 mph, and two cars were built for the Targa Florio. One started, and failed to finish, but it was notable to break into international competition so soon after the war.

Macklin, however, soon parted from the Eric-Campbell, and next attempted to market an even more sporty light car, the Silver Hawk, produced in the three-car garage and workshop behind his house in Surrey. The project was abandoned after a year.

Now Macklin decided to experiment with steam, and bought both Stanley and Doble steamers for trial purposes. Sundry conflagrations and scalds convinced him that steam and the average motorist would not mix, so he decided to develop a petrol car whose lazy top-gear performance would emulate the desirable characteristics of steam as closely as possible.

Three prototypes of the new car, which Macklin called the Invicta, were built in the garage at Cobham in 1924; however, their 2.5-litre Coventry Climax six-cylinder engines did not have the flexibility that Macklin sought. A fortuitous meeting with Henry Meadows of Wolverhampton resulted in the supply of 2.6-litre Meadows sixes for subsequent Invictas; these power units gave the top-gear performance which Macklin was seeking, at the expense of maximum speed, which the overall gearing restricted to just over 60 mph. The cars could, however, climb the one-in-four Brooklands Test Hill in top.

Production versions of the Invicta were built in a new factory on the Fairmile at Cobham; finance for the venture was provided by Oliver Lyle (of Tate and Lyle) and Earl Fitzwilliam, formerly the power behind Sheffield-Simplex. The designer was W. G. Watson.

The handsomely square-cut radiator of the new car recalled both the Silver Hawk and the Eric-Campbell, and rivets down the bonnet-hinge line emulated Rolls-Royce. To improve the top speed, the engine was bored out to 3 litres for 1926, giving a maximum of around 70 mph. To gain publicity for the new model, Macklin arranged a remarkable endurance test at the Monza Autodrome. Even in the 1920s, they were using sex to sell motor cars, for a pretty young lady driver, Violette Cordery, headed the Invicta team.

Starting on 1 March 1926, the car averaged around 60 mph—stops included—for four days. Then, one of the drivers nodded off at the wheel, and the car overturned into the iron railings edging the track. After extensive repairs at the Isotta-Fraschini factory, a fresh start was made at midnight on the 9th, and the car ran until Sunday 21 March, covering 25,000 kilometres at an average speed of 55.78 mph, breaking 33 Italian and four international records, despite frame fractures caused by damage sustained in the crash.

A few months later, the irrepressible Violette was off again, this time with her sister, Evelyn, on a 10,000-mile round-the-world tour, which won Invicta the coveted Dewar Trophy for 1927.

At Olympia in 1928, Invicta Cars showed their

Left: the Invicta badge; Invicta is the Latin for 'unconquered', which was quite a challenge for a car to meet

Above: seen at a Vintage meeting at Oulton Park, a 4½-litre Invicta

latest model, the 30 hp 4½-litre; the chassis price was £985, and the Meadows power unit developed over 100 bhp. In mid 1929, a number of these cars were acquired by Scotland Yard's Flying Squad, as the Invicta's rapid acceleration made it ideal for chasing smash-and-grab raiders.

In September 1929, three men were tried at the Old Bailey after a chase by one of the Flying Squad Invictas. They had driven off at high speed in their 30/98 Vauxhall (which had eluded a police car by its sheer speed on a previous occasion), when signalled to stop in Victoria Street, just down the road from the 'Yard'. The Invicta drew alongside the 30/98 in Buckingham Gate, and one Inspector Ockey jumped on to the Vauxhall's running board. A desperate fight ensued: the Inspector was hit on the back of the head with a jemmy, and rolled into the gutter outside

Wellington Barracks. The two cars raced down Ebury Street at 70 mph, until the Vauxhall skidded, ripped off two tyres and crashed into a wall. After a hand-to-hand struggle on the pavement, the criminals, well known smash-and-grab raiders, were arrested; at their trial, they were sentenced to penal servitude: 'Since these really fast cars were added to the fleet, the police have been successful in capturing a number of alleged motor bandits,' commented *The Motor*.

In mid 1929, Violette and Evelyn Cordery were off again. This time they travelled over 30,000 miles in 30,000 minutes, driving round and round Brooklands over a two-month period. Their average running speed was 61.5 mph, the car used a gallon of petrol every 18.47 miles, and needed no more than routine maintenance throughout the run, which took place in atrocious weather conditions. This triumph of reliability won Invicta their second Dewar Trophy.

By the autumn of 1929, production was entirely concentrated on the 4½-litre, and the 3-litre had been dropped. However, as the larger engine had been fitted in a virtually unmodified 3-litre chassis, it became obvious that the extra power was too much for the frame. So, at the 1929 Motor Show, an entirely new chassis was introduced. This was the Type NLC, the most expensive Invicta model that had then been produced, with a chassis price of £1050, and finish and fittings to Rolls-Royce standards. Lower and more rigid than the old chassis, the NLC also had longer springs and a wider track.

For speed merchants, however, Invicta had a new thrill in store, and one that was not to be seen at the

Below: an S-type 4½-litre of 1931 at Lewes, near Brighton, for speed trials

Show. This was the new S-Type sports chassis, which appeared at the very end of 1929. It was exceptionally low-built, with sidemembers which were dropped behind the radiator and then continued backwards beneath the rear axle. The top of the engine was at the same level as the top of the radiator, and the steering was sharply raked to keep the overall height down. A

massive cast-aluminium dashboard carried reserve oil and petrol tanks, and there was a twenty-gallon fuel tank at the rear of the chassis. The engine was endowed with two massive bronze SU carburettors and dual magneto and coil ignition, with separate plugs for each system. The twin exhaust pipes emerged spectacularly from the bonnet sides, clad in chromed conduits like those of the contemporary Mercedes sports models, and then burrowed beneath the side valances, where a massive silencer and tailpipe were

fitted to take away the roar of the engine.

On the radiator of the new model was a distinctive badge, with the word 'Invicta' vertically on a gold 'I'-shaped ground, supported by red, green and blue wings in iridescent enamel like some fantastic butterfly. The car's performance was sufficiently high for the new model to be nicknamed the '100 mph Invicta', although

its makers described it only as the 4½-litre Sports; the top speed was certainly well into the 90s, and the car could go from 10 to 90 mph on top gear in 32.5 seconds and from 10 to 60 mph in 15 seconds.

Almost as newsworthy as the performance of the new Invicta Sports was the marque's massive price reduction during 1929, achieved mainly by production economies such as the use of aluminium instead of Elektron for chassis castings, and the substitution of chromed brass for German Silver brightwork. The

cost of the high chassis was cut from £1050 to £650, the new sports chassis sold at £750, the high chassis saloon cost just £765 and the sports four-seater was £875 complete.

In a complete reversal of all that the Invicta stood for, the Cordery sisters drove their '30,000 miles in 30,000 minutes' high-chassis tourer from London to Edinburgh in top gear during 1930; Donald Healey then used the same car to win his class in the Alpine Trial that summer.

More spectacular was Healey's performance in the 1931 Monte Carlo Rally. Driving an S-Type, he started from Stavanger in Norway, slid off the road soon afterwards and demolished a telegraph pole, bending the chassis and putting both axles out of alignment. Despite this, Healey won the Rally outright *and* beat all his competitors in the Mont-des-Mules hill-climb which followed the event. Healey repeated the Mont-des-Mules success the following year, but only managed to take second place behind Vasselle's Hotchkiss in the Monte. His car, however, already had 50,000 miles on the clock before the rally started.

Long-distance reliability trials of this type were more within the Invicta's compass than track events, although S-types appeared in the 1931, 1933 and 1934 Tourist Trophies. The leading Invicta track driver was George Field, but the racing Invictas rarely stayed the distance. In the 1931 Brooklands Double-Twelve, Field's car was the fastest car around the sharp curve from the Members' Banking into the Finishing Straight (the race was being run the wrong-way-round), but holed a piston. A new set was fitted over-

Far left: a 1926 streamlined occasional four-seater

Near left: a 1928 4½-litre Invicta, fitted with a Harrison body

Left: a superb example of a 1933 low-chassis 4½-litre

Right: another example of a 1933 4½-litre; the 4½-litre cars were able to accelerate from 10 to 90 mph in top gear in just 32.5 seconds

night and, by the middle of the second day, the car was lapping at 90 mph. It was still running at the end, but failed to complete the distance.

A special single-seater was built for the 1931 Brooklands 500-mile race, but was written off during practice. More successful was Raymond Mays's White Invicta, which did well in sprints, hill-climbs and sand races. However, it was rumoured that the low-chassis Invicta was liable to become tail-happy under racing conditions, a contention that seemed amply borne out in the summer of 1931, when S. C. H. Davis wrapped his S-Type round a telegraph pole at Brooklands. That same summer, Donald Healey was back in the news: driving an S-Type, he completed the International Alpine Trial without a single penalty point, winning one of the coveted Coupe des Glaciers awards and making the fastest climb of the Galibier Pass. He repeated the Coupe des Glaciers feat the following year; two other Invictas also gained the coveted trophy for their performance in the Trial.

The 1931 Olympia Motor Show saw a new small Invicta, designed to bring the marque's appeal to a wider market. Priced at just £399, the car had a dropped frame along similar lines to that of the S-Type. Its power unit was a six-cylinder single-overhead-camshaft Blackburne engine.

However, the car turned the scales at nearly 24 cwt, which meant that to get any sort of performance from the engine, the depressingly low final-drive ratio of 6:1 had to be used, resulting in engine speeds of over 5000 rpm in normal use.

The Motor, testing a rather tired example which could only reach 67 mph instead of the 70 mph-plus claimed by enthusiastic owners was, nonetheless, impressed: 'Here is a car with altogether exceptional roadholding qualities and superb springing, capable of excellent hill-climbing and rapid acceleration, besides having a very fair turn of speed, and all this, mark you, for the very modest upkeep and running charges of the smaller and more-conventional type of light car'.

Even then, a few months after the model's introduction, Invicta must have realised that the engine was not really up to the task of moving this car around with the traditional reliability and speed for which the marque was renowned, so, in July 1932, a supercharged 1½-litre with 80 mph performance was announced. It was not particularly successful, due to carburation problems; the 14/120 announced at the end of 1932 had a similar supercharged power unit, this time of 1660 cc, but, although it was listed as available, it is unlikely that the model ever reached the public. Stillborn, too, was the 5-litre twin-overhead-camshaft SS-Type, with three valves per cylinder: two prototypes were apparently built, with Reid Railton as consultant designer, and there was talk of a team, headed by Humphrey Cook, for Le Mans, but nothing came of the car or the competition version.

In any case, Invicta production was virtually at an end. In 1933, Macklin sold the company to Lord Fitzwilliam, and perhaps half-a-dozen Invictas were assembled from spare parts at the company's London depot in Flood Street, Chelsea. They were the last of perhaps 1000 examples of the marque, of which 77 were the low-chassis S-type.

Macklin had retained the Fairmile works and soon they were busy with 'a new departure in motor-car construction', the Railton Terraplane, which was the remarkable Essex Terraplane adapted into a characteristic English class car by the designer of the *Bluebird*, and the experimental staff of a famous British sports car. In fact Reid Railton had not had much to do with the design of this first of the Anglo-American sports cars, but his was an impressive name to have on the square-cut radiator shell, which had a distinct family resemblance to that of the Invicta (and, of course, rivets down the bonnet).

There was talk in 1938 of reviving the Invicta name for a range of rebodied French Darracqs assembled in London, but it came to nothing.

From 1934, the Railton had a Hudson 8 engine (Hudson sixes became available in 1938) and there was also a 10 hp standard-engined version from 1938. Hudson Motors acquired the company in 1940—they had been assembling the cars for some time anyway—but production of Railtons was minimal after that, and ceased entirely in 1949.

Noel Macklin died in 1946, having received a wartime knighthood for his work as head of a gunboat factory; a few weeks before his death, a new Invicta was announced, but he had nothing to do with this new venture, which originated from the Invicta Car Development Company of Virginia Water, Surrey. The designer was, again, W. G. Watson, and power was by a Meadows six-cylinder engine, but there the resemblance ended. The 1946 Invicta Black Prince had all-round torsion-bar independent suspension and a complex Brockhouse hydrokinetic automatic transmission. During the new company's four-year life, production amounted to between twelve and twenty Black Princes, and then the moribund company was acquired by AFN Ltd, makers of the Frazer Nash, but no more Invictas resulted from the takeover.   DBW

INNES IRELAND WAS ONE OF THE LAST of the great characters of motor racing, for after he gave up racing in 1966 the amount of sponsorship money hanging on race results precluded any of the all-night pre-race parties and escapades in which Ireland often indulged. Although he was a professional racing driver, his approach was that of a gentleman amateur to whom the sport was simply a well paid means of assisting him to enjoy life.

Born Robert McGregor Innes Ireland at Kirkcudbright, Scotland, in 1930, he was the son of a veterinary surgeon who attempted to give him a good education. However, Innes was more interested in sport and motor cycles, so his father bowed to the inevitable and apprenticed him to the Rolls-Royce aero-engine division in Glasgow. His engineering talent was obvious, but he went to great lengths to hide this by becoming involved in various pranks and other anti-establishment activities. His departure from Glasgow was precipitated when he managed to blow up an expensive aircraft engine during power tests, so he was switched to the car division in London. In London, he met various people interested in motor racing, and before long, he was working on vintage cars, which naturally introduced him to the race track. His first race, at Boreham in 1952, was in a 4½-litre Bentley but before his racing career could develop any further he was called up for military service, joining the Parachute Regiment, where he was commissioned as an officer.

On his discharge from the Army, he went into partnership in a garage business and soon got back into racing with a pre-war Riley, with which he scored several wins and good placings. He really began to come to public notice when he acquired a Lotus 11 for the 1957 season. He picked up several wins with the car, principally at Goodwood, finally winning the Brooklands Memorial Trophy as a result of his success in club racing at Goodwood in 1957. Already, he was developing a reputation as a 'hairy' driver, for his Lotus spun quite regularly on its way to victory. By now, his rather long name had been shortened by race reporters and public alike to Innes Ireland, and that is the way it remained.

In 1958, he drove both his own Lotus and those of other entrants in a large number of races, winning the 3-hour Circuit of Auvergne race in France as well as a number of other minor events. By 1959, he had been invited to join Team Lotus as a works driver both in Formula One and sports cars, although he also drove an Ecurie Ecosse Jaguar at Le Mans. In Formula One, he was number two to Graham Hill, but the front-engined car he drove was not very competitive and his only result all season was a fourth place at the Dutch Grand Prix. However, he picked up several wins in the 1½-litre Lotus sports car.

He stayed with Lotus in 1960 when they produced the new rear-engined Mk 18 F1 car. With it, he won the Glover Trophy at Goodwood and the International Trophy at Silverstone but, in Grand Prix races, he was less fortunate because the car often broke down, and his only places of note were second in the Dutch and US GPs. In the F2 Lotus, he won the Lavant Cup at Goodwood and the Oulton Park Trophy race.

Staying with Lotus in 1961, Ireland had another poor year, partly because of a crash in the Monaco Grand Prix when he changed into

A Grand-Prix typewriter

Above: Innes Ireland, *inset,* in the UDT-Laystall Lotus, chases car number 8, racing in the 1962 Belgian GP at Spa-Francorchamps

the wrong gear in the famous tunnel, receiving serious leg injuries. However, he came back to top form later in the year, winning a furious battle for the Solitude GP in Germany, following up with the non-Championship F1 race at Zeltweg in Austria, and then, in October, he won the United States Grand Prix; not only was it his first, and only, Championship win, but it was also the first Championship win for Lotus.

Despite his success in the US GP, he was dropped from the Lotus team in favour of Jim Clark, a decision which still rankled Ireland years after. He joined the private UDT-Laystall team which ran Lotus-BRMs but, from then on, he was equipped with out of date machinery and, although he drove particularly hard in 1962, his only major win was in the London GP at Crystal Palace. He had more luck in the team's Lotus 19 sports car with which he won the Nassau Trophy in the Bahamas and a whole string of British sports-car races. He also won the Tourist Trophy at Goodwood in a Ferrari 250GTO.

The UDT team was renamed BRP for 1963, and Ireland stayed with them, winning the Glover Trophy at Goodwood, in their Lotus-BRM. When he switched to their new BRP-BRM

car, he was often fast, but the car seldom lasted the distance. However, he was put out of racing for a long while when he crashed a Lotus-Ferrari in America; he received multiple injuries, including a very badly smashed hip. He returned to racing in 1964 with the BRP once more, winning the Daily Mirror Trophy at Snetterton, but, in Grand Prix races, he either crashed or retired in most events.

By now, he was unable to command a place in a works team and, in 1965, he drove a rather uncompetitive Lotus-BRM for the Parnell team which brought him no success at all. In 1966, he raced only spasmodically, taking in the last two races of the season in Bernard White's old 2-litre BRM. His last race was the Mexican Grand Prix of that year.

Ireland retired from the sport soon afterwards to take up farming, but he was tempted by *Autocar* magazine to come back into the sport as their sports editor, reporting on Grand Prix racing. He also wrote an amusing autobiography called All Arms and Elbows and, later on, returned to competition in such events as the London to Sydney Marathon, about which he also wrote a book.   MT

ITALY'S DOWN-MARKET SUPERCARS

The Rivolta family set out to build cars that would be better suited to everyday driving than other exotic Italian machinery

THE ISO COMPANY has never belonged to the same set as Ferrari, Maserati and Lamborghini, the surviving great names in the performance-car business. Ferrari and Maserati road cars have been offshoots of motor racing; Lamborghini was born of the desire to be better than Ferrari, at a time when Ferrari road cars played very much second fiddle to the competition side. Iso, on the other hand, was the product of people who saw an opportunity, had the money and moved in for a killing with what they believed would be a far more suitable car for the well-heeled performance advocate, rather than the highly-strung machinery already dominating the scene. In a way, they succeeded, but in 1974 they found difficulties in producing cars which were that much cheaper than their V12-engined counterparts, simply because Isos were still Italian supercars. This meant that they had supercar interiors and supercar finish. However, the company was still confident that the small saving was worth it.

Iso was the creation of a family business run by Renzo Rivolta. The initial wealth came from the production of mopeds and other two-wheelers after the war, at a time when Italy was in urgent need of transport but could not afford four wheels. Rivolta saw that the demand for two wheels was only a transient thing and that future progress would depend on super-economy four-wheelers. As a logical extension of their existing business, the Rivoltas designed and developed the Isetta bubblecar just at the very moment that the Arabs upset the Suez applecart for the first time. Later, the Arab situation was to work savagely against Iso, but at that time it paved the way for the future production, because BMW saw the Isetta as being exactly what was needed to counter the fuel crisis in increasingly affluent Germany. The resultant deal did the Rivolta fortunes a lot of good and moved them into the field of the big-time GTs.

However, as the Rivoltas quickly found out, it was a field full of nettles: expertise is needed even for the first tentative steps. The idea was that the first GT had to be essentially practical and uncomplicated, something that would appeal to the buyer who thought that with every Ferrari or Maserati a prerequisite for ownership was to have a full-time mechanic travelling in the luggage compartment. They knew they needed a proprietary engine since the cost of setting up an engine plant, to say nothing of the trauma of designing and developing a unit from scratch, was prohibitive. There was no shortage of Chevrolet engines, so a supply of V8s was arranged, some with automatic transmission already attached and others ready to be fitted with ZF manual boxes. That part was easy enough; so was the consultation with the Bertone organisation, on the outskirts of Turin. They agreed to supply the Rivolta establishment with some ideas for bodies that would not be too revolutionary and that would carry four adults comfortably enough, plus a reasonable quantity of luggage. At almost exactly the

Above: the first Iso car was the Iso Rivolta coupé, styled by Bertone, which was announced in 1962; the car pictured is a 1963 model. The Rivolta was fitted with a 5.3-litre Chevrolet V8 and a choice of power outputs was offered: 300 or 350 bhp

Left: in 1973, Frank Williams began to enter Formula One Racing cars known as Isos; these cars, which were used in modified form in 1974, were powered by Cosworth V8 engines. In fact, the cars were not built by Iso, but acquired that name as a result of heavy sponsorship. Here, Arturo Merzario is seen in action during the 1974 Monaco Grand Prix

same time, the British Gordon-Keeble company was commissioning Bertone to style a body for its very similar project. The important difference was that the Gordon-Keeble team already had a chassis and they took it to Bertone so that the prototype could be built.

When a chassis was eventually delivered to Bertone for the Iso prototype, it was very similar indeed to the Gordon-Keeble's. It had a tubular frame, discs all round, de Dion rear end and so on. In fact, they were very close to being interchangeable. Whatever the reason for this surprising coincidence, they were good chassis that worked efficiently in their role as four-seater GTs.

The very first Iso Rivolta, as the new Italian car was named, appeared before the public in the autumn of 1962. It was greeted with enthusiasm. After all, it was a practical, good-looking car, capable of 150 mph or so, and ideally suited to markets outside Europe, where

Above: Iso's big saloon was introduced in 1967 as the S4; the name was changed in 1968, however, to Fidia. The Chevrolet V8 produced either 300 or 365 bhp and the bodywork was styled by the house of Ghia, now a wholly owned subsidiary of the Ford Motor Company. Unfortunately, the Fidia has not enjoyed the success of the Lele, which it joined in the Iso range, perhaps because it is just too big and too thirsty for the strife-torn industrial times of the late sixties and early seventies

big American engines were commonplace and were understood by most mechanics. In other words, the Iso Rivolta was successful from the outset. It may have lacked the development and engineering finesse of some of the more sophisticated, long-standing makes, but it was a prestige car—at a prestige price—and it found buyers waiting in the Americas, and even as far away as Hong Kong and Australasia.

The original trauma of getting the car off the ground had given the Rivoltas a nasty fright. They were well aware that they needed additional expertise if the Iso Rivolta were not to be the first and last of the line. Certainly they needed help if they were to catch the US market, particularly while it was in the grip of Corvette Stingray fever. The Americans were intoxicated by the hairy sports-car image typified by the 'Ray.

Salvation appeared in the form of a young engineer named Giotto Bizzarini who had previously been working on some of Ferrari's GT projects and who was later to build cars under his own name before having a brief and disastrous flirtation with American Motors. As he had done before and was to do later, Bizzarini quickly grasped the problem at Rivolta's establishment (on the grounds of the family estate outside Milan) and set to work designing the muscle-car of the line, the Iso Grifo. Again Bertone styled, the Grifo was a great success in the places where the Iso Rivolta had been such a good car to own. The measure of the car's success is in its longevity: the last few were rolling off the line at the beginning of the summer, 1974, after close on a decade of continuous production. Engine capacities fluctuated upwards to as much as seven litres, but were always either Chevrolet or Ford V8s. Good aerodynamics and the sheer beefy performance ensured that the Grifo was one of the fastest of road cars, its top speed being a claimed 186 mph; even allowing a fair percentage for the optimism inherent in Italian specialist-car builders, the Grifo was a fast car and just the thing for upstaging your Stingray-owning next-door neighbours.

Having outgrown the little factory on the family estate, the Rivolta entourage moved camp to a site in an

industrial estate at Varedo, on the northern edge of Milan. With the expansion were to come the labour difficulties which later brought the company to its knees. However, the more immediate problems were related to getting some new models rolling. Although the concept of the original Iso Rivolta was not dated, its looks certainly were, when it was placed against rivals which had grown from strength to strength. The Gordon-Keeble was extinct by then, but Jensens were doing well outside Europe and Maserati, Ferrari and Lamborghini had by then put a lot of effort into the GT field.

With the demise of Maserati's big Quattroporte saloon, there was an obvious gap in the market for a large, prestigious four-to-five-seater saloon, both for the Italian market itself and for non-European countries. Despite Fiat's valiant attempts with their 130 saloon (and later the coupé), rich Italians were preferring Mercedes-Benz rather than home-grown products. Even the Pope was using a Mercedes!

The Lele was launched to replace the Iso Rivolta. A similar package to its forebear, the Lele was again styled by Bertone and, despite its coupé-like stance, revealed itself to be a full four-seater, having a top speed nudging 150 mph, and optional automatic transmission and ZF power steering. Again, it was aimed at traditional Iso buyers: all the exotic-car cosmetics without the alleged hang-ups of sophisticated engineering.

The big saloon, the Fidia, followed a similar design philosophy. Unlike the Lele, which has had predictable success in predictable places, the Fidia has not enjoyed the same fortunes, mainly because it was the wrong car at the wrong time. The perpetual uncertainty in Italy militated against sales there (it is a brave tycoon who is seen to be driving a big, thirsty luxury car when he arrives at his strife-ridden factory) and more recently the energy crisis has done sales of big cars no good at all. Nevertheless, Fidias have been finding a measure of success in the US, where their size and thirst is rather smaller than that of the typical American full-sized saloon, which resembles two European cars.

Other, more subtle, forces had been working against Iso, however. High labour costs, pushed to even greater heights by strikes and increased material costs, drove prices of the Isos ever-closer to those of the more sophisticated vehicles. Advanced management techniques by the new owners of Maserati (Citroën), Ferrari (Fiat) and Lamborghini (the Swiss family Rosetti) helped keep their prices down to competitive levels, but Iso and, to some extent, de Tomaso, with similar design philosophies have been the loners, miraculously surviving against soul-destroying odds that would have killed lesser companies.

The strain of trying to manufacture cars or anything else constructive in Italy, no doubt contributed to the death of Renzo Rivolta in the late 1960s. His son took over and again called upon the services of Bizzarini, who, following the debacle with American Motors, had retired to his small vineyard at Livorno to grow wine instead of making cars. The outcome of this fresh liaison was a mid-engined two-seater called the Varedo. envisaged as a Grifo replacement. When it was shown at the Turin Motor Show, in 1972, it was far from complete and, in fact, was never finished, because it

just did not seem a practical proposition.

In order to get a new-model programme under way, Rivolta had also retained the services of Ing. Dallara, the young, bespectacled engineer from Parma, who designed the Lamborghini Miura before going into semi-retirement to pursue his own interests. However, he emerged from time to time to handle the Pantera and Deauville projects for de Tomaso, as well as to turn the futuristic Lancia Stratos from a very good idea into a rally winner.

However, the difficulties of keeping the business going drove Rivolta to such despair that he sold out to an American refrigeration tycoon, Dr Iro Pera, who put his youthful Sicilian son-in-law, Carlo Beltiore, in charge of Iso. In 1974, he was bearing the burden of the labour problems and trying to rationalise production techniques in the hope of getting a generally bad situation onto a safer part of the tightrope. Meanwhile, the Varedo project had been killed off, along with the new-model programme. In other words, the new management was just about starting out afresh, with the determination to get a tottering organisation firmly back on its feet.   IF

Top: the Bertone-styled Iso Grifo was introduced in 1965 with the usual choice of Chevy V8 power outputs (300 and 365 bhp); with the more powerful unit, this was one of the fastest cars in the world, having a maximum of 160+ mph

Above: the Lele was announced in 1969 to replace the Rivolta—in fact it used many components from that car; this 5.3-litre four-seater was a quick success

ISO LELE

The Iso company uses the same formula for building cars as the De Tomaso concern: lavishly equipped bodies that give nothing away to the other Italian 'supercar' manufacturers, but sacrificing the light-alloy, multi-cam power units for a more tractable and essentially cheaper form of engine, namely an American V8, still with enough power, though, to compensate for the fewer cams and fewer carburettors.

The Iso Lele, one of the company's three models in production in 1974, is a Bertone-bodied two-door four-seater that is powered by a Ford Cobra Jet 5762 cc V8. It is available in either 325 bhp or 360 bhp (SAE) form, the more powerful version being designated the Lele Sport. Either a five-speed manual or three-speed automatic transmission is available.

The suspension is of the independent front type, by means of wishbones, coil springs, an anti-roll bar and telescopic dampers. The rear is of the non-independent type by a de Dion axle, twin trailing radius arms, a transverse linkage bar, coil springs and telescopic dampers. Braking is taken care of by servo-assisted disc brakes on all wheels.

The Lele comes with power-assisted steering, air conditioning, electric windows, tinted glass, leather or cloth upholstery and metallic paintwork (if wanted) as standard. As in most luxury cars, the price for the manual and automatic versions is the same, as is the price of the Lele Sport.

ENGINE Front-mounted water-cooled V8. 101.6 mm (4 in) bore × 88.9 mm (3.50 in) stroke = 5762 cc (351.6 cu in). Maximum power 325 bhp (SAE) at 5800 rpm (Lele), or 360 bhp at 5800 rpm (Lele Sport); maximum torque 349 lb ft at 3800 rpm (Lele), or 360 lb ft at 3000 rpm (Lele Sport); Cast-iron cylinder block and head. Compression ratio 8.6:1. 5 main bearings. 2 valves per cylinder operated by a single camshaft at the centre of the V.1 single Motorcraft downdraught 4-barrel carburettor.

TRANSMISSION Single-dry-plate clutch and five-speed manual gearbox, or torque converter and three-speed Ford automatic gearbox. Ratios of manual ZF unit. 1st 2.900, 2nd 1.780, 3rd 1.220, 4th 1, 5th 0.845, rev 2.630; Ratios of automatic. 1st 2.400, 2nd 1.470, 3rd 1, rev 2:1.

Hypoid-bevel final drive with limited-slip differential. Ratio 3.310:1.

CHASSIS Integral.

SUSPENSION Front—independent by wishbones, coil springs, an anti-roll bar and telescopic dampers. Rear—non-independent by a de Dion axle, twin trailing radius arms, a transverse linkage bar, coil springs and telescopic dampers.

STEERING Power-assisted recirculating ball. Turns from lock to lock 4.

BRAKES Twin-circuit, servo-assisted discs all round.

WHEELS 7 in × 15L.

TYRES 215/70 VR 15.

DIMENSIONS AND WEIGHT Wheelbase 106.30 in; track—front and rear 57 in; length 183.60 in; width 69.09 in; height 52.36 in; ground clearance 4.72 in; dry weight 3200 lb (Lele), or 3131 lb (Lele Sport); turning circle between walls 42 ft; fuel tank capacity 22 gals.

PERFORMANCE Maximum speed 140 mph (Lele), 132 mph (Lele automatic), or 150 mph (Lele Sport); fuel consumption approximately 15 mpg for all models.

NOVELTY OFFSET BY STAGNATION

Isotta Fraschinis were renowned for clever innovations, but eventually the company seemed to run out of ideas

One of the many versions of the type 8, the 8A four-seater sports model of 1927, with Cesare-Sala coachwork

SINCE THE VERY NAME Isotta Fraschini excites the salivary glands by its suggestion of some exotic Italian dish, a culinary analogy may be appropriate to summarise its place in car-making history. Like a new restaurant, Isotta Fraschini began by trying out all sorts of fresh and exciting dishes and garnishing them with novel ideas, and that is how it was for the first fourteen years, 1900–1914. Then came wartime meals to feed the troops, and after that the restaurant sought to please an exclusive clientele with one basic menu, scarcely changed thereafter except for the rich sauces and dressings. Ultimately, money became short and the wealthy customers, mostly from the USA, withdrew their patronage. Nothing much was done to modernise the establishment, nothing at all to widen its inducements socially; another fourteen years, and it had to close the doors. After another war, and under new management, a brave attempt to reopen was frustrated by problems in the kitchen.

Cesare Isotta and Vincenzo Fraschini (later joined by their brothers Stefano Isotta, and Oreste and An-

tonio Fraschini) got together in 1899 to import single-cylinder Renault voiturettes, Mors cars and Aster engines from France. Next, they brought in the parts to assemble in their Milan premises, and gradually more and more locally made components were incorporated until the product could be called an Isotta Fraschini. Then in 1902, when the Renault derivative had grown into a 12 hp twin-cylinder car, the brothers forsook the Renault formula with its neat transmission through cardan shaft and live axle, and went in for bigger things with cruder but more versatile chain-drive. The first true Isotta Fraschini was a 24 hp four with separate T-headed pots. By 1904, the range had expanded to three models of 12, 16 and 24 hp. Strong financial backing paid for the erection of a new factory in Milan's via Monterosa, and an able young design engineer named Giustino Cattaneo was engaged; he was to remain with the firm through to 1933.

By 1905, Cattaneo had found time to create a vast racing car, the 120 hp Tipo D, with a 17-litre, four-cylinder engine having its overhead valves operated by

an overhead camshaft. In September that year, two of these monsters were entered, with drivers Le Blon and Trucco, for a three-lap road race round a 104-mile circuit embracing Brescia, Cremona and Mantova, but both failed to get very far. Finances must still have been somewhat tenuous, for in 1907 the French De Dietrich company were able to buy a controlling interest, an alliance that lasted only three or four years. No Milan-made Lorraine-Dietrichs seem to have left the via Monterosa, only a few IFs wearing the wrong badge on the radiator.

No doubt the Gallic intrusion was prejudiced by a string of Isotta Fraschini competition successes on both sides of the Atlantic during 1907–8. A four-car team of side-valve IFs, based on a stock chassis, was entered for the second Targa Florio in Sicily, with drivers Trucco, Minoia, Tamagini and Sorel; Tamagini crossed the line in seventh place, Minoia in tenth. Then in June 1907, Minoia finished seventh in the German Kaiserpreis over the tricky Taunus circuit, this time in a bigger car with an overhead-camshaft engine within the 8-litre capacity limit prescribed by the regulations. The same driver was outright winner of the Coppa Florio later that year round an abbreviated circuit centred on Brescia, his team-mate Trucco (who, twenty years later, was to win the first Mille Miglia) finishing fourth.

In 1908, Trucco carried off the Targa Florio in Sicily; in the USA, overhead-camshaft, 7.9-litre IFs had a whole string of successes that established the make commercially in that country, opening the main outlet for future production. The 7.9 somehow qualified as a 'stock' chassis, although this model was not apparently marketed in Europe. Its most notable achievement was Lewis Strang's second placing, behind a Locomobile with more than twice the cylinder capacity, in the Vanderbilt Cup race held in October, over a circuit on Long Island. Strang also won the Savannah, Briarcliff and Lowell races, Lytle the Long Island Parkway Sweepstakes, and Poole other track events and a major hill-climb.

Recent historians have tried to read a Bugatti influence into this period of association with De Dietrich, because Ettore Bugatti had certainly known the Isotta and Fraschini brothers since before the turn

of the century through racing against them, and had been employed by De Dietrich during the years 1902–4. They have noted certain similarities between his designs and the intriguing 1208 cc overhead-cam racer entered by IF for the 1908 voiturette race at Dieppe, comparing this with Bugatti's own *petit pur-sang* prototype (65 × 110 mm, 1456 cc) which did not appear for some time later. As Cattaneo is on record confirming that he designed the little Isotta in conjunction with Stefanino, it seems more probable that Le Patron (Bugatti) might have drawn inspiration from their work than vice versa.

Although the baby Isotta, like other four-cylinder

contenders at Dieppe, was defeated by a formula favouring otherwise impractical weirdies with ultra-long-stroke singles and twins, it certainly merits close attention and sets one wondering why the commercial brains in the via Monterosa did not exploit it further, especially bearing in mind that the home market in Italy was too poor to buy their bigger cars in any numbers. It was put into production as the 10 hp, with the cylinder bore enlarged from 62 to 65 mm (1327 cc), but only for about two years. Its four-speed gearbox, incidentally, had a geared-up, or overdrive, fourth speed for cruising.

For 1909, the IF range comprised five models, including the 10 hp, all the rest having side-valve four-cylinder engines with the blocks cast in pairs. Multi-plate clutches, four-speed transmissions and fixed wooden wheels were common to all, but only the smallest two had shaft drive as standard. Shaft or chains were optional on the 20–30 hp and 30–40 hp, chains being used on the huge 10½-litre 50–65 hp. Late that year, Isotta Fraschini introduced four-wheel braking, designed by Oreste Fraschini, but these were not fitted to all models for some years to come. As in the early Austin Sevens, front and rear systems were uncoupled, so that some skill was required to get the best fore-and-aft balance, especially on slippery surfaces. In retrospect, the general lack of interest in four-wheel braking—or was it, rather, fear and trepidation because early systems were dangerously unpredictable?—seems incredible, since the problems of slowing or stopping a 2½-ton limousine riding on 3-inch-wide tyre treads from, perhaps, 50 mph on autumn leaves must have given many a chauffeur long, spine-chilling moments. Four-wheel brakes were by no means universal fifteen years after Oreste Fraschini put them on the market.

1910 was notable for another overhead-cam design, this time a huge 100 hp car, with enclosed chain drive, front-wheel brakes and water-cooled transmission brakes for the rear wheels. The Tipo KM engine was a long-stroke four (130 × 200 mm, 10.6 litres) said to deliver about 125 bhp at 1800 rpm. The

Left: a 12 hp Renault derivative of 1902

Below: one of the first true Isottas, the 12 hp of 1903

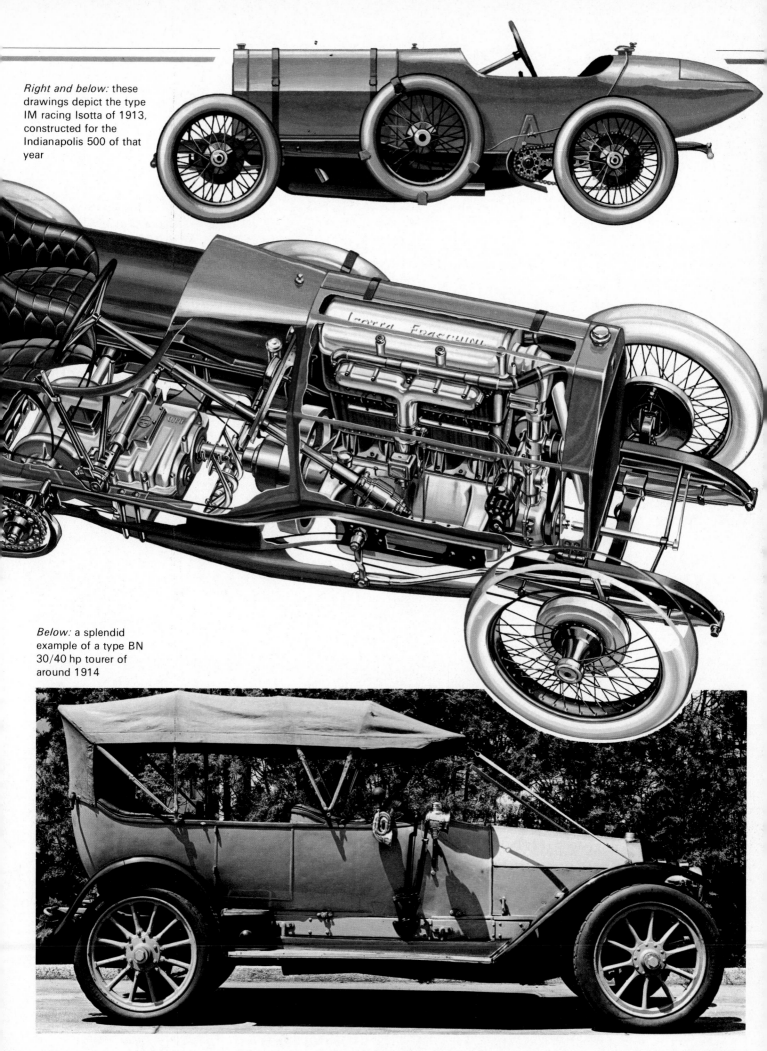

Right and below: these drawings depict the type IM racing Isotta of 1913, constructed for the Indianapolis 500 of that year

Below: a splendid example of a type BN 30/40 hp tourer of around 1914

cylinders were cast in pairs, and there were four valves per combustion chamber; the camshaft was driven by a vertical shaft from the nose of the crank, with skew gears. Most of the KMs had sharply pointed Mercedes-style radiators, giving them an awesome appearance, but some seem to have been less aggressively contoured. Already Cattaneo was involved with aero engines, and the cross-breeding between the two elements was clear in the KM. A smaller derivative, the 6.2-litre Tipo TM, differed in having a monobloc cylinder casting.

Surprisingly, these were the last Cattaneo cars to have overhead camshafts, and the rest of the story centres round one design that promised great things when introduced shortly after World War I, but became progressively more stolid by comparison with its competitors. The nigger in the woodpile, so far as Cattaneo's Tipo 8 was concerned, was the Swiss Marc Birkigt's 32CV Hispano-Suiza, made in Paris and first shown at the 1919 Paris Salon. This had a 6¼-litre, overhead-camshaft engine, much more compact and daintier than Cattaneo's eight-cylinder 5.9-litre, in a chassis that combined excellent roadholding with easy steering and matchless brakes assisted by a mechanical servo. There was also the threat of two rival Italian super-cars from the Lancia and Fiat factories, both with large V12 engines but, fortunately for Isotta Fraschini, neither of

these two were ever to be put into production.

Although announced in August 1919, the Tipo 8 took a year or two to get off the line, due to labour problems affecting all Italian industry. Even so, it has a strong claim to being the world's first true production straight-eight. The massive engine was a joy to look at and was beautifully constructed, but as a dynamic object it was more noted for long life and reliability than for power or refinement, in the marine rather than the aviation idiom. The monobloc aluminium cylinder casting was topped by two three-cylinder heads, and the overhead valves were opened by pushrods and rockers. Nine main bearings supported the vibration-damped crankshaft, which was arranged like two fours in series in the Bugatti manner. This layout was claimed by Cattaneo to provide better mixture distribution, although it was inherently less well-balanced than the 2–4–2 disposition later adopted by Bugatti, in line with US designs. Cylinder proportions were strictly small bore/long stroke (85×130 mm, 5902 cc) and the original output was a modest 75–80 bhp at 2200 rpm. It breathed through two Zenith side-draught carburettors and was fired by a Bosch magneto. Transmission was through a multi-plate clutch and a wide-ratio three-speed gearbox, with centre ball-change, in unit with the engine.

With neither the power and manoeuvrability of the Hispano nor anything approaching Rolls-Royce

Opposite page, top to bottom: an 8A landaulette, with coachwork by Cesare Sala; a sports saloon 8A with Castagna coachwork; a convertible 8A with bodywork attributed to Figoni & Falaschi; a type 8B of 1932, with a Worblaufen of Berlin body; a 1931 type 8S with special sports bodywork by Touring of Turin

Right: yet another Castagna-bodied type 8, this time a tourer

Below: one of the many coachbuilders to clothe the Isotta type 8 was Farina, who constructed this convertible car, one of the few with disc wheels

unobtrusiveness, it is difficult to understand how the Tipo 8 was such a success. It was not even a pleasant car to drive. The answer probably lay in the huge chassis, with its 12 ft-plus wheelbase, which formed a wonderful platform for the specialist coachbuilders of Italy and the USA in particular. Some of their creations behind that noble radiator were amongst the most magnificent ever conceived, and the majority were expressly for paid drivers to handle (who would not complain) while the owners sat in the mobile drawing-room behind a winding glass division. Italian houses, like Sala, Castagna, Stabilimenti, Farina and Touring, were then at their peak in both style and execution, and in America, England and France, the IF became a symbol of aristocratic dignity.

Just as the Tipo 8 was coming to fruition, in 1920–1, Oreste Fraschini died, and his brother Vincenzo and Cesare Isotta left when new management, with much-needed capital backing, took over; but the faithful Cattaneo stuck to his post. Towards the end of 1924, after about 400 Tipo 8s had been sold, he released the 7.4-litre Tipo 8A (93 × 135 mm) which gave 110–120 bhp at 2400 rpm, much of the extra power no doubt being absorbed by heavier coachwork. It had a stouter chassis frame and larger brake drums with vacuum-servo assistance, and rode on larger-section tyres. The 8A was soon supplemented by Spinto and then Super Spinto versions with higher compression ratios and other tuning devices. These still failed to match Birkigt's new 46CV 8-litre Hispano, although a short-chassis 8ASS with sporting bodywork could allegedly exceed 100 mph (one such car finished sixth in the 1927 Mille Miglia, driven by Count Maggi and Bindo Maserati).

Although the world slump around 1928–30 nearly put paid to IF, in April 1931 they launched the 8B, a great improvement, on paper at least. A lot of development had gone into its engine, which now gave up to 145–160 bhp at 3000 rpm; the chassis was deeper again and with added cross-bracing; hydraulic dampers replaced the friction Hartfords and a four-speed Wilson pre-selector gearbox was optional. There were very few takers, however, and only about thirty were sold before the close-down in 1935. That was when aeroplane manufacturer Gianni Caproni took over, with enthusiastic encouragement from the belligerent Fascist government; there was great prosperity then from aviation and marine engines, and from trucks of German design built under licence.

After the war, Caproni initiated two parallel projects to get back into the private-car market. One was to be a small car for the common man, for which Ing. Fessia chose a platform frame with all-independent suspension, the front wheels driven by a 1250 cc ohv flat-four engine. Called the CEMSA-Caproni, it appeared at shows in the late 1940s, but never got off the ground. In 1953 it very nearly became a Belgian Minerva, but nothing came of that either. Ultimately, Fessia went to Lancia, and the result was seen when in 1960 out popped the Lancia Flavia.

The other more ambitious venture was a luxury model called the Isotta Fraschini Monterosa, dreamed up by Ing. Rapi. The only things in common with the 8B were its eight cylinders, arranged in a 90-degree V and placed behind the rear wheels in a platform frame with all-independent suspension employing rubber in compression. The overhead-camshaft engine progressed through successive shows from $2\frac{1}{2}$ to 3.4 litres, and it appeared in a variety of bodies of varying aesthetic merit before Monterosa was finally closed down in 1950, perhaps because the Brave New World was not yet brave enough for Fessia and Rapi.   RB

British Leylands industrial revolutionary

SIR ALEXANDER ARNOLD CONSTANTINE ISSIGONIS, KBE, will be marked in the history books as the man who added a new word to the English language: Mini. This readily smiling, impish man has had many engineering achievements in a lifetime as a designer, but none has made such an impact on the world as the small car which started life as a scribble on the back of an envelope and was translated into a running vehicle in only nine months.

He is a man of great personal charm who gives the impression to anyone with whom he is talking that that person is of great importance, that the conversation they are enjoying is of great import, and that they are engaged in something as fascinating as anything he has ever done. This may be because he is an enthusiast who throws himself heart and soul into the job of the moment; he usually starts sketching away in great sweeping lines to illustrate his theories and beliefs. No journalist ever comes away from an interview

without a portfolio of sketches in the inimitable Issigonis manner—like Leonardo da Vinci, some admirers say.

Issigonis is a man who likes the good things of life, gourmet food, fine wine, conversation in words which are weighed with care. He is a model-steam-locomotive enthusiast, and spends his holidays in Monte Carlo drinking dry Martinis, swimming, and sunbathing.

Although so successful as an engineering designer, he holds no degrees, but has an engineering diploma from Battersea Polytechnic and honours from the Royal Society of Arts, the University of Surrey and the University of East Anglia, as well as holding the Leverhulme Medal of the Royal Society, of which he is a Fellow. He received the CBE (Commander of the British Empire) in 1964 and was knighted in 1969, when he was made KBE (Knight Commander of the British Empire). The great irony is that his most famous contribution to the motor-engineering scene, the Austin Seven or Morris Mini-Minor, has not made much money for its makers although it is a world-beater in sales, trendsetting, competition success, and was number

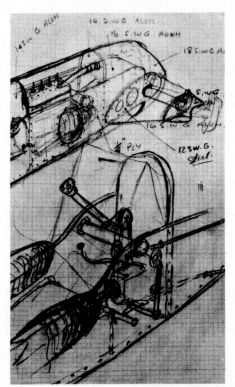

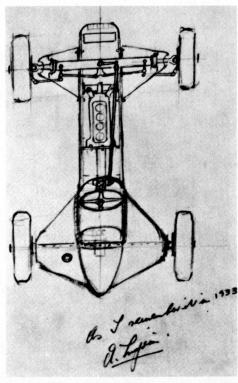

two in the British sales charts during 1974.

Issigonis's father was a marine engineer and constructor, a Greek with British nationality. Alec's mother was a Bavarian, born in the days when Bavaria was an independent kingdom associated with Germany. He was born in 1906 in Smyrna, then the second city of the Ottoman Empire, which had a population of one million in and around it, more than half of them Greek.

Top: some of Issigonis's sketches for the pretty Lightweight special, planned in 1933

Far left: Issigonis's collaborator, George Dowson, with the Lightweight at Prescott in 1939

Above: Dowson plus Lightweight

Alec Issigonis came from a cosmopolitan background and travelled widely in Europe with his parents, who were comfortably off and had many English friends. When Smyrna was overrun by the Turks in 1922, Alec and his parents were evacuated, with other British subjects, by the Royal Navy, but his father died in Malta on the way to England. Alec, then sixteen, was sent to Battersea Polytechnic, where he completed the course but failed to win the required qualification to go on to university and study for an engineering degree.

He continued his studies, then travelled in Europe, and finally took his first job at 22 with a man called Edward Gillett, who was trying to produce a forerunner of automatic transmission by making the clutch work automatically as the throttle was opened and closed. Two British companies, Rover and Humber, were interested in this device, which led to Issigonis leaving Edward Gillett in 1934 and joining the design staff of Humber.

At Humber he was concerned with front-suspension design at a time when independent front suspension was in its infancy with some attempts at design which are perhaps better forgotten. From Humber, he moved to Morris Motors, a company which also made MGs and Wolseleys. It was at Morris, in 1936 at the age of thirty, that he became a specialist in suspension design and experimented with some of the earliest attempts at all-round independent suspension for mass-production cars. The war put a stop to this, but one of his designs was eventually

adopted on the 1¼-litre MG Y series of heavy-weight saloons with tiny engines. This can be seen as the parent of the independent front end still in use on the MGB today. Parallel with his official work, Issigonis was playing with sports cars and sports-car design and produced the now well known 750 cc Lightweight Special, which has really only achieved fame due to the recognition, so many years later, of its designer/driver.

The crux of the layout of the Lightweight Special was that all four wheels were independently suspended by spring/damper units, using rubber rings for both springing and damping. The camber of both front and rear wheels could be changed quickly, and by ringing the changes on rear-wheel camber Issigonis learned that this can be the key to getting the power of an engine down on the road.

Issigonis made his mark, however, as a designer of mass-production cars made at a low price for the man in the street, and this foray into sports/racing cars was not repeated once the burdens of office were laid upon him. He was over forty years of age by the time his first design was on the market, this being the Morris Minor.

Looking back from this distance we can perceive that the Morris Minor was relatively as big a trendsetter and market leader as the Mini was to be later. It was in production in various forms from October 1948 to July 1971 and was a pioneer of the modern small car with good handling and reasonable comfort for four people allied to low running costs and adequate performance. In all, 1.6 million Morris Minors were

Sir Alec Issigonis with his most famous creation, the British Leyland Mini; this car made the Issigonis name a household word and led the way for a whole series of British Leyland models, not to mention rival copies

made during the car's twenty-three-year life.

The Minor had the Issigonis stamp, yet was a very different car when it reached the market place from the idea first envisaged by its individualistic designer when he put pencil to paper. He started planning it during the war when he was project engineer for Morris. One of the car's novelties was the use of torsion-bar suspension at the front, with the bars running lengthwise down the car. It is now a commonplace which has come and gone, but at that time it was something new and untried. Another hallmark was the use of 14-inch-diameter wheels when everyone else was on 16-inch or at the smallest 15-inch.

The story has been too often told to repeat in detail of how the final prototype was thought to be too tall and narrow, until Alec had the brainwave of cutting it down the middle and inserting a 'gusset' ten inches wide to produce much better proportions and the classic beetle-like shape which became familiar in millions on the roads of the world. Some of the other ideas, like the flat-four air-cooled engine, were also lost along the way, but the ultimate result was a design which was, in its day, head and shoulders ahead of the opposition in terms of value for money, ride comfort, handling and servicibility. When Austin and Morris joined in 1952 to become the

British Motor Corporation, it was a logical step to put the 863 cc ohv pushrod Austin engine into the Minor, in place of the earlier 918 cc side-valve unit inherited from the pre-war Morris 8 Series E. This improved performance and there was no need for other major changes, as the model continued to sell well right up to its dis-continuation, although the engine size was increased on two occasions.

Meanwhile, Issigonis was not happy with things moving along quietly without innovation and experiment, and by 1951 he was playing with a front-wheel-drive version of the Minor, which had its influence eventually on the Mini, but never saw the light of day in its original form because the two partners in the new giant com-bine were more interested in consolidating than in investing in any way-out schemes for peculiar cars which might not sell.

The Morris Minor has been so much over-shadowed now by its 'son', the Mini, that we are apt to forget what an impact it made in its day, but by the time the Minor appeared Issigonis was already thinking far ahead, towards a newer concept which eventually made his name as familiar a household word as Ford or Rolls-Royce. In fact no motor-car designer in the history of the art has become as well known to the general public, although it is Sir Alec's second brain-child, the Mini, which led to this universal acclaim and recognition and eventually to his knighthood.

In between designing the Morris Minor, which was such a hit with the man in the street, and the later Mini, which swept the world, Alec Issigonis left the British Motor Corporation and went off to produce an entirely new motor car, a project which was much more exciting to him than being king of a production empire and turning out the same item day after day. So in 1952, not long after the big merger of the two major British factories, he took his leave of Cowley and moved over to Alvis at Coventry, then producers of a luxury sporting car with a reputation for quality and a long-honoured name in the history of the British motor industry.

His brief was to produce an all-new car in this luxury-performance bracket, to succeed the cur-rent Alvis offering. He produced a V8 engine with overhead camshafts, giving 130 horsepower from 3.5 litres. He mounted this in a monocoque structure and used a novel type of transmission. Issigonis had, as we have seen, been involved in an attempt at a two-pedal transmission back in his twenties, and he now produced a two-speed box allied to an orthodox mechanical overdrive unit working on both ratios to give a spread of four gears. The theory was that the third-top change would be on the electrically controlled overdrive switch, so eliminating the clutch-and-lever change once the car was rolling on the open road. The transmission unit could also be moved farther back away from the engine to reduce the gearbox tunnel in the front of the car.

Just as the earlier experience of Issigonis in transmissions was used in the Alvis design, so he began using there techniques in suspension which ultimately were a cornerstone in the suc-cess of the still-to-come Mini. His friend Alex Moulton, who designed the Hydrolastic suspen-sion which came later on the Mini and other BMC cars like the 1100 and 1800, produced a

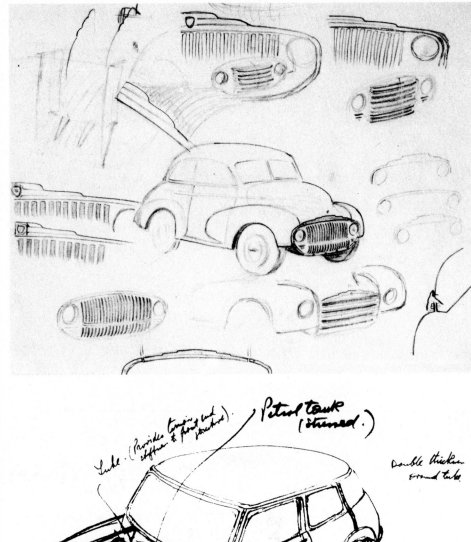

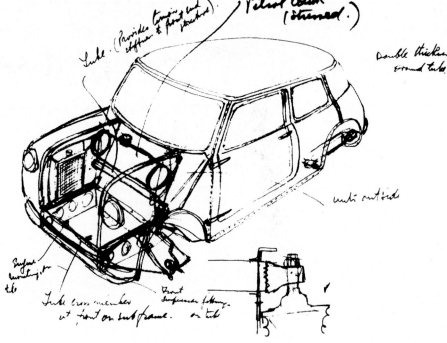

design for the Alvis company, linking the front and rear suspension systems hydraulically to a common spring.

Alec Issigonis was pleased with his Alvis design, but the company were dubious about tooling up for such an unorthodox vehicle, which would have involved them in raising extra capital. Cars were a small part of their business, which was also concerned with the production of armoured cars and aircraft engines, and even-tually the Alvis car was allowed to die. After long consideration and some expenditure on the Issigonis dream-car project, they decided not to produce it and, after four years' wasted effort,

Top: a series of early sketches for the Morris Minor introduced in 1948; in its original form, the Minor was 4 inches narrower than the production car.
Above: the famous BMC baby; note the front fuel tank

Issigonis moved back to BMC to work on new ideas with his previous employers.

When Issigonis returned to his old masters, he took with him designers from both Alvis and his old days at Cowley. This time his headquarters were on Austin territory at Longbridge, in the building known jokingly as The Kremlin. He

reported directly to the late Sir Leonard Lord, then in charge of the combined operation. Sir Leonard wanted a forward-looking design which would sell. The Issigonis brief was rather different from the one he had had at Alvis, although similar in that he was to produce a new car from the ground up. In this case, though, it had to be practicable, cheap to make and a best-seller.

He brought with him from Alvis the Moulton suspension idea and that of divorcing the gearbox from the engine, and also chose what might have been half of his old 90-degree Alvis V-engine, a 1500 cc all-alloy ohc power plant. However, the Suez crisis, which brought petrol-rationing to Britain, put paid to this somewhat esoteric design, and the new brief in 1957 was for an economy car, in tune with the times, which must be on the market quickly.

Sir Leonard Lord, a man not given to mincing his words, told Issigonis he could use any engine he wanted so long as it was in current production in the BMC range. The rest is history. Issigonis went slightly outside his orders by chopping an 1100 cc engine in half and trying to run with two cylinders, but it was a rough and nasty result. His problem was space. He wanted a tiny car—what was to be the Mini—and there was not much room for the power unit. Eventually he hit on the obvious solution, so obvious that no-one in seventy years of motor cars had thought of it, of putting the gearbox underneath the engine and saving space that way. So the Mini was born.

It was the BMC A-series engine from the old Minor which was finally chosen; Moulton provided the simple suspension, and eventually a drive-shaft steering problem was solved. Before that, Issigonis had to sell his ten-inch wheels—no-one had gone that small before—to the

management, and the engine had to be turned round east-west instead of north-south across the car. The radiator went to the side with the air pushed out through it instead of sucked in, and the car was ready, at a cost of £100,000, for mass production.

Problems came later: the ignition flooding with the exposed distributor, the water inside the floor of the car and so on. These were readily solved, however, once the reasons had been discovered. The original engine came down from 948 cc to 848 because the tiny car was considered too fast, then later it went up again in the Cooper and Cooper S versions, finally reaching 1275 cc. Then came vans and station wagons and Mokes and beach cars. A new car was born, which won all the races and rallies, and a new word was added to the English language—and many other languages too.

The Mini, however, was just the foundation stone for a succession of other vehicles, further up the size and price scale, but all having basic east-west engine and front-wheel drive. The four-door 1100 arrived in 1962, with a 1098 cc version of the A-series power unit. Again, like the Mini, the 1100 possessed remarkable road-holding and handling qualities that many advanced, conventional-drive vehicles have been unable to match. The 1100 then received the 1275 cc engine as an option, being named the 1300. Also, a GT version followed in 1970, with even more power that the chassis was still well able to cope with.

The BLMC organisation certainly got their fair share of success from Issigonis's basic design, not least from the Hydrolastic suspension system that was first employed on the 1100, and later tried on the Mini. At the same time, Riley, MG

It did not take long for the Mini to become a competition success; this is a rally-modified version of the Cooper S, with a highly tuned engine and modified body

and Wolseley, as well as Austin and Morris, also captured buyers in their own sectors of the market which was all icing on the BMC Mini cake.

The 1800, equipped with the BMC B-series engine came along in 1965, looking like a stretched version of the 1100 and being slightly ungainly. Next was the five-door Maxi, with an overhead-camshaft 1500 cc engine; this power unit was later stretched to 1748 cc.

It would be fair to say that Sir Alec Issigonis truly revolutionised the motor industry: Fiat and Renault, two other advanced car manufacturers, were not too proud to copy the Mini concept and find their own transverse niche in the market, albeit some years after.

Sir Alec was not content to rest on his many laurels, though, and continued to experiment in his own design shop at the Longbridge works. One of his experiments was with a steam-engine design that was meant to fit into a Mini body. Issigonis was told by many noteworthy sources that it was impossible to make such an engine efficient enough. He said himself: 'I don't see much hope for it'. However, he carried on with the project and expressed disappointment when it failed to turn out as planned; he expected the impossible to be made possible. Many people who know Issigonis would not have been surprised if he had succeeded; he is that sort of engineer. **GB**

BLMC MINI

Sir Alec Issigonis's Mini brought a new word into the English language and proved to be an institution, a cult car, an ideal town car and a winner in most forms of competition that it entered; no mean achievement for one fairly simple design of motor car.

The Mini's career has not been all roses, however. When it first appeared, in 1959, even though the younger generation flocked to it like bees to honey, most of the older dyed-in-the-wool generation of 50s drivers cried out that the Mini was so small as to be dangerous, going as far as to christening them 'death traps'. They did not realise that the Mini was inherently safe, and could out-corner and handle better than most of the contemporary racing cars. However, as time went on, the Mini proved beyond a shadow of doubt that it was definitely a force to be reckoned with.

In 1974, the Mini range, now separate from the guises of Austin and Morris, comprised the 850 and 1000 saloons, the Clubman 1000 cc saloon and estate (a slightly revised Mini with a restyled interior and nose) and the Mini 1275GT.

The Mini's power unit is the well proven A-series engine that powered Issigonis's first BMC success, the Morris Minor. The suspension is now of the dry type using unequal-length arms, with the upper unit operating against a rubber cone spring, and telescopic dampers for the front, while the rear is by a trailing arm, operating a rubber cone spring via a lever and strut and telescopic dampers. Between 1964 and 1969 the ingenious Hydrolastic 'wet' suspension, borrowed from the 1100, was used.

An interesting option for the 1275GT is the Dunlop Denovo tyre, which is fitted to the car's 12 in wheels; other Minis still use the 10 in variety. With the addition of this 'run-flat' option, the Mini has further enhanced its position as one of the most inherently safe cars available.

ENGINE Transverse, front-mounted, water-cooled straight four. 63 mm (2.48 in) bore × 68.4 mm (2.69 in) stroke = 848 cc (51.7 cu in) (850), 64.6 mm (2.54 in) bore × 76.2 mm (3 in) stroke = 998 cc (60.9 cu in) (1000), or 70.7 mm (2.78 in) bore × 81.4 mm (3.20 in) stroke = 1275 cc (77.8 cu in) (1275). Maximum power 33 bhp at 5500 rpm (850), 39 bhp at 4750 rpm (1000), or 54 bhp at 5250 rpm (1275); maximum torque 44 lb ft at 2900 rpm (850), 52 lb ft at 2700 rpm (1000), or 68 lb ft at 2500 rpm (1275); cast-iron cylinder block and head; compression ratio 8.3:1 (850 and 1000), or 8.8:1 (1275). 3 main bearings. 2 valves per cylinder operated, via pushrods and rockers, by a single camshaft, side. 1 SU HS4 semi-down-draught carburettor.

TRANSMISSION Single-dry-plate clutch and 4-speed manual gearbox, or torque converter and 4-speed automatic, with possible manual selection. Ratios of 850 and 1000, 1st 3.525, 2nd 2.218, 3rd 1.433, 4th 1, rev 3.544:1. Ratios for 1275, 1st 3.330, 2nd 2.090, 3rd 1.350, 4th 1, rev 3.350:1. Optional for 1000s only, automatic gearbox. Automatics have a high compression 41 bhp engine as standard. Maximum ratio of converter at stall 2. Ratios 1st 2.690, 2nd 1.845, 3rd 1.460, 4th 1.269, rev. 2.690:1. Helical-spur final drive. Ratio 3.765 (850), or 3.44 (100 and 1275).

CHASSIS Integral with front and rear auxiliary frames.

SUSPENSION Front—independent by unequal length arms in conjunction with a rubber cone spring and telescopic dampers, while the rear is independent also by trailing arm operating a rubber cone, via a lever and strut, and telescopic dampers.

STEERING Rack and pinion. Turns from lock to lock 2.33 (850 and 1000), or 2.72 (1275).

BRAKES Drums all round (850 and 1000), or front discs and rear drums (1275).

WHEELS 3½ × 10 (850 and 1000), or 4½ in × 12 (1275).

TYRES 145 × 10 (850 and 1000), or 155 × 12 (1275). Optional for 1275 155/65 SF 310 Dunlop Denovo safety tyres.

DIMENSIONS AND WEIGHT Wheelbase 80.16 in (all models except estate), or 84.15 in (estate); track—front 47.82 in (all models except 1275), or 48.77 in (1275), rear—46.4 in (all models except 1275), or 47.43 in (1275); length 120.25 in (850 and 1000), 124.64 in (Clubman saloons), or 133.92 in (Clubman estate); width 55.5 in; height 53 in (850, 1000 and Clubman saloons), or 53.5 in (Clubman estate and 1275); ground clearance 6.2 in (850, 1000 and Clubman saloon), 6.3 in (Clubman estate), or 6.55 in (1275); kerb weight 1357 lb (850 and 1000), 1406 lb (Clubman saloon), 1514 lb (Clubman estate), or 1488 lb (1275); turning circle 28.5 ft (saloons), or 29 ft (estate); fuel tank capacity 5.4 gals (850, 1000 and Clubman saloon), 6.0 gals (Clubman estate), or 7.5 gals (1275).

PERFORMANCE Maximum speed between 73 mph (850) and 87 mph (1275); fuel consumption approximately 40 mpg

CHASING JAPAN'S BIG THREE

The Isuzu company is now linked with General Motors, but for many years the organisation had to exist and attempt to survive in the shadow of 'giants' like Honda, Nissan and Toyota

EVERY COUNTRY HAS SPECIALISTS in its motor industry, not only in car production but in the commercial field as well. Isuzu has as much standing in the Japanese motor-manufacturing field, as the names of Scammell and Dennis have in Britain. Although Isuzu produces a small range of cars, it is essentially a commercial truck and chassis manufacturer.

In 1916, vehicles were built under the company name of Tokyo Ishikwajima Dockland Company Ltd. This changed in 1937 to the Tokyo Jidosha Kogyo (Automotive Industry) Co Ltd; it was this company which was the beginning of Isuzu Motor Ltd.

Truck production began in 1939 and by 1943 the diesel engines which the company had designed and developed were being fitted to its vehicles; Isuzu had established the formula which was to make it a leader in the post-war era.

In order to market cars, Isuzu signed a ten year agreement with Rootes Motors to assemble Hillman Minx saloons. These cars were built up from 'knocked-down form' between the early fifties and 1957, by which time they had become completely Japanese manufactured.

Primarily, Isuzu has been a truck manufacturer and, in 1974, held some 62% of the medium-heavy truck market in Japan. Besides this, 40% of all heavy trucks and 45% of all light commercial transport in Japan were also Isuzu products. The remainder went for export to South-East Asia, Africa and America. The truck range was extensive in 1974, and Isuzu offered its operators a huge choice of cabs, frames, and special bodies, not to mention multiple-axle combinations and four and six-wheel drive for off-road vehicles. To power the whole range there were no less than two four-cylinder and five six-cylinder diesel engines, the largest being 732 cubic inches in swept volume.

At the lower end of the 1974 truck range was the KB30LU which was built by Isuzu for distribution in the USA by General Motors. The very popular Chevy LUV (light utility vehicle), as it was called, made large inroads into the leisure-vehicle market. It was powered by a single-overhead-camshaft, four-cylinder, in-line, water-cooled engine of 110 cubic inches, producing 75 bhp.

Isuzu were also manufacturing a large number of four-wheel-drive and six-wheel-drive 2½-ton military trucks for the Japanese Self Defence Force (Army). Similar to American tactical trucks of the same class, these military vehicles were available commercially, with special bodies for earth moving and logging.

In the late 1960s, Japanese car makers began to threaten Detroit's 'big three'. Toyota, and Nissan, Japan's two largest automobile producers, were not only cutting into the US market, but were also beginning to dominate the Asian markets. To meet the challenge, General Motors began to look for a new Pacific production base.

US antitrust laws precludes the purchase of Toyota

or Nissan, and the Japanese government did not favour GM building its own plant. So, GM began to evaluate several of Japan's smaller auto makers, thinking it might acquire one of them.

The American giant's knowledge of Isuzu was, at that time, limited. GM knew that the Japanese company was one of its country's fifty largest manufacturers and one of its country's oldest motor manufacturers. Its reputation was for building high-quality, heavy-duty trucks, but its management was somewhat suspect. As a result, by 1969, the company was in need of working capital.

Large Japanese companies rarely go bankrupt; usually the government and the company's bankers

Top: the sleek Bellett RO Spider, as seen at the eighteenth Tokyo Motor Show

Above: again at the Tokyo Motor Show, the 1600 Florian saloon of 1967

Top: the Isuzu Sport Wagon prototype, which was powered by a twin-cam, twin-carburettor 1.8-litre engine; it never went into production

Above: the Ghia-styled 117 Coupé, looking rather like the series II Fiat 124 Coupé

force a merger with other, more profitable, Japanese firms. Isuzu, at that time, was being guided towards a merger with Fuji, Mitsubishi Heavy Industries or Nissan. Isuzu's management, although they have had little choice in the end, resisted the idea, in order to retain their own independence.

After extensive negotiations, General Motors acquired 34.2% of Isuzu Motors, for $56 million. The integration of East and West created some interesting situations while the early ground work was being covered. The co-operation between the various Japanese industrial companies, as well as the suspicion of the GM consultants by the Isuzu management, was something that took the Americans by surprise. The Japanese guarded their future plans very closely, as GM were potential customers for many of the Isuzu company's various products.

In 1974, the car-production side ran to three main models, all built along with the light trucks in Isuzu's newest factory at Fujisana.

At the bottom of the range was the Bellett saloon, a simple two or four-door model of not very handsome lines. The power plant was by a conventional in-line, four-cylinder, 1584 cc, water-cooled unit with a five-bearing crankshaft and single carburettor. A two-door, twin-carburettor 1817 cc version was also built. The next model in the range, and successor to the Bellett was the larger Florian. Built in four-door saloon and estate-car versions, the Florian was powered by a similar 1600 cc engine to the Bellett. The most exciting Florian built was the 1800 TS, with a single-overhead-cam, 110 bhp 1800 cc engine and a pair of SU-style carburettors. This engine was also available in single-carb 100 bhp form.

Finally, there was the very stylish Isuzu coupé, with its Ghia-designed, two-door, 2+2 body. The 117 coupé had no less than four forms—XE, XG, XC, and XT. Heading the line was the XE, powered by a twin-overhead-cam, 1800 cc unit with fuel injection and a claimed 140 bhp (Japanese rating). The twin-cam, two-carb XG was rated at 125 bhp. The XC and XT 117s were twin and single-carburettor versions of the 1800 cc single-overhead-cam engine and these were rated at 115 and 100 bhp respectively, the latter having a Rochester carburettor.

The car-construction side began to bear fruit after GM's involvement, as both companies were working closely on a new Isuzu car based on a GM Opel model. Isuzu was expected to build some 120,000 of these units in 1975 of which half were to be exported to the US to be marketed under the Oldsmobile banner. Thus Isuzu had become used to GMs influence, for only in Japan could a German-designed car, built by one GM subsidiary company, be produced for the United States and then be sold as a home-bred American model. RP

THIRTY YEARS OF AUTOMOTIVE HISTORY

Itala is a name remembered with awe and respect, and yet the company was hard pressed to stay in business for as little as a thirty-year period

Above right: now in the National Motor Museum is this famous Itala: the 1907 120 hp, 14-litre Grand Prix car. This won the Grand Prix-formula race of the Coppa Florio at Brescia. The cylinder dimensions of the car are an enormous 175 × 150 mm

THE ITALA COMPANY was founded in the summer of 1903 by Matteo Ceirano, a member of a family famous in the history of Italian industry. In November of the same year he left the family firm, Filli Ceirano, and set up Matteo Ceirano & Company in Via Guastalla, Turin, with his associates Angelo Moriondo, Leone Fubini, Guido Bigio and Giovanni Carenzi. In the following year, he added the marque name 'Itala' to his company's title, and this one ran until the troubles of 1929, as 'Itala Fabbrica Automobili', then became just 'Itala' from 1929–31, and finally 'Itala Società Anonima Costruzioni Automobilistiche (SACA)' from 1931 to 1934, when it all came to a sad end.

Itala started off with racing cars, a policy pursued more or less up to World War I with some success. They made their debut in the Coppa Florio in 1904, and in the same year Matteo Ceirano ran a 24 hp, four-cylinder, 4.5-litre with shaft drive—something of a novelty then—in the Susa–Mont Cenis race, winning the light-car class. This was the first of a long line of successes. In the autumn, Giovanni Battista Raggio, the Marquise Raggio of Genoa and a gentleman amateur, finished second in the Circuit of Brescia, and Guido Bigio won the Padua–Bovolenta event.

Then came the first reorganisation. In September 1904, a Genoese financial group, headed by the bankers G. B. Figari, were persuaded to put up some

cash and the firm became a limited company under the new name of Itala Fabbrica Automobili, with capital of three million lire, half of which was paid up. The engineer Guido Bigio, who was also a works racing driver, became Managing Director, and other directors included Matteo Ceirano, who left the following year to found the Ceirano-Ansaldi concern with Michele Ansaldi, which eventually became SPA. The lawyer, Grosso Campana, who had been with Matteo at the start, was also a director.

The policy of building only racing cars continued, and in 1905 the engineer Alberto Balloco was appointed Technical Director, a job he held right up until 1919, when he moved to Savigliano. On being promoted, he at once launched the 14-litre, 100 hp racer with which Giovanni Raggio won the Coppa Florio on the Brescia Circuit, beating all the powerful foreign entries.

The 100 hp racer also ran in the 1905 Circuit des Ardennes, which was won by Héméry in an 80 hp Darracq. Also in 1905, the 24 hp Itala driven by Raggio again won its class in the Susa–Mont Cenis race. In 1906, Alessandro Cagno won the first Targa Florio, over three laps of the full Madonie Circuit, at an average speed of 29.07 mph for the 277.3 miles. More dramatic was the fact that Itala filled four of the first five places, the other cars being driven by Graziana, Rigal, and de Caters. Sadly they never won again,

Above: an Itala 25/35 hp tourer of 1913. This car was powered by the 5401 cc (115 × 130 mm) four-cylinder engine. Note the stylish horn mounted on the wing at the front

Above right: a poster drawn by Carlo Biscaretti, founder of the Automobile Museum in Turin, depicting the sporting activities of the Itala company

although they finished third and fifth in the following year's Targa Florio.

It was also in 1906 that Itala achieved another kind of record, when H. R. Pope made the fastest run in the London–Monte-Carlo race. However, the Targa was a much more interesting affair: the race was promoted by Cavaliere Vincenzo Florio, a wealthy Sicilian vineyard owner, who had sponsored the Coppa Florio on the Brescia circuit, and had decided to organise a major race around his own island. It was said that during the first race round the 93-mile circuit of the mountains, the competitors were shot at by brigands, so the Cavaliere appointed the three most important mafiosi as stewards of the meeting, to stop this happening again. Cars entered had to be standard production models, on sale to the public under a fixed price limit.

1907 was in some ways an even more successful year for Itala. The famous Targa victor, Cagno, distinguished himself again by winning the Grand Prix formula race of the Coppa Florio at Brescia, driving the 120 hp, 14-litre racer. He was held up for eight minutes with magneto trouble early on, but ran right through the field in a race which lasted only half an hour, averaging 71.8 mph on one lap of the twisty 38-mile circuit. The year before, the Italian government had refused to provide troops or police to keep spectators off the course, so the race was not run. In 1907, Cavaliere Florio provided his own marshals and ran two events over a shorter course, the Grand Prix and the Kaiserpreis.

The big event of the year for Itala was their victory in the Peking–Paris race, during which Prince Scipione Borghese, with his mechanic, Ettore Guizzardi, and his co-driver, Luigi Bargini, covered the 10,000 miles in his 35/45 hp Itala between 10 June and 10 August, overcoming the most formidable obstacles in China, Russia and a great deal of Europe. Prince Borghese arrived in Paris three weeks ahead of his rivals, after being dragged by camels and coolies and running on railway lines part of the way. He said: 'By utilising only the engine of a motor car, it is impossible to go from Peking to Paris without ceasing to be comfortably seated on the cushions of the said motor car'.

The Peking–Paris Itala was rediscovered in the 1920s by Carlo Biscaretti, partially restored and placed in the Turin motor museum.

Encouraged by their racing successes, the company went on making competition machines, but seemed to have shot their bolt, although they produced a variety of sporting models before the first closed car appeared in 1920. This was the Type 50 coupé de ville, a four-cylinder, 2.8 litre (Locatti & Torretta had fitted a landaulette body to a 1909 model 20/30). There was also an Alession-bodied tourer on the 50/65 chassis in 1911.

To review their models from the start, 1904 saw the famous 24 hp which did so well in competition. This was a four-cylinder of 4562 cc with shaft drive, which was the Itala hallmark from the very early days. This car was produced up to 1906, and had meanwhile been joined by three other models. They were the four-cylinder 50 hp, the four-cylinder 18 hp, and the formidable 100 hp racer, originally of 14,759 cc and later (1906) bored and stroked to 16,666 cc, which had an inlet-over-exhaust layout.

Then came the 14/20, still a four, of only 2610 cc, virtually a mini-car for those days, but still with shaft drive and costing 10,500 lire. This hit the market in 1907, and at the same time we had the 35/45 which did Peking–Paris, and the 35/40 which seemed to have the same specification at 7433 cc, although the catalogued model could revolve at 1500 rpm against 1250 rpm for the Peking model. There was also the 60 hp, a six of 11,148 cc with the same dimensions, so presumably a plus-two-cylinder version of the same engine. These models ran on to 1915, and a top speed of 90 kph was claimed for the 35/40 and 100–105 kph for the 60. They cost respectively 18,000 and 28,000 lire in 1908.

At the same time, we had the 120 hp racer, with which Roth won the 1909 Mar del Plata race, equipped with a four-cylinder 12,076 cc motor and again inlet-over-exhaust valves. In 1907, the same car was catalogued with 14,432 cc, but the later engine revved to 1800 rpm instead of only 1200 rpm and was said to give the same power, although it was quoted ambiguously as '100 to 120'.

There was also, from 1908 to 1910, a 20/30 hp four

1915 unchanged in specification, but was joined from 1908 to the end by a 75 hp six of 140 mm—140 mm making 12,930 cc and another 'mini', the 16/20 four of only 2799 cc (90 mm × 110 mm). To confuse us even more, 1910 brought the 12/16 (75 mm × 110 mm) of only 1944 cc, and from 1911 to 1916 we had the 14/18 (2235 cc) and the 14/20 again, but this time of 2235 cc. There was also the 18/24 of 3308 cc and then the 18/30 of 3308 cc, which were the last before we come to the so-called 'valveless cars', except for the 50/70 of 8107 cc.

The valveless or 'Avalve' machines had rotary or sleeve valves, the first being the 25 hp of 1912–13, with the same 3308 cc engine as the 18/30. They went on in various sizes right up to 1922, with a 25, 35 and 50 hp ranging from just under four litres up to 8.5, and included a racer which ran in the 1913 French GP, and also finished second in the Targa Florio in the hands of Moriondo who covered the 268.5 miles of the medium Madonie circuit over four laps in 8 hours 21.46 minutes. Curiously enough, he drove not the 8-litre racer, but the so-called 35 hp of only 5195 cc. Giulio Foresti also won his class in the Targa in 1921 on a Type 51S (2813 cc) and Moriondo finished in seventh position overall.

In 1916, confusion became worse when type numbers joined the numerical designations, and we had Tipo 39 (2614 cc) and later (1919 to 26) Tipo 50, 51, and 55. The 50 and 51 had the same dimensions and capacity (2813 cc from 83 mm × 130 mm) but the Tipo 51 was called 'Sport' and was faster with a 100 kph maximum. The 55 was a 'valveless' four-litre. Type 54 was a taxi, and Type 56 the same two-litre size, while Type 61 was almost the same engine size, but a six.

Type 65 Sport, the last listed, was a six, again of two litres, but with overhead valves as a variation from side valves, inlet-over-exhaust and sleeve valves. All the Italas had very clean-looking engines, like a Bugatti or a Talbot, with few external pipes, wires or other excrescences. Bodies came from the coachbuilders already mentioned and also from Garavini, Farina, and many others.

Having waded through the morass of model names and numbers, let us return to the fortunes of the company. In the 1913 French Grand Prix, three sleeve-valve cars ran, driven by Felice Nazarro (borrowed from Fiat for the event), Moriondo, and Pope, but they did not finish in the money. This was their last grand prix appearance, which was partly due to the tragic death of managing director Guido Bigio, who had been a great believer in racing to improve the roadgoing breed, no matter what the make.

Top left: the 5401 cc Itala engine that was used in the 20/30 and 25/35 hp cars from 1908 onwards

Top right: Materassi pushes his Itala to the limit on the Circuito del Mugello

Above and left: the amazing 1.5-litre supercharged V12 Grand Prix car of 1926, which was designed by Cappa. This wooden-framed front-wheel-drive car's supercharger was used to scavenge exhaust gases from the cylinder on one stroke and to compress an over-rich mixture on another. Unfortunately, the car never ran under its own power and is now in the Biscaretti museum

of 5401 cc, with side-by-side valves, and, just to confuse matters, from 1911 to 1915, we had a 25/35 of the same dimensions (115 mm × 130 mm) and capacity (5401 cc) as the earlier 20/30, with no power output quoted for either. Just to make sure that no possible combination of numbers was left out we had, from 1908 to 1915, a model called the 50/65; in 1908 it was 150 mm × 150 mm, giving 10,604 cc, and then went to 140 mm × 150 mm, giving 9236 cc, but remained otherwise the same, except that the price went down a little from 24,000 lire to 21,500.

Parts and service must have been a nightmare for all these similar models with slightly different engine sizes, all made in small numbers. If we fight valiantly on with our statistics, we find that the 120 went on to

Three versions of the six-cylinder, overhead-valve type 61s. *Above left* is a saloon with coachwork by Garavini, now in the Rinaldi-Cuttini collection; *above right* is a cabriolet with coachwork by Lavocat & Marsaud; *right* is another saloon, this example being in the Quattroruote collection

After World War I, Itala again took up racing, but with sports versions of production models rather than purpose-built racing cars. Back in 1906, they had moved to larger premises in Corso Orbassano, Turin, and pressed on with the four and six-cylinder touring models, with the shaft drive which they had adopted. In 1910, they had made 350 cars, and they doubled this in 1911. The factory was now 80,000 square metres in area, employing 1000 people, plus 250 at Caluso where they made bicycles.

At that year's Turin Show, Alberto Balocco first presented his sleeve-valve engine, and another novelty —an engine with a variable stroke, which was supposed to be able to run without a gearbox, but does not seem to have worked. When the war came, production was switched to personnel carriers, and then in 1915 the factory was completely redesigned to produce V8 Hispano-Suiza aero engines under licence for a consortium of Italian companies including SCAT, which was a leading partner.

Tooling was scheduled for the 200 hp Hispano, which was not a great success and was replaced by the 300 hp model, but this cost a year in time switching the tooling, and it was 1918 before units came off the line. Itala and its partners had tooled up for 3000 units, but the government cut orders by fifty per cent and the group was in financial trouble. It sold off bought-out and semi-finished parts, but also had labour

troubles and the workforce fell to 180 by 1920. It began to make the sleeve-valve cars again and Moriondo's Targa second place in class helped the morale of the Itala concern.

The post-war models designed by Baloco and his assistant Alberto Orasi appeared and a Type 51 Sport won an Alpine Cup, while Foresti's Targa class win with this model also helped the factory. By 1925 the hand-to-mouth existence of Itala became too difficult and a receiver was called in, under a government scheme to help ailing companies. The engineer Giulio Cesare Cappa was appointed technical consultant, a man of experience with Aquila and Fiat. He produced the last-but-one Itala, the Type 61, with overhead valves in place of sleeve valves. He also produced a prototype GP light car (voiturette) with a wooden chassis, front-wheel drive and a supercharged V12 engine of 1100 or 1500 cc, but the model remained experimental.

In 1929, Itala amalgamated with Officine Metallurgiche e Meccaniche di Tortona (OM), with new headquarters and capital of 35 million lire. They hoped to sell to Poland, but this was not a success and the company was liquidated in 1931.

The following year the automotive section was reformed as the new firm Itala SACA, which lasted until the end came in 1934, completing 30 years of automotive history.   GB

A STYLE ALL OF THEIR OWN

Giorgetto Giugiaro and his Ital Design organisation have been responsible for some of the most excitingly-styled motor cars the world has ever seen

IT WAS ONLY BY CHANCE that Giorgetto Giugiaro, co-founder and co-head of Ital Design, got involved in cars. As a somewhat impoverished student of painting at the Liceo Artistica, which is part of Turin's Accademia Albertina, he did some sketches of cars in the hope of selling them (a strong possibility, for Turin is the headquarters of Italy's car industry). His work was spotted by a professor who was a close relative of a certain Dante Giacosa, then head of Fiat's engineering section. The professor suggested to Giacosa that the young man might be a candidate for Fiat's Centro Stile. So, at nineteen years of age, Giorgetto (christened Giorgio, but preferring Giorgetto which translates as Georgie) was painlessly absorbed into Italy's biggest car company, to learn his craft.

The Turin Salon, the showcase for the world's stylists, of 1958 was a fateful one for Giugiaro. He cornered Nuccio Bertone to show him some plans he had devised, and Bertone, singularly impressed, formed an association that was to last until 1965. The first fruit of this new liaison was the Alfa Romeo 2600 Sprint, which was a sensation then and has since turned into something of a collector's item. After that came the Alfa Romeo 1600 Sprint (which was still in production in 1974 as the GTV2000), the Fiat 850 Spider (eventually replaced by the X1/9), the experimental Alfa Canguro, some Mazdas, the Iso Rivolta, the Gordon Keeble, the Simca 1000 Coupé, the NSU Sport Prinz and the NSU Spyder, which was the first production car to be Wankel powered. Among the more spectacular cars, Giugiaro styled the Lamborghini Miura, the Iso Grifo, the Bizzarini and the classic Fiat Dino.

By the time he left Bertone, Giugiaro had left an unmistakable mark on the entire motoring scene. The move to a different camp was another step towards Ital Design, but first there was a spell at Ghia, which he joined in 1965. The split with Bertone was not an idealogical one: Ghia offered more money.

In the two years he was with Ghia, Giugiaro saw the company fall into American hands (Ford of America), but he was there long enough to design the Fidia for Iso, the Ghibli for Maserati, the Mangusta for de Tomaso and a variety of one-offs.

It sounds heady stuff, working with such exotic cars, but Giorgetto Giugiaro did not have hubcaps for eyes. He was not fanatically enraptured by the automobile nor did he have love affairs with them. 'Form is what counts', he said. 'I like to think that I can see beyond the car.'

The break with Ghia finally resulted in Giugiaro and two others—a production engineer and a body engineer—setting up in business under the banner of Ital Design. Their purpose was not just to design car shapes, but to productionise them as well; in other words, produce a complete package, from the styling through to the actual planning of the manufacture. Unlike designer organisations such as Pininfarina and Bertone, Ital Design from the start made it clear that they were not in business to manufacture bodies for customers. They set up their facilities to do one-offs and prototypes, but that was all.

In 1974, Ital Design moved to a new building on the outskirts of Turin. Until then, the operation had been conducted from an unlabelled, smallish office building in suburban Turin. Indeed, complete prototypes had usually been stored in garages under adjoining blocks

Below: the Alfa 33-based Iguana of 1969, showing a resemblance to the Ital-designed Maserati Merak and Bora

Bottom: the Maserati Boomerang of 1972

This page and opposite top: the Porsche 914/6 Tapiro, which was a particularly successful attempt at combining head-turning style with the certain amount of practicality that is essential for a road car. This car features four gull-wing doors, the front pair giving plenty of room for access to the stylish interior, and the rear pair for access to the engine compartment and luggage space. One of the problems of having gull-wing doors is the fact that in the event of a roll the occupants will not be afforded the protection of a conventional car, due to the large glass area in the roof

of flats. There were no great clanking gates and uniformed guards behind high wire fences. When strangers were shown through, there was a scurry for tarpaulins to cover the prototypes and mock-ups, which seemed just as effective as more formal methods of ensuring security.

Ital Design were obviously satisfying their customers. They had contracts with Maserati and produced for that company the Bora and the Merak, although the Khamsin was done by Bertone. It was Ital Design that turned the Audi 80 into the VW Passat, and followed this with the Scirocco, the VW Golf and the Audi 50. There was no known connection with Fiat—who remained loyal to Pininfarina and Bertone—but there was a very strong link with Alfa Romeo. For them, Giugiaro had designed the Alfasud and the Alfetta GT, besides having a substantial hand in the

Alfetta saloon. In 1974, the fruits of Ital Design's contract with Skoda, were yet to be seen, as was the two-seater they were designing for Lotus. The interior of the Lotus Elite was Giugiaro's, but the design was too advanced when it went to Ital Design, for the exterior to be changed much.

Of course, like everyone else, Ital Design needed to advertise. To this end, Giugiaro has built a number of spectacular one-offs, based on a variety of components from Maserati, to Alfasud to Porsche 911, to Lotus. A feature of these is that they have been cars that are driven around the roads of northern Italy. As Giugiaro pointed out, the hard part about designing was creating a form that was also practical. He believed totally in the necessity of making those two ends meet, as he exemplified in the gracious shape and fine aerodynamics of the Alfetta GT, which was far

more of a four seater than the vast majority of its rivals.

The success of Ital Design's work has been largely due to Giugiaro getting his priorities right in the first place. The perspective drawings of new models have always been done after the plan drawings, so that neither he nor his staff lose their objectivity. Furthermore, Giugiaro has never believed in working with scale models. Mock-ups are done one-to-one (life size) so that proportions can be gauged exactly, rather than visualized. He has broken his rule, however, when it has been necessary to solve aerodynamic problems; then, models have been made for wind-tunnel use.

Giugiaro and Ital Design, have been largely responsible for giving coupés a respectable name, making them four seaters and not a sort of two-plus-toothbrush and so on. In 1974, there was still plenty to come from this enterprising styling house.   IF

Above: based on the Alfasud is this rather garish design called the Caimano. The rectangular pattern on the wheels does little to complement the design

FORMULA ONE ITALIAN STYLE

Motor racing is, by nature, scintillating and stimulating and few nations respond to the sport quite like the excitable Italians

TO A MOTOR-RACING ENTHUSIAST, the Italian Grand Prix means 'Monza'. In turn, Monza means 'motor racing' to many people. Each September, tens of thousands of Italians flock to Monza to cheer their favourites, or jeer if they fail. The atmosphere of the place is reckoned to be second to none, the heat is usually unbearable and the slipstreaming cars have, over the years, provided the exciting spectacle of split-second finishes.

Yet, the first Italian Grand Prix, in 1921, was not at Monza. It was at Brescia. Three Ballots opposed three Fiats on the triangular 10.75-mile Montichiari road circuit. The cars set off at one-minute intervals, and for the first thirteen of the thirty laps, Pietro Bordino set a scorching pace in his Fiat, but tyre problems beset his heroic drive and ultimately the two French Ballots of Jules Goux and Jean Chassagne cruised home to a one-two victory with Louis Wagner's Fiat eventually finishing in third place.

Monza came into being the following year. The Milan Automobile Club won permission to build an autodrome in the disused Monza royal park, some 12 miles from Milan. Vincenzo Lancia and Felice Nazzaro laid the first stone of the circuit on 26 Feb-rurary 1922, but two days later the Government issued an order to stop work. Their grounds were that the 'landscape had to be preserved', but opposition to the order was weighty and, by April, the authorities had to give way. On 3 May, work eventually commenced, the contractors undertaking to complete work by 15 August. By courtesy of 3500 workmen, 200 carts, thirty lorries, three miles of Decauville railway (with two engines and eighty trucks), the work was accomplished in record time.

By July the first cars had set forth on the track and in August racing took place. The Autodromo Nazionale di Monza was unique in that it combined a 'speed bowl' with an artificial road track. The 'speed bowl', 2.796 miles in length, comprised two straights of 0.665 mile each, joined by two banked curves; the road course, 3.418 miles long, had slightly banked curves. The two tracks crossed each other via a tunnel under the northern curve of the 'speed bowl' and by using a common length of track in front of the pits twice a lap distance of 10 km (6.214 miles) could be achieved by the competitors.

The 1922 Italian Grand Prix, however, was not over-exciting, although the 100,000 crowd cheered Pietro Bordini's victory with a 2-litre Fiat 804. So superior were the Italian machines that the team's only challenge was offered by one Bugatti! In 1923, Fiat's new 805s found much stronger opposition in the shape of Voisin, Miller and Benz but were still superior, Carlo Salamano leading Felice Nazzaro to a comfortable one-two finish ahead of Jimmy Murphy's Indianapolis Miller.

Alfa Romeo took over where Fiat left off in 1924, although the strategy of postponing the race until October in the hope of attracting tougher opposition failed. Antonio Ascari led his team-mates, Louis Wagner and Giuseppe Campari, to an overwhelming one-two-three Alfa triumph. Mercedes offered some challenge, but when Polish driver Count Louis Zborowski crashed fatally on the 44th of the 80 laps the remaining team cars were withdrawn in respect. Despite Duesenberg opposition, it was Alfa Romeo again in 1925 with Gastone Brilli-Peri leading home Giuseppe Campari.

Only two finishers from five starters made the 1926 race one to forget, chiefly due to lack of support for the new 1½-litre formula, and the following year saw no real improvement, with four survivors from six

Left: the first Italian Grand Prix was held not at Monza, but at Brescia, in 1921; the track was the triangular 10.75 mile Montichiari road circuit. The two French Ballots of Jules Goux and Jean Chassagne finished first and second, while Louis Wagner's Fiat finished third. Our picture shows a car passing the main grandstand during the event

Bottom: the start of the 1968 Italian GP at Monza; on the front row are the red Ferrari of Chris Amon, the orange McLaren of Bruce McLaren and the white Honda V12 of John Surtees. Victory eventually went to the howling Japanese car of Surtees

starters. French cars swept the board. There were, however, 22 cars on the grid for the 1928 race when a confused formula, based on weight limits and race distance, was imposed. It developed into a contest between Bugatti, Alfa Romeo and Talbot, but on the eighteenth of the sixty laps tragedy intervened when Emilio Materassi's Talbot swerved along the finishing straight and ploughed through the safety netting and protective ditch into the spectators. Twenty-seven were killed and twenty-one injured, Materassi receiving fatal injuries. The race continued—minus the Talbot team who withdrew—with Frenchman Louis Chiron's Bugatti T35C trouncing the Alfa Romeo P2 shared by the Italians Achille Varzi and Giuseppe Campari.

There was no Italian Grand Prix again until 1931. Meanwhile, safety facilities at Monza were improved to placate the public outcry after the 1928 tragedy. The ten-hour race fell to Alfa Romeo, the winning machine driven by Giuseppe Campari/Tazio Nuvolari covering 967.94 miles on a revised 4.263-mile circuit using only one of the banked corners of the 'speed bowl'. The following year the same pair triumphed in the five-hour Italian Grand Prix, covering 520.46 miles and successfully fending off a strong attack from the 4.9-litre Maserati Tipo V5 of Luigi Fagioli/Ernesto Maserati. The old 10 km full circuit was back in use now.

Alfa Romeo won their third successive Italian Grand Prix in 1933, with Luigi Fagioli's P3 conquering the two Maserati 8CM-3000s of Tazio Nuvolari and Freddie Zehender. The Grand Prix was held in the morning and the *formule libre* Monza Grand Prix in the afternoon. During the latter event Giuseppe Campari, Baconin Borzacchini and Count Stanislas Czaykowski were involved in fatal accidents. Although drivers reported that oil on the already slippery track was the cause of the tragedy, an inquiry ruled the track itself was dangerous and the 10 km combined road/'speed bowl' circuit was abandoned. For 1934, the first year of the 750 kg maximum-weight formula which brought the German Mercedes-Benz and Auto Union teams to the forefront, a tortuous 2.678-mile circuit was evolved using part of the road circuit and one banking, with chicanes on the two fastest corners to reduce speeds. From 1935 until 1938 (with the exception of 1937 when the Grand Prix was held at Leghorn), a circuit varying from 4.281 to 4.350 miles in length (depending on the number and severity of the chicanes) was utilised, this comprising most of the road circuit plus one banking of the 'speed bowl'.

Up until the outbreak of World War II, the German cars swept the board in the Italian Grand Prix. A Mercedes-Benz W25, crewed by Rudi Caracciola/Luigi Fagioli, triumphed in 1934 at the low speed of 65.35 mph, while in 1935 Hans Stuck's Auto Union B-type conquered an Alfa Romeo driven by René Dreyfus and Tazio Nuvolari. The following year Nuvolari's Alfa was once more beaten into second place, this time by Bernd Rosemeyer's Auto Union C-type.

The 1937 Grand Prix was run on the Montenero circuit at Leghorn, usually the scene of the Coppa Ciano. The Italian Automobile Club prayed that Nuvolari's great skill would outweigh the superior power and speed of the German teams on this street circuit (he had, in fact, beaten them in the 1936 Coppa Ciano), but it was not to be. After a start delayed while spectators were cleared off the course, the race developed into a duel between Mercedes drivers Hermann Lang and Rudi Caracciola, much to the consternation of team manager Alfred Neubauer, which

Caracciola won, also gaining the European Championship. German cars filled the first six places with an Alfa Romeo shared by Giuseppe Farina and Nuvolari in a distant seventh position.

Back at Monza, 46-year-old Nuvolari triumphed in 1938—this time driving an Auto Union D-type. Farina's sixteen-cylinder Alfa Romeo was a game second, ahead of the best of the troublesome Mercedes-Benz W154s, driven by Rudi Caracciola and relief driver Manfred von Brauchitsch. After this race, the banked circuit was taken down and the road circuit slightly extended to give a lap distance of 3.915 miles. However, war intervened and 1940 to 1945 saw Monza, occupied by the forces, falling into disrepair.

In 1948, the Milan Automobile Club negotiated with the Milan and Monza town councils and obtained permission for the track to be rebuilt. Meanwhile, the 1947 and 1948 Italian Grands Prix were run at Milan Park and Turin's Valentino Park respectively. The all-conquering Alfa Romeo 158s triumphed both times, Carlo Felice Trossi heading Achille Varzi, Consalvo Sanesi and Alessandro Gaboardi to a crushing one-two-three-four success in 1948, and Jean-Pierre Wimille conquering Luigi Villoresi's Maserati 4CLT in Turin; third in this race was a brand new machine, the first Ferrari Grand Prix car, driven by Raymond Sommer.

In 1949, back at Monza, it was a Ferrari that won. Alberto Ascari's 125 V12 model vanquished Philippe Etancelin's Lago-Talbot by more than a lap. After sitting out the 1949 season, Alfa Romeo returned in 1950—the first year of the World Championship series—but winner Giuseppe Farina was troubled by the speed of the new 4½-litre Ferraris. Indeed, the following year Ascari and Froilan Gonzalez scored a Ferrari one-two, easily beating Alfa Romeo.

Run to the 2-litre Formula Two regulations, the 1952 and 1953 Italian Grands Prix saw victory go to Ascari's Ferrari 500 and Juan Manuel Fangio's Maserati A6SSG respectively; in fact, Ascari's Ferrari appeared set to win the 1953 race as well, but was involved in a controversial last-corner pile-up. Stirling Moss, then 24, had the honour of Italy on his shoulders in 1954 when his Maserati 250F successfully fought off the challenge of Fangio's Mercedes-Benz W196. In the closing minutes, however, Moss's Maserati lost its oil and ground to a silent halt, leaving Fangio an untroubled victory.

Monza underwent improvements before the 1955 season, a new banked circuit being built to replace the pre-war one. Running on the combined road/track circuit, Fangio's Mercedes-Benz triumphed once more in 1955 and Stirling Moss's Maserati 250F scored in 1956. However, the circuit proved tough on the machines and the road circuit was brought back into use, now 3.573 miles in length following the construction of the new banked circuit. The British Vanwalls enjoyed superior speed and Stirling Moss drove one to victory in 1957, Tony Brooks repeating the dose in 1958. In 1959 Moss really upset the apple-cart by winning with his tiny Cooper T45-Climax, the more powerful Ferraris being handicapped by having to change tyres.

In 1960, it was back again to the original road/track combination, a move which upset the British teams whose lightweight cars were not suited to the rough bankings of the 'speed bowl'. But the race went on, despite British abstention, with a Ferrari walkover. In 1961, a new 1½-litre Grand Prix formula came into being and again the combined road/track circuit was utilised, this time with British teams in full attendance. Ferrari were superior anyway that year and as the flag fell the season-long battle for the World Championship between Ferrari drivers Wolfgang von Trips and Phil Hill continued. However, on the second lap von Trips was involved in an accident with Jim Clark's Lotus: entering the Parabolica bend on the road section on lap two, von Trips cut across Clark and the two cars touched. The Lotus spun along the grass verge to a safe halt, but the Ferrari ploughed up the bank and slammed into the 'protective' wire fencing twice before bouncing back on to the grass, a total wreck. Fifteen spectators—plus von Trips—perished in the accident.

For 1962, the safety measures had been improved and the race was held on the road circuit, providing BRM drivers Graham Hill and Richie Ginther with a one-two victory. In 1963, it was planned to hold the Grand Prix on the combined road/track circuit again, but in practice it was obvious that the banking had become too rough and bumpy for modern-day Grand Prix cars and a revertion was made to the road circuit where the race was then run every year. Clark's Lotus averaged 123.62 mph in 1963. Every subsequent year until 1972 speeds rose and the race had the reputation of being a slip-streaming classic, with strings of cars battling for honours. For the spectator the excitement was intense, but for the drivers it was positively dangerous. With closely matched, tightly packed cars constantly changing places at speeds approaching 190 mph, the threat of a major accident was always there. The worst accident fortunately did not involve spectators, nor was it a result of a multi-car pile-up; during practice for the 1970 Italian Grand Prix Jochen Rindt crashed fatally and, because his points tally could not be overtaken, became the first posthumous World Champion.

Monza's fastest Grand Prix was in 1971 when Peter Gethin of Britain took only 1 h 18 m 12.6 s to cover the 196.51 miles, an average of 150.75 mph. Gethin's BRM P160 won by mere inches—officially one-hundredth of a second separated it from Ronnie Peterson's March 711-Ford. It was both the fastest and the shortest Grand Prix in the history of World Championship motor racing and also featured the closest-recorded finish.

For 1972, two temporary chicanes were swiftly incorporated for the Grand Prix, increasing the lap distance to 3.588 miles. Gone were the slipstreaming tactics which were part and parcel of Monza; gone, too, was much of the excitement, but it was 'safe'. The crowds were appreciative of good racing and in 1972 and 1973 cheered home the winning John Player Special/Lotus 72-Fords of Emerson Fittipaldi and Ronnie Peterson respectively. Peterson also won in 1974, in a race which probably cost Ferrari the World Championship; the quick-tempered Latin spectators did not forget that quickly.   MK

Left: cars enter the Parabolica Curve shortly after the start of the 1971 event. The picture shows Clay Regazzoni's Ferrari leading the STP March of Ronnie Peterson, the dark blue Tyrrell of Jackie Stewart and the white Yardley-BRM of Jo Siffert. The race was eventually won by Peter Gethin, in a BRM, who beat Peterson by one-hundredth of a second!

A CAT MAY LOOK AT A KING

The Jaguar recipe for success is simple. Backed by a successful racing history they make high quality cars and sell them at almost unbelievably modest prices

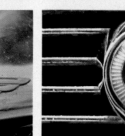

'NINETY PER CENT OF THE MOTORING POPULATION', said Lord Stokes of Leyland in 1970, 'would like to have a Jaguar XJ6; the other ten per cent would like the same thing with a Daimler grille and badges'. It was a pardonable exaggeration, but no more than an exaggeration; for the Jaguar, which had begun life a quarter of a century earlier as a car for cads, boulevardiers and poodlefakers, had matured into an extraordinarily impressive car that was capable of giving the most demanding drivers and the most sensitive passengers equal satisfaction. The Jaguar, whatever model you consider, was never by absolute standards a cheap car, and this made the ownership of one in itself something in which to take a certain pride. By comparative standards, the Jaguar was never anything but a cheap car, and this was the other element that made it so incredibly popular. For decades the question was 'How do they do it at the price?' Only in the most recent years, with demand so far outstripping supply that newly delivered cars might change hands at vastly inflated prices in what was tantamount to a black market, did the question change to '*Why* do they do it at the price?'

The man who could answer these questions but has always tended to keep his own counsel is Sir William Lyons, the Chairman of the company until 1973 and best described as one of the most outstanding men in the motor industry. When Mr Lyons began his business life, it was in Blackpool in partnership with Bill Walmsley. They set up the Swallow Sidecar Company in 1922 to manufacture sidecars for motor cycles, but Lyon's flair as a body stylist soon found expression in the Swallow-bodied Austin 7, after which he turned out a succession of cars based upon mechanical components made by Standard, but so well styled and so competitively marketed that SS Cars, as the company became known in 1935, never looked back, until 1945. There has been argument as to whether the initials stood for Swallow Special or for Standard Swallow—Lyons has never said. In any case, by 1945, with World War II uppermost in everybody's memories, the initials were more likely to be associated with the *Schützstaffel*, and the name of the company was changed to Jaguar Cars Limited. The Jaguar title was supposedly chosen by Lyons from a list of 500 animal names, because it had power, speed and courage. The name-change made no difference to the way Lyons ran the company. He was completely autocratic: there was not one board meeting until 1965, despite the fact that the company had acquired Daimler in 1960, Guy Motors in 1961 and Coventry Climax Engines in 1963. The year 1965 was one in which negotiations got under way for the merger of Jaguar Cars with the British Motor Corporation; when eventually these talks reached their fruition, it was only on the strict understanding that Lyons remained virtually as autonomous and autocratic as before. Although he was so quiet and so gentlemanly in his conduct (he never addressed even

Almost as famous as the Jaguar cars themselves, the Jaguar badges, from the emblem of the old SS cars to the insignia of the XJ series. Most famous, though, has to be the leaping cat, the centre of attraction for most enthusiasts and the prized possession of many unscrupulous badge collectors

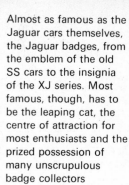

his Vice Chairmen by anything other than their surnames), he was extremely strong in business. When British Motor Holdings (the company which represented the merger of BMC and Jaguar) were in turn acquired by Leyland to form part of the new BLMC group in 1968, Lyons became the deputy chairman under Stokes and, during the dealings leading to the completion of the merger, he is recorded as having addressed the board in terms so powerful that they were, by agreement, left out of the minutes of that

meeting. Jaguar, in effect, belonged to Lyons, and he would countenance nothing that challenged his control.

The name Jaguar was already well known and closely associated with the company's products when it was adopted in 1945. It had been applied to a series of SS models introduced in 1936 and popularly acclaimed as a kind of poor man's Rolls-Bentley. In 1945, the Jaguar that was prepared for production in the following year was substantially the same as the pre-war design, subject only to the adoption of hypoid gearing in the back axle. There were three versions, with engines of 1½, 2½, or 3½ litres, the two larger six-cylinder versions being mounted in chassis of 10 ft wheelbase, and the four-cylinder engine in one that was eight inches shorter. Before the war, all these pushrod engines had been made for SS by Standard; soon after it, Standard's Managing Director, John Black, told Lyons that, with his company's commitment to the new Vanguard car, the production of engines for Jaguars could not be maintained. Offering to sell the necessary plant to Jaguar, he was prompted to have second thoughts upon the prompt arrival of transport for the equipment and a cheque to pay for it; but Lyons, having secured for himself yet more independence, was not one to surrender it again, being content merely to let Standard continue with the four-cylinder engine, for which he had no long-term plans.

As might be expected from a company which owed its commercial success to concentrating on appearances, the mechanical realities beneath the fashionably glamorous Jaguar bodies were essentially humdrum. A simple girder chassis carried beam axles on half-elliptic leaf springs, the modestly rated engines drove the car through four-speed gearboxes having synchromesh on the upper three of some well spaced but not so well engaged ratios, and the car was stopped by Girling rod-operated brakes. None of this was as important as the fact that in 1946, the smallest of the three Jaguars

could be bought for £684, and the largest for £991.

No sooner was the production of these cars established again than adventurous plans were made for future cars. Some massive re-tooling was indicated, and an entirely new engine prepared; and all this would take more time than the pre-war designs could be expected to remain attractive to the customers. An interim design was therefore developed, which came onto the market in 1949 as the Jaguar Mk V, with the same choice of six-cylinder engines in a chassis brought mildly up to date by the incorporation of independent front suspension and hydraulic brakes, while the body was elaborated and smoothed—faired headlamps and a new style of fenestration being the most important features. The cars were not particularly fast, not very responsive and, by the standards of the kind of cars they purported to be, they were not even very good; but neither were they very expensive, the 2½-litre Mk V costing only £1247 in 1950, when the cost of real quality was £3000 for a 2-litre Bristol or even more for a 4½-litre Bentley.

By this time, the world had already been given a taste of the new generation of Jaguars that was to come, and for so long to endure. It was at the London Motor Show of 1948 that the XK 100 and XK 120 sports cars were first publicly shown. The 100 was to be a four-cylinder, 2-litre affair that would do 100 miles an hour or so, the 120 being a six-cylinder 3.4-litre version that would surely do 120; but they looked identical, and at the time it seemed improbable that either could have been improved by looking different from the other. At a time when the average sports car looked like an agglomeration of RSJs and flying buttresses, the XK 120 (the 100 was never seen again) was as smooth and svelte a creation as ever bore witness to the fluency of Lyons' styling, even though the design was fairly obviously derived from that of the 1940 Mille Miglia 328 BMW.

Top: the SS I model of 1934; it was fitted with an in-line six-cylinder engine of 2143 cc

Above: the SS company's first sports car appeared in 1935. It was the SS 90 model and was fitted with a six-cylinder 2.7-litre engine. The car featured a short chassis and slab-tank two-seater bodywork

What mattered even more than the body—and much more than the chassis which was merely sturdy and had little but the use of torsion bars for the front independent suspension wishbones to distinguish it—was the engine. Engineering Director William Heynes, with Walter Hassan and Claude Baily, put more work into this than into the whole of the rest of the car; and the fact that the engine was still, *mutatis mutandis*, in production in 1974, shows how well worthwhile the work was. At least as much as the body design, it brought entirely new standards to the production sports car, while nevertheless remaining quite old-fashioned in its basic elements. It was tantamount to a Grand Prix engine of 1930, with twin overhead camshafts, a long stroke and a robust crankshaft generously furnished with a main bearing between each two adjacent crank throws. The hemispherical cylinder heads in which the two inclined valves were seated (Heynes presented a famous paper on the virtues of this shape) combined with well-shaped inlet and exhaust tracts to ensure high performance, and only the tremendous weight of the massive iron crankcase would have disqualified it from being competitive as a Grand Prix engine twenty years earlier. As it was, tuned for the revoltingly bad petrol of the times, the XK 120 engine developed 160 bhp, and could safely be run up to 6000 rpm. This was an extraordinary power output for a two-seater in those days, and the effectiveness of the engine/body combination was demonstrated by a timed run on the motorway from Jabbeke to Aeltre in Belgium, when an almost standard XK 120 was timed at over 132 mph—after which it was driven with pardonable ostentation past the timekeepers and observers at 10 mph in top gear. It was a wonderful engine—although it was not without its faults, for the vast iron block soaked up a great deal of heat that the engine could hardly dissipate (you could burn your fingers on the dipstick) and its lubrication system had

the unfortunate habit of delivering more oil to the camboxes in the head than the return system could handle, with the result that the surplus simply had to find its way past the valve guides into the combustion chambers. The sump could be emptied in the course of a fast run up the motorway from London to Birmingham; but nobody minded at the time, for the motorway was not yet built.

In fact, it was not intended that many XK 120s should be built. The 100 was forgotten almost as soon as it was displayed; the four-cylinder XK engine had been usefully employed in Goldie Gardner's record-breaking MG streamliner to take some international speed records in the unsupercharged 2-litre class, and then quietly shelved. The six-cylinder engine was intended to power a big new Jaguar saloon, and the sporting XK 120 was no more than a small series of aluminium-bodied cars that would get the engine into production, earning money and kudos, while the saloon was readied.

In 1949, we were shown just how impressive the XK 120 could be. At Silverstone for the Daily Express one-hour race for production cars, there appeared a team of three two-seater Jaguars, one in red for Peter Walker, one in white for Leslie Johnson, and one in blue (with touches of yellow to complete the Siamese royal palette) for Prince Birabongse. It was an Allard that led away from the run-and-jump Le Mans start, but between the first and second corners it was swamped by the team of Jaguars rushing past to lead the race in disciplined line-ahead formation. The demonstration was wonderfully convincing; the cars might have rolled like yachts, but they still seemed to get around the corners pretty well, and their speed down the straights was blisteringly fast. In fact, one of the tyres on Bira's car did blister its inner tube (an ordinary one had been fitted inside the Dunlop racing cover on one of the rear wheels) and the car retired three-legged onto the grass where its jack proved use-less. So the hour ran out with Johnson winning from Walker, a comfortable distance ahead of the 2-litre Bristol-engined Frazer-Nash that was there to show us how a proper sports car should go around corners.

This impressive performance did wonders for morale at a time when it was universally accepted that

section members with a triangulated tubular super-structure, while the front suspension was largely standard, the rear axle was carried in a simple but ingenious three-link mechanism sprung by a trans-verse torsion bar anchored in the middle. The engine had been tuned by conventional methods to produce 210 bhp at 5800 rpm, sufficient with a light and pretty

Above: the SS 100 of 1936, one of the world's most classic sports cars. The SS was capable of 100 mph (hence the designation 100) and was fitted with a 2.7-litre six-cylinder engine

Britain could not make a proper racing car. However, even in sports-car racing, it would be seen that an hour around Silverstone was one thing but 24 at Le Mans was a very long way indeed. One of these Jaguars was brought up to third place for a while in the 1950 race before retiring with its single-plate clutch disinte-grated, while Johnson managed fifth place in the Mille Miglia that year, a much better effort. For a car that was never supposed to go into quantity production, it was an unexpected effort—but the demand for the XK 120 was quite fantastic, and Lyons sanctioned a steel-bodied version that was to open up the American dollar market for the company and establish the Jaguar reputation so firmly that, roll and brake fade and soggy low-geared steering notwithstanding (and after all the Americans were never accustomed to anything else), nobody would hear a word said against it. Not until 1955 was the XK 120 updated, and the changes then were superficial; heavier bumpers and more extensive chrome altered the appearance little, the fixed-head coupé profiting more than the open roadster from the change, and the new drophead coupé looking uncommonly graceful. Now that petrol was better, the output of the engine could be raised to 190 bhp at 5600 rpm—and it remained pegged at that level two years later when a rebodied XK 150 came along. The XK 150 was later to get disc brakes, which at last made it feasible to use that prodigious perfor-mance fully on winding roads.

Those disc brakes had made Jaguar famous in 1953, when they helped the XK 120 C (or C-type) cars to win Le Mans for the second time, despite the greater speed and power of the rival Ferraris. The C-type had already won Le Mans when it made its competition début in 1951—inspired apparently by the perfor-mance in 1950 of the supposedly standard but actually very specially prepared XK 120s there. The chassis of the C-type was based on generously drilled channel-

streamlined body to give it a maximum speed of about 150 mph.

Three of these cars went to Le Mans in 1951, two retiring because of oil-pipe fractures, but the third, driven by Peter Whitehead and Peter Walker, sur-viving to win by 77 miles from a Talbot at a record average speed of 93.5 mph, and with a new lap record to the credit of one of the other Jaguars at a speed of 105.24 mph. It was a great occasion for British devo-tees of motor sport, giving Britain its first Le Mans win since the Lagonda success of 1935, and it did every-thing that was intended in the way of publicising Jaguard competence. Any remaining doubts were dispelled by the C-type's victory later in the year at the TT, while more ordinary XK 120s took a gold cup in the Alpine Rally and ran for 24 hours at an average of 107 mph around the banked track at Montlhéry.

So successful was the 1951 season that Jaguar were tempted to treat the following year a little too casually. A half-hearted attempt at the Mille Miglia, in a C-type equipped with the first disc brakes to be used by Jaguar, was a failure. While driving the C-type in Italy, however, Stirling Moss was given food for serious thought when his car was passed easily along a straight by one of the Mercedes-Benz 300 SL coupés. When he reported this to the Jaguar factory, it was agreed by all concerned that something had better be done to increase the top speed of the Jaguar lest it suffer similar humiliation at Le Mans. In great haste, a new body was devised with longer bonnet and tail, and the cars were sent off to France, only to prove during practice that the smaller radiators fitted in the shallower noses of the new cars were inadequate. Despite the substitution of standard radiators in two of the cars, producing hideous bulges in the bonnet tops that had been so carefully profiled, the entire team succumbed to overheating early in the race. A few weeks later (with standard bodywork again), the factory team was once again roundly defeated in the nine-hour sports-car race at Goodwood, but when the C-type was put into production and appeared in the market place at a basic price of £1495 (plus tax) in August 1952, there was no shortage of willing customers. Road tested by *The Motor*, the C-type, in its production form, accelerated from rest to 100 mph in 20.1 seconds.

The factory team of C-types that returned to Le Mans in 1953 were faster and a lot better·prepared. Once again, they had to contend with formidable Ferrari opposition, but what the Jaguars lacked in the ability to go (although the power output had risen to 220 bhp with the aid of triple twin-choke Weber carburettors) they made up for in their ability to stop:

Right: a later version of the SS 100, this being a 1938 model; this time the original 2.7-litre engine had been replaced by a more-powerful 3485 cc unit. This new engine was also a six-cylinder and developed 125 bhp

Below: front view of the 3½-litre SS 100; the price of these machines when new was £445. Jaguar has long been famous for marketing high-quality cars at extremely reasonable prices, a policy the company still pursued in 1974

Dunlop disc brakes were fitted to all the team cars, allowing them to leave their braking dramatically later than the drum-braked Italian cars at the end of the long straights. With a five-link rear-axle location and flexible fuel tanks to forestall any repetition of failures noted in the past, the team of three cars finished first, second, and fourth, with a privately entered car in ninth place, and their honour was popularly vindicated.

Although the disc brakes that made it all possible were not to feature in a quantity-production Jaguar until 1958, the car that most needed them from the outset was introduced in 1951, in the same year as the C-type appeared. This was the Mk VII saloon, the car for which the XK engine had been prepared, and for which it had mainly been intended. It was a big and bulbous pachyderm, with a 10 ft wheelbase and a vast heavy body that could only by the greatest stretch of imagination be thought a sports saloon, as its predecessors often were. It was a frankly luxurious carriage, opulent in all its interior appointments and almost obscene in the grossness of its exterior contours. Despite its great weight, its soft suspension, its barge-like proportions, and its severely taxed brakes, the Mk VII could go very quickly, thanks to that wonderful engine, and quietly. Nor was it beyond the wit of Jaguar's engineers, despite the distractions of a move to larger factory premises in Allesley, on the outskirts of Coventry, to produce a firmly sprung, highly tuned aluminium-bodied and substantially lightened facsimile version which swamped the opposition in the production-car race at Silverstone, successfully giving the public the quite false impression that this Mk VII was the finest and fastest saloon on the market.

In any case, most customers did not buy it to go fast, but to be comfortable and to swank. By 1955, the Mk VII had succeeded well enough to develop into the VIIM, now with 190 bhp at its disposal and with a basic price tag of £1616, £340 more than in 1951.

Another two years, another couple of hundred pounds, and another 20 bhp, not to mention a great proliferation of chromium beading and two-toned paintwork, made it into the Mk VIII, with a curved windscreen suppressing some of the lines of old age evident in the angular two-piece screen of the earlier models. The really significant change came in 1959 when the Mk IX acquired Dunlop servo-assisted disc brakes on all four wheels, and an enlarged XK engine of 3781 cc, from which 220 bhp was claimed. Not all these horses might reach the rear wheels, for by now many of these cars were fitted with automatic transmissions, comprising an epicyclic gearbox and converter coupling that took its toll of the torque it transmitted. Automatic transmissions were first fitted to the Mk VII as an optional extra, and this choice remained open to the buyer of virtually any production model thereafter.

The one that could least afford such deprivations was the 2.4 saloon, a complement to the grandiose Mk VII and some sort of compensation for the loss of quasi-sporting attributes lamented with the passing of the Mk V and its predecessors. The new engine displacement of 2483 cc was arrived at by shortening the stroke of the XK engine from 106 to 76.5 mm, and the corresponding shortening of the cylinder block made a welcome reduction in the weight of cast iron in the nose of the tubby little car. Unfortunately, the engine did not respond as well as had been expected to the shortening of stroke, its power output being a rather undistinguished 112 bhp at 5750 rpm. Since the

car was by no means light in weight, the engine could not propel it at any great speeds, and since it was particularly narrow in the rear track (where the wheels were enclosed by spats, as had those of the early XK 120) and the road holding was mediocre, it was probably just as well. To be fair to the car, one example, driven by Paul Frère, won the touring class of the Belgian production-car race at Spa in 1956, but it pays to remember that the factory-entered saloons of this period were as far from standard as the regulations of each event would allow. The very special specification of the racing Mk VII, has already been mentioned, and that of the Mk VII which won the Monte Carlo

Rally in 1956 might be arrived at by inspired guesswork. In competition, Jaguar did not believe in accepting unnecessary handicaps.

In fact, it was because of a handicap system, that applied to the results of the Dundrod TT, that the little 2½-litre engine was first tried in competition, in an early version of the beautiful and otherwise generally successful D-type competition car.

Without a doubt the loveliest, the fastest, and (after the end of its production run) the most cherished Jaguar, the D-type is even more important to the critical student of the make's history as the Jaguar which, better than any other, demonstrated the ability

Top: a 1948 XK120 coupé, clearly showing the cat-like elegance of the body styling

Centre: the 1955 XK140, which was powered by a 3442 cc 190 bhp version of the famous XK engine

Above: another XK120 of 1949, now in the Medici collection

Right: the Jaguar XK engine proved quite popular in the mid 1950s with racing-chassis builders, this engine taking the laurels from the previously popular Bristol units

Below: the 1957 XK150 convertible

Bottom: the fabulous D-type which proved so successful in the late 1950s. A D-type won Le Mans three times in succession, from 1955 to 1957

of the firm's engineers to do things properly. Perhaps the most accomplished of these gentlemen was their ex-Bristol aerodynamicist, Malcolm Sayer, whose work on the D-type earned the unstinted approval of the experts at Farnborough. The shape he created for the car, basically elliptical in longitudinal and transverse sections, was an evolved form of the special body built for record-breaking purposes in 1953—the record-breaker being known as the C/D prototype which reached nearly 180 mph in October of that year when driven by Jaguar's well known tester, (and occasional racing stand-in) Norman Dewis. The refined contouring of the final D shape did more than reduce aerodynamic drag: it also encouraged the adoption of constructional techniques that had hitherto been foreign to the firm. The centre section was an elliptical-section tub of stressed 18-gauge magnesium-alloy sheeting, suitably stiffened by bulkheads at front and rear and welded to a multi-tubular frontal frame carrying the engine and front suspension.

In 1954, when the D-type first appeared at the Le Mans practice weekend, the engine was the well proven 3.4-litre XK now tuned to develop nearly 245 bhp. To get it into the surprisingly low D-type body, it had been converted to dry-sump lubrication and further lowered by being canted eight degrees on its side. The front suspension and the rack-and-pinion steering came without much change from the new XK 140, and the rear suspension consisted of a five-link location for the live axle, sprung as in the C-type. Between that axle and the special racing clutch at the back of the engine was an entirely new four-speed gearbox, designed and made by Jaguar and furnished with synchromesh on all forward ratios. The Moss gearbox that had served in all previous Jaguars, and was to be a notorious feature of ordinary production models for some years to come, was very strong, but in other respects rather nasty, with a hideously slow and heavy change that was not improved by the rapid decay of the synchromesh serving the topmost three ratios. Behind this new gearbox was an interesting little detail, often overlooked—a Plessey pump driven by the output shaft to provide servo assistance for the disc brakes, an example of powered hydraulic application.

Right: the large Mk VII saloon of 1955

Below right: the Mk 2 Jaguar that was available with either 2.4, 3.4 or 3.8-litre engines. This car proved popular with the British Police Force, because of its fairly small size and weight, and its powerful engine

Bottom right: the XK engine was still being used well into the 1970s, although outwardly, it had been modernised by way of smart new cam covers

This meant that Jaguar antedated the classic Citroën DS design by no less than twelve months.

In 1953, it had been the Jaguar's ability to stop that had brought it victory at Le Mans and earned it such fame. In 1954, things were different: thanks to Sayer's body, the new D-type was the fastest thing yet seen on the roads of the French circuit, being timed on the Mulsanne straight at a new record 172.97 mph. It was not, alas, sufficient to win the race, for all three team cars had troubles and only one survived, fighting through foul weather to finish the 24 hours just 105 seconds behind the winning 4.9-litre Ferrari. The fact that the stupendously powerful Italian was nearly 13 mph slower than the D-type proves how well the latter was shaped. In the twelve-hour race at Reims, a month later, D-types finished first and second, despite opposition from Ferrari and Gordini. It was in the D-type's next venture, the TT in Ulster, that a 2.48-litre engined car was tried, finishing fifth and presumably supplying some kind of reasssurance for the production engineers preparing the 2.4 saloon for 1956.

Before then, there was to be another season of earnest competition endeavour, and the prelude thereto consisted of some furious redesign and development of the D-type. The redoubtable engine itself had not been without its problems, but the most notable change was a new cylinder head, made to accommodate larger valves by increasing the included angle between the banks of inlet and exhaust poppets from 70 to 75 degrees. This change that was instrumental in raising the output from 245 to 270 bhp, still at 6000 rpm. This was as much as the 2.4 could run up to in safety, developing 193 bhp for the 1954 TT. What caused Jaguar more concern than engine performance, however, was the car's vulnerability to accidental damage. A lot of time had been lost at Le Mans, for example, in repairing the ravages of an excursion into the sand banks. Some very intelligent alterations were accordingly made so that localised damage could quickly be repaired, especially in and around the nose of the car, where the radiator and other

Above: the large Mk X saloon of 1961; it was powered by the 3.8-litre engine at first, but acquired the 4.2 unit in 1964. The car was renamed the 420G in 1965, when it was updated

major elements of the cooling system were carried in their own independent sub-frame. The best change of all was in the design of the tubular half-chassis which carried the engine and front suspension ahead of the stressed-skin tub amidships: in place of the original light-alloy tubing that was made integral with the tub, and which partially penetrated it in rather inept fashion to constitute a spinal reinforcement connecting the engine with the rear bulkhead, an entirely new steel sub-frame was built up in a triangulated shape of the utmost elegance, designed so that it could be bolted to, and unbolted from, the middle portion of the car, as an aid either to survival or to cannibalisation.

More apparent and almost equaly beautifully done was the reshaping of the body's contours. A longer nose was designed to give cleaner air entry, a new tail fairing with integral fin replaced the headrest and bolted-on fin of the previous year, and the wraparound windscreen was extended to merge with this fairing, to create a sort of conning tower that was about as well streamlined as an open car could hope to be. All told, the 1955 D-type was a beautiful thing, improved even further by the adoption of 16-inch wheels of light-alloy, in place of the 17-inch ones used the year before.

These things being thus, the D-type promised to have a very good season in 1955. Perhaps it did, for it won the race at Le Mans, which was its prime objective, but it is arguable that it won because of the withdrawal of the Mercedes-Benz team after the ghastly accident that occurred there, and which cast such a shadow over subsequent races that in truth nobody could have had a really good season. Nevertheless, Jaguar went on trying at such venues as they were able, but elsewhere than at Le Mans the D-type was trounced by opposition from Mercedes-Benz and Aston Martin. In fact, it was beginning to look as though the D-type was so highly specialist that it was fit for Le Mans and precious little else. There was certainly no question of entering this fragile little beauty for something as stern and uncompromising a test of road-going ability as the Mille Miglia, while on closed circuits that could not offer the billiard-table smoothness of the Le Mans surface the Jaguar seemed to lack something in the roadholding department. A necessary corollary of its shape was that it was narrow in the track, which meant in turn that its suspension movement had to be somewhat limited, and Dunlop had to do a lot of hard work in developing tyres to suit the car. Still, it must be recognised that Jaguar were not campaigning a team of cars for the sake of enjoying motor racing, but for the sake of publicity; and all the other sports-car races of the year could not, when put together, equal in importance the publicity value of the 24-hour race at Le Mans—which is what the D-type won in 1955, as the earlier Jaguars had in '53 and '55.

The trouble with establishing such a pattern is that it tends to become habit-forming, and true to form Jaguar had a pretty disastrous year in 1956. The only thing of any consequence that the factory cars won was the 12-hour event at Reims—but by that time, there were a lot of D-types about, a production line having been established to build a total of 67. It was one of the cars sold to private owners (at what must have been a nominal price of £3878, with a 55-page handbook thrown in) that, entered by the Ecurie Ecosse, won the Le Mans event after the works' cars had run into trouble, two of them crashing and the third having trouble with its new fuel-injection system. The Scots

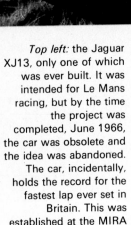

Top left: the Jaguar XJ13, only one of which was ever built. It was intended for Le Mans racing, but by the time the project was completed, June 1966, the car was obsolete and the idea was abandoned. The car, incidentally, holds the record for the fastest lap ever set in Britain. This was established at the MIRA test circuit when David Hobbs drove the car to set a lap speed of 161 mph

Top right: power unit of the rear-engined XJ13 was a four-camshaft V12 engine of 4993 cc capacity. It produced 502 bhp at 7600 rpm

did the same again in 1957, when the factory had withdrawn from official participation, and this was at a record average speed that was not to be beaten until 1961. This time the car had an engine of 3.8-litres displacement, achieved by the expedient of increasing the cylinder bore by 4 millimetres. This was first tried by American tuners, preparing a D-type for Sebring, and it served to raise the bhp to 306, which was 30 more than the 3.4-litre engines of the previous year.

The Americans, who had numerous associations with Le Mans, dating back to the 1920s, but had never shown any enthusiasm or aptitude for less-refined forms of torture, such as the Mille Miglia, were very keen on the D-type. In an effort to widen the car's appeal, Jaguar embarked on a batch of cars to be known as the XK SS, tantamount to a D-type with full width windscreen, interior trim, and reasonably comprehensive roadgoing equipment for the US market. Sixteen of these cars were completed before the whole service department and the D-type end of the factory were destroyed by fire in February 1957. Jaguar could hardly be criticised for withdrawing from racing in these circumstances, especially when they had so many important developments coming to fruition in their bread-and-butter range. Of these, by far the most important was the evolution of the little 2.4-litre saloon, which had appeared the year before. It was not long before its rear spats disappeared to make room for an axle of sensibly wider track. With the increased stability that came from this, it was little longer before the same compact and handsomely curvacious car acquired the regular 3.4-litre engine, which by now was attributed with the ability to give 210 bhp, as did the contemporary Mk VIII saloon, profiting from the improvement in the quality of petrol available. Little more time was to pass before the body was revised, most notably by the enlargement of the rear window, and a number of refinements created what became known as the Mk 2, at first with 2.4 and 3.4-litre engines. By 1960, the car could also be had with the 220 bhp 3.8-litre engine, and in all forms was braked by Dunlop discs on all wheels.

The Mk 2 was a phenomenally successful Jaguar. Anybody reluctant to spend a fortune could hardly conceive of a better proposition among sporting saloons, combining as it did the legendary XK engine with up-to-date brakes and traditional standards of

interior décor. Enthusiastic motorists loved it; so did the police, who found that in motorway service, the engine would run for a quarter of a million miles and so did the club racers, who found that the 3.8 version was able to dominate saloon-car racers in a splendid flurry of roll and slide. It was a car that went with pride and with avarice, prompting envy and the sour-grapes syndrome among those who were not honest enough to admit that they would like to have one. Thus, 'Jag' became an accepted term in English usage.

Compared with the crisp manners and phenomenal performance of the larger-engined Mk 2 cars, the bulbous Mk IX no longer seemed so magnificent. The time had come for a new big car to deal with the pomp-and-circumstance end of the market, and when the Mk X was introduced, in 1962, it became apparent that the Mk IX was in truth as much of a stop-gap as it felt. Rounder in its contours, wider in its track, more expansive in its interior, and in every respect more luxurious than ever, the Mk X was distinguished by a very fine piece of independent rear suspension, in which the geometry of wheel motion was that dictated by double unequal unparallel wishbones, but in which the duties of the upper wishbone were undertaken by the universally jointed half-shaft, devoid of slip joints so that the universals could define the motion of the hub carrier. Within a couple of years, the suspension of this £2400 car had also been grafted onto the rear of the Mk 2 saloons to create the S types in 3.4 and 3.8-litre forms, softer-riding and bigger-booted but less sporting successors to those compact cars that had set so many new performance standards in their time.

Hardly anybody noticed. Since the year before the birth of the Mk X, the word 'Jaguar' had acquired a new connotation. Everybody was obsessed with the E-type. It would have been unpardonable to react in any other way; the very idea that it was possible to buy in 1961 for less than £2100 (apart from tax) a mass-produced two-seater of modest size, dramatic appearance, and quite fantastic performance, smote the entire motoring world with a sense of awe that it had not felt since the unveiling of the original XK 120.

Of course the ones you bought from your local dealers could not match the 150 mph reached by the carefully prepared cars road-tested by the motoring journals. Of course it was cheaply made and finished, and it got very hot inside, and the brakes were a bit

Top: the Jaguar E-type was introduced in 1961 and immediately caused a sensation. Here was a superfast, ultra-sleek sports car available at a very modest price. The original power unit was Jaguar's six-cylinder 3.8-litre motor. By 1974 the E-type was still going strong, but by then was powered by a 5.3-litre V12 engine

Above: a 1969 Jaguar XJ6. Graceful, luxurious and extremely quick, the XJ6 was available with a choice of either 2.8-litre or 4.2-litre six-cylinder engines

Right: the XK100 engine first shown at the 1948 London Motor Show. The engine was a four-cylinder 2-litre unit. However, the six-cylinder XK120 proved so popular that the XK100 model was quietly dropped

fit to do otherwise.

For their part, Jaguar discovered that most of the people who could afford their cars could also afford to waste time, but on the other hand were not well-endowed either with co-ordination or energy. The 265 bhp (a gross figure, as Jaguar's commonly were) 3.8-litre engine was supplanted in 1965 by a 4.2-litre version in the E-type and the Mk X. Extensive redesign of the cylinder block relocated the bores so that they could be enlarged to 92.1 millimetres and, whilst the maximum power remained the same as before, the torque was increased, as was the flexibility. However, you cannot go on indefinitely making an established engine bigger and bigger in capacity: it is more than likely that, some time before the limit of feasibility has been reached, the limit of advisability will be passed. This was what happened to the XK engine. The 3.8 had been phenomenal in view of the size of its pistons and the length of their stroke; it was crisp, responsive, tractable, and safe up to 6000 rpm. The enlarged version of 1965 and the years that have followed was more flexible but rougher in its running, and severely limited by structural considerations so that it could not safely be run at more than 5000 rpm continuously, and indeed was unpleasant beyond 4500. In the E-type, to cruise at those revolutions would have involved going much faster than most drivers were prepared to undertake, so nobody really minded. It was simply assumed that a bigger engine must be better, and people thought it was nice not to have to do so much gear-changing. So much then for Jaguar's long-overdue admission that the Moss gear-box was obsolete, and that their own all-synchromesh device should replace it.

There were lots of other changes too: room was found for taller drivers, brakes were devised that would stop the car properly and radial-ply tyres that improved the ride and promised reasonable durability replaced the high-speed nylon cross-plys that had given the earliest 3.8 E-types such uncommonly good handling characteristics.

Of course, people were not content with the two-door fixed-head coupé, the roadster, and the hard-top. They wanted two extra seats in the back, and more luxurious interior trim, and crash-safe switches, and power steering, and their heads examined. Without going so far as to usurp the prerogatives of the National Health Service, Jaguar did absolutely everything demanded of them.

Thus, the 4.2 E-type begat the 2+2 with high roof, steep screen and long wheelbase; and that begat the second series E-type which was a face-lifted variant beginning to suffer, as were all Jaguars and most other

problematical when cold, and the seats would not accept anybody taller than about 5 ft 9 inches. It did not matter; here was a refined roadgoing son of the D-type, a car that made the higher-priced Aston Martins and exotics seem faintly ludicrous, a car that was quite simply the most glamorous and eye-catching object one could possess. Lots of people bought it simply as a cosmetic, and were content to drive it slowly. Lots more bought it as an ego booster, and discovered in a few frightening and perhaps final seconds of unfamiliar experiences that they were not

cars, from the legislative strictures of the US anti-pollution and safety lobbies. The weight was going up and the power was going down, but the car was still a lot faster than most customers, particularly in those many countries beset by new levels of speed limitation. In time, there would be a new E-type of a third series, based on the long-wheelbase chassis of the 2+2, but with wider track and squatter tyres and so much boiler pressure that lack of steam would cease to be an objection even among the heavy-footed minority.

The third series was given a new V12 engine of 5343 cc displacement. Made mostly in light alloys, the twelve weighed about the same as the old iron-bellied six—which was such a ponderous six hundredweight that the achievement was less meritorious than it sounded. Gone was the hemispherical combustion chamber, its place taken by a Heron-type head with half the depth of the chamber sunk in the piston crown. The valves were worked by a single camshaft above each head, the plugs were sparked by an electronic system built into a big distributor that sat and fried in the angle between the banks, the power was an entirely adequate 254 bhp at 6000 rpm, and the flexibility was outstanding. It looked a splendid engine, if you could see it; most of the time it has been hidden from view beneath the festoons of supplementary plumbing for detoxing devices such as air injectors, gulpers, bypassers, and so Gadarenely on.

Its devolution from a four-camshaft racing engine that never raced was a fairly well kept secret for a good many years, although rumours of a new rear-engined Jaguar sports/racer reached a few ears in the middle 1960s. It was made, and it was beautiful in the Sayer tradition, and it mustered something like 500 bhp, which the designers (Walter Hassan and Harry Mundy) thought inadequate. It went very fast, but it never raced. In fact, the sole example was written off in a high-speed accident, to be rebuilt later as a showpiece exemplifying all that Milton had to say in his *Areopagitica* about fugitive and cloistered virtue.

So much for the XJ 13, which is what the hypersports car was called. The XJ Saloon series is much more important: it is the model for which the V12 engine in its production form was intended. Employing the all-independent suspension of the E/S/Mk 10

Above: the Jaguar E-type V12 of 1974. Although by this time the E-type had been in production for thirteen years its image was still one of luxury, high speed and dateless styling. The engine was a single-overhead-camshaft-per-bank V12 unit of 5343 cc, producing 272 bhp at 5850 rpm

refined until its ride quality set standards by which anything could be judged, heavily and expensively insulated (as was the engine) by a generously finished body of consummate good looks and unmistakable Jaguar breeding, the XJ saloon was meant to be powered by either the V12 or a curious V8 version of it, but the car was ready before the engines, and went well enough with the 4.2-litre XK engine under the broad bonnet. Quite well enough, in fact, for the XJ6 to become immediately the most outstanding of its year (1969) and for a time to appear to make redundant any saloon costing more than £2254 before tax. The detuned XK engine was down to 170 bhp, but the car would do 120 mph or more despite its formidable weight, and its roadholding on new 70-series radials was as good as the wide track and low build suggested. For those content to motor more gently, and perhaps constrained by other countries' fiscal arrangements to do it behind a smaller engine, there was a 2.8-litre version (the stroke was shortened to 86 mm) that managed 140 bhp and looked just as handsome.

So well did the XJ6 sell that there seemed no point in hurrying the XJ12 into production. The V12 E-type was therefore allowed to go before it in 1971; the following year, when at last the flagship was launched, was by no means too late for it to impress all who sailed in her. Very fast, very thirsty, very quiet and very smooth, it was exactly what all manner of people persuaded themselves they wanted. It was not long enough ago from the time of writing for a fair judgment to be pronounced on it in this historical context, but it was long enough for long-wheelbase versions (making life more tolerable for back-seat passengers) and two-door 'coupés' to evolve, for good air-conditioning systems to be developed, and for the price to rise to an all-inclusive £5768 or thereabouts. It was long enough for Sir William to retire gracefully, for his successor Mr England to be displaced rather less ceremoniously, and for the new incumbent—a Mr Robinson—to take command. It was also long enough for a successor to the E-type to slip quietly into the 'open secret' category as the F-type. And if things were to change . . . why, there was always the XK-engined Alvis lightweight tank to maintain a tradition that looked like lasting a very long time.   LJKS

E-TYPE

In 1961, Jaguar announced a new model to replace the XK150. The new car turned out to be a whole new concept in motoring, a car with performance that was usually set aside for the race tracks: 0–50 mph 4.8 secs, top speed 150 mph, all produced by a 3.8-litre twin-cam straight six.

Wherever motoring enthusiasts got together and the talk turned to cars, the 'E-type' would be mentioned and the talking would cease: the E-type was the ultimate, there was nothing quicker, no greater status symbol, no other car that girls would rather be whisked away in. True or not, people from 7 to 70 were happy to believe; and of course Jaguar were happy to sell.

The edge was taken off the performance by the introduction of the 4.2-litre power unit that was less happy to rev into the regions that would bring the magic ton and a half. Emission requirements took their toll too,

as did the large 2 + 2 version and the automatic. The car now had to give best to the new superstar: the Lamborghini Miura.

In 1971, the E-type received a new lease of life, a splendid 5.3-litre V12 engine that re-captured almost all of that lost performance of the early '60s. Twice as many cylinders and almost half the capacity again. The V12 was not brutal and hairy, though, it was smooth and silent.

Gradually, the 2 + 2 and coupé versions of the car were dropped, the roadster being the only model available in 1974. Also, the six-cylinder version was dropped, the 1974 range thus consisting of the V12 roadster, with a choice of automatic or manual forms.

ENGINE Front-mounted, water-cooled 60° V12. 90 mm (3.54 in) bore × 70 mm (2.76 in) stroke = 5343 cc (326 cu in). Maximum power 272 bhp at

5850 rpm; maximum torque 304 lb ft at 3600 rpm; light-alloy cylinder block and heads; compression ratio 9:1. 7 main bearings. 2 valves per cylinder operated by a single overhead camshaft per cylinder head. 4 Stromberg carburettors.

TRANSMISSION Single-dry-plate clutch and 4-speed manual gearbox, or torque converter and 3-speed automatic gearbox. Ratios for manual 1st 2.933, 2nd 1.905, 3rd 1.389, 4th 1, rev 3.378:1. Ratios for automatic 1st 2.400, 2nd 1.450, 3rd 1, rev 2:1. Hypoid-bevel final drive and limited-slip differential. Ratio 3.310 (manual), or 3.070 (automatic).

CHASSIS Integral, with front and rear auxiliary tube frames.

SUSPENSION Front—independent by wishbones, longitudinal torsion bars, an anti-roll bar and telescopic dampers. Rear—independent by wishbones, semi-

axles acting as upper arms, trailing lower radius arms, 4 coil springs and 4 telescopic dampers.

STEERING Servo-assisted rack and pinion. Turns from lock to lock 3.50.

BRAKES Servo-assisted discs all round, inboard at the rear; handbrake on rear wheels.

WHEELS 6 in × 15 steel.

TYRES E70 VR × 15.

DIMENSIONS AND WEIGHT Wheelbase 105 in; track—front 54.25 in, rear—53.25 in; length 184.38 in; width 66 in; height 48.40 in; ground clearance 5.92 in; dry weight 3232 lb; turning circle 36 ft; fuel tank capacity 18 gals.

PERFORMANCE Maximum speed 147 mph; acceleration 0–50 mph 4.9 secs; fuel consumption 15.5 mpg.

XJ SERIES

No car, no matter what sector of the market it is aimed at, can ever be perfect. The Jaguar XJ series, though, has probably come closer to the ideal than most cars: it is handsome, quick —especially in V12 form—spacious and graceful, and it has that conservative English appearance with the bite of a thoroughbred engine and the handling qualities of a thoroughbred chassis. Voted Car of the Year in 1969, the XJ6 proved so popular that there was a waiting list of many months for it. Despite this, the Jaguar company announced that they would not increase production.

The car the public was clamouring for was a four-door luxury limousine powered by the trusty twin-cam, six-cylinder engine that had given the company much success since the 1950s. The XJ6 was available with either a 2.8 or 4.2-litre version of the same basic unit. A four-speed manual gearbox was standard, while a three-speed automatic was optional.

It was noted by many people that, although the XK engine was powerful and provided the XJ with plenty of speed, there was sufficient room in the engine compartment to accommodate an engine of somewhat

larger proportions. The XJ12 was duly announced in 1972.

If this was not enough to keep Jaguar enthusiasts mouths' watering and customers making the queue ever longer, long-wheelbase and two-door coupé versions followed, the 2.8-litre being quietly dropped on the British market, although still available for export. The XJ range in late '74 thus consisted of the XJ6 coupé, manual or auto, XJ6 long-wheelbase, manual or auto, the XJ12, available only in long-wheelbase automatic form and the XJ12 coupé auto.

ENGINE Front-mounted, water-cooled straight-six or 60° V12. 92 mm 3.63 in) bore × 106 mm (4.17 in) stroke = 4235 cc (258.4 cu in) (XJ6), or 90 mm (3.54 in) bore × 70 mm (2.76 in) stroke = 5343 cc (326 cu in) (XJ12). Maximum power (DIN) 180 bhp at 4500 rpm (XJ6), or 250 bhp at 6000 rpm (XJ12); maximum torque 232 lb ft at 3000 rpm (XJ6), or 301 lb ft at 3500 rpm (XJ12); cast-iron cylinder block and light-alloy head (XJ6); or light-alloy block and heads (XJ12). Compression ratio 7.8:1 (XJ6), or 9:1 (XJ12). 7 main bearings. 2 valves per cylinder operated by twin over-

head camshafts (XJ6) or by a single overhead camshaft per head (XJ12). 2 SU carburettors (XJ6), or 4 Stromberg carburettors (XJ12).

TRANSMISSION Single-dry-plate clutch and 4-speed manual gearbox plus overdrive, or torque converter and 3-speed automatic gearbox. Ratios for manual 1st 2.933, 2nd 1.905, 3rd 1.389, 4th 1, overdrive 0.799, rev 3.378:1. Ratios for automatic 1st 2.400, 2nd 1.450, 3rd 1, rev 2:1. Hypoid-bevel final drive. Ratio for manual 3.540, ratio for XJ6 automatic 3.070, or ratio for XJ12 automatic 3.310. Limited slip differential optional on XJ6 or standard on XJ12.

CHASSIS Integral, with front and rear auxiliary sub-frames.

SUSPENSION Front—independent by wishbones, lower trailing links, coil springs, an anti-roll bar and telescopic dampers. Rear—independent by wishbones, semi-axles acting as upper arms, trailing lower radius arms, 4 coil springs and 4 telescopic dampers.

STEERING Power-assisted rack and pinion, with adjustable

steering wheel. Turns from lock to lock 3.30.

BRAKES Servo-assisted discs all round.

WHEELS 6 in × 15 steel.

TYRES E70VR × 15 (XJ6), or 205/70 VR × 15 (XJ12).

DIMENSIONS AND WEIGHT Wheelbase 108.80 in (coupé), or 112.80 in (saloon); track— front 58 in, rear—58.60 in; length 190.70 in (coupé), or 194.70 in (saloon); width 69.70 in; height 54.10 in; ground clearance 7 in; dry weight 3947 lb (XJ6L), 3861 lb (XJ6C), 4128 lb (XJ12L), or 4046 lb (XJ12C); turning circle 36 ft (coupé), or 37 ft (saloon); fuel tank capacity 20 gal.

BODY Either 2-door coupé or long-wheelbase 4-door saloon. 5 seats.

PERFORMANCE Maximum speed 117 mph (XJ6 versions), or 140 mph (XJ12 versions); performance: 0–50 mph approximately 6.5 secs (XJ6 manual), 7.1 secs (XJ6 auto), or 5.5 secs (XJ12s); fuel consumption approximately 19 mpg (XJ6s), or 12 mpg (XJ12s).

This magnificent four-color encyclopedia is brought to you by Columbia House
in cooperation with Orbis Publishing Ltd., one of Great Britain's most enterprising publishers.
Rather than change any of the encyclopedia's authoritative international automotive text, we have
included a glossary of terms that will give you immediate American equivalents, a conversion table
for the international metric system, and a conversion table for equivalent monetary values.

Glossary

BRITISH	AMERICAN	BRITISH	AMERICAN
Aerial	Antenna	Motor	Engine
Aluminium	Aluminum	Number plate	License plate
Apron	Skirt	Overrider	Bumper guard
Big-end	Rod (conrod) bearing	Paraffin	Kerosene
Blower *(colloquial)*	Supercharger	Parking brake	Parking lock
Bonnet	Hood	Petrol	Gasoline, "gas"
Boot	Trunk	Petrol pump	Gasoline or fuel pump
Brake servo	Power brake	Production car	Stock car
Bulkhead	Firewall	Propellor shaft	Drive shaft
Capacity	Displacement	Quarter light	Door vent
Carburetter; carburettor	Carburetor	Rear lamp	Tail light
Check strap	Door stop	Rear seat squab	Rear setback or backrest
Clutch release bearing	Clutch throwout bearing	Reverse lamp	Back up light
Control box	Voltage regulator	Roof lamp	Dome light
Crown wheel and pinion	Ring gear and pinion	Saloon	Sedan
Cylinder block	Cylinder crankcase	Scuttle	Cowl
Dip switch	Dimmer switch	Selector rod	Shift bar
Door pillar	Door post	Servo-assisted	Power assisted
Drop arm	Pitman arm	Side lamp	Parking light
Drop-head	Convertible	Side member	Side rail
Dynamo	Generator	Spanner	Wrench
Epicylic gearbox	Planetary gearbox	Sparking plug	Spark plug
Exhaust silencer	Muffler	Starting handle	Crank handle
Facia panel	Dashboard	Steering column	Steering post
Gear lever	Gear shift lever	Steering relay	Steering idler
Gearbox	Transmission	Stub axle	Steering knuckle
Gearbox housing	Transmission casing	Sump	Pan
Gearchange	Gearshift	Swivel pin	King pin
Glassfibre	Fiberglass	Toe board	Toe pan
Grease nipple	Grease fitting	Track	Tread
Gudgeon pin	Piston or wrist pin	Track rod	Tie bar or track bar
Half shaft	Axle shaft	Two-stroke	Two-cycle
Handbrake	Parking brake	Tyre	Tire
Hose clip	Hose clamp	Valance	Rocker panel
Ignition harness	Ignition set	Wheel arch	Wheelhouse or housing
Kerb	Curb	Wheel brace	Wheel wrench
Layshaft	Counter shaft	Windscreen	Windshield
Main shaft	Output shaft	Wing	Fender
Marque	Brand, make	Wishbone	A-arm; Control arm
		Works	Plant, factory

Metric Equivalents
(Based on National Bureau of Standards)

Length

Centimeter (Cm.)	=0.3937 in.	In.	=2.5400 cm.
Meter (M.)	=3.2808 ft.	Ft.	=0.3048 m.
Meter	=1.0936 yd.	Yd.	=0.9144 m.
Kilometer (Km.)	=0.6214 mile	Mile	=1.6093 km.

Area

Sq. cm.	= 0.1550 sq. in.	Sq. in.	=6.4516 sq. cm.
Sq. m.	=10.7639 sq. ft.	Sq. ft.	=0.0929 sq. m.
Sq. m.	= 1.1960 sq. yd.	Sq. yd.	=0.8361 sq. m.
Hectare	= 2.4710 acres	Acre	=0.4047 hectar
Sq. km.	= 0.3861 sq. mile	Sq. mile	=2.5900 sq. km.

Volume

Cu. cm.	= 0.0610 cu. in.	Cu. in.	=16.3872 cu. cm.
Cu. m.	=35.3145 cu. ft.	Cu. ft.	= 0.0283 cu. m.
Cu. m.	= 1.3079 cu. yd.	Cu. yd.	= 0.7646 cu. m.

Capacity

Liter	=61.0250 cu. in.	Cu. in.	= 0.0164 liter
Liter	= 0.0353 cu. ft.	Cu. ft.	=28.3162 liters
Liter	= 0.2642 gal. (U.S.)	Gal.	= 3.7853 liters
Liter	= 0.0284 bu. (U.S.)	Bu.	= 35.2383 liters

$$\text{Liter} = \begin{cases} 1000.027 \text{ cu. cm.} \\ 1.0567 \text{ qt. (liquid) or } 0.9081 \text{ qt. (dry)} \\ 2.2046 \text{ lb. of pure water at } 4 \text{ C} = 1 \text{ kg.} \end{cases}$$

Weight

Gram. (Gm.)	=15.4324 grains	Grain	= 0.0648 gm.
Gram	= 0.0353 oz.	Oz.	= 28.3495 gm.
Kilogram (Kg.)	= 2.2046 lb.	Lb.	= 0.4536 kg.
Kg.	= 0.0011 ton (sht.)	Ton (sht.)	=907.1848 kg.
Ton (met.)	= 1.1023 ton (sht.)	Ton (sht.)	= 0.9072 ton (met.)
Ton (met.)	= 0.9842 ton (lg.)	Ton (lg.)	= 1.0160 ton (met.)

Pressure

1 kg. per sq. cm.	=14.223 lb. per sq. in.
1 lb. per sq. in.	= 0.0703 kg. per sq. cm.
1 kg. per sq. m.	= 0.2048 lb. per sq. ft.
1 lb. per sq. ft.	= 4.8824 kg. per sq. m.
1 kg. per sq. cm.	= 0.9678 normal atmosphere

$$1 \text{ normal atmosphere} = \begin{cases} 1.0332 \text{ kg. per sq. cm.} \\ 1.0133 \text{ bars} \\ 14.696 \text{ lb. per sq. in.} \end{cases}$$

Approximate Values of the Pound (£)
in terms of U.S. Dollars ($)

1914-1919	$4.76
1935	4.90
1936	4.97
1937	4.94
1938	4.89
1939	4.46
1940-1949	4.03
1950-1967	2.80
1968-1970	2.40
1971-1972	$2.40/2.60
1972-Present	2.60/2.10